The Bibliotherapy Toolbox

100+
Creative and Playful Story-Based Interventions to Help Kids Create Safety, Overcome Challenges, and Build Resiliency

Tammi Van Hollander, LCSW, RPT-S™

THE BIBLIOTHERAPY TOOLBOX
Copyright © 2024 by Tammi Van Hollander

The materials provided in this book of children's therapeutic interventions are intended for mental health professionals, parents, and teachers alike. While teachers may utilize these interventions as a supplementary resource, it is crucial to recognize that they are not a replacement for professional therapy or counseling. Parents, teachers, and mental health professionals utilizing this book are responsible for assessing the appropriateness of the interventions for their specific context. Professional judgment and discretion should be exercised when implementing these techniques. Additionally, individuals are encouraged to seek guidance from licensed mental health professionals when encountering interventions or activities that may be outside their expertise or comfort zone.

Published by
PESI Publishing, Inc.
3839 White Ave
Eau Claire, WI 54703

Cover and interior design by Emily Dyer
Editing by Jenessa Jackson, PhD

ISBN 9781683737759 (print)
ISBN 9781683737766 (ePUB)
ISBN 9781683737773 (ePDF)

All rights reserved.
Printed in the United States of America.

As I Walk into the Playroom

By Tammi Van Hollander, LCSW, RPT-S

I walk into my playroom and what do I see?
I see toys and puppets calling to me.
I walk into the playroom and how do I feel?
I feel so at peace with the power to heal.
I sit with the child so open and clear,
I have no agenda
but quiet their fear.
We may build a fort
to create a safe space,
then read a book
where they feel so embraced.
We may play a game where I always lose.
I feel like the winner
for the child does choose.
The sand is so soft as we bury each hand.
I wait for their journey
to a faraway land.
There are dragons and villains
and so much to fear.
They conquer their demons
without shedding a tear.
Imagination goes deeper
and the healing begins.
Through humming and stories,
I reveal a slight grin.
As I know what I've witnessed
and I'm part of their play.
Their work in the playroom
gives them something to say.
Their language is play
and a toy is a word.
Yes, dear child, I promise,
"You're heard."
Magic and wonder, the world of play.
I am so blessed,
what more can I say!

Table of Contents

Introduction ix

1. Expression of Anger and Other Big Feelings 1
    The Rabbit Listened 3
    "I Am Human" Collage 4
    Anger Stones 5
    I See, I See 6
    "Terrible, Horrible, No Good, Very Bad Day" Drawing 9
    Mixed-Up Animals 10
    Shrink Your Monsters 11
    The Magic Home 13
    Monster Simon Says 15
    Monster Puppet Play 16
    Monster Feelings Sandtray 17
    Color Monster Creation 18
    The Very Hungry Worry Monsters 19
    Shame Monster 20

2. Resilience and Self-Esteem 23
    The "Never Give Up" Tank 25
    Create Your Opportunity 26
    Doing Hard Things 28
    Everyone Poops 30
    I've Got This 32
    The Rosebush Drawing 34
    Happiness Doesn't Come from Headstands 36
    There's More to This Story: Telling the Tale of Resiliency and Growth 38
    The Reflection in Me 40
    Sense of Self with Animal Projections in the Sand Tray 42
    Greatness Sticks 44
    I Love You the Purplest 47

3. Diversity, Equity, and Inclusion 49
    Red Crayon I 52
    Red Crayon II 54
    What Color Is Your Shadow? 55
    Your Body Can 57
    My Unique Body 62
    The Beauty Within 63
    Hair Love 65
    Chocolate Me! 66

4. Neuroscience for Kids 101 67
    Flip Your Lid 69
    NowMaps Adventure 72
    The Power of Neurons 73
    Sensory and Somatic "Ception" Party 75
    Polly Vagale and the Vagus Nerve Superhighway 77
    Mirror, Mirror 80
    My Seven Sensational Senses Self-Care Kit 82

5. Neurodiversity 85
    Red Light, Green Light Scribble Drawing 87
    My "About Me" Book 89
    Brain Power 90
    My Neuro Is Not Typical 92
    Animal Allies 97
    What's Your Question? 99
    Funneling and Focusing BIG Energy 101
    When Things Get Too Loud 102
    Feeling Feelings from the Inside Out 104
    My Calming Snail Fidget 106

6. Trauma and Attachment 109
    A Safe Circle for You 112
    Understanding Neglect 113
    When a Grown-Up You Love Hurts You 116
    Plucking the Peacock 119
    Riding Daddy's Waves 121
    We Are Still Family 122
    Maybe Days 125

Catch the Feather 127
"My Grief Is Like the Ocean" Mantra 128
Grief Parts 130
Family Forest 133
The Heart and the Bottle: Heavy and Light 136
Heart to Heart 138
In Grandpaw's Pawprints 140
Jungle Journey: Grieving and Remembering Eleanor the Elephant 141
The Gifts They Left Us 143
Searching to Belong 145
The Magic Rainbow Hug 147

7. Separation, Divorce, and Sibling Rivalry 151
A Paper Hug 154
I Can Love and Be Loved by Both of My Parents 156
Two Homes 158
A Piece of My Heart 161
"Silly Bone" Chart 163
My Bombaloo 165
The Epic Battle 167
Here and There 169
Feel-Better Glue 171
Peeling Feelings 172
Cooperative Jenga 174
Maple and Willow Fairy Houses 176

8. Anxiety, Fear, Perfectionism, and OCD 179
My Wonderful Warrior 182
Bravery Ladder 184
Face My Fears with Coping Skills 187
Washing Our Worries with Soap's Superpowers 191
Having the Courage to Find Beauty in Imperfection 194
Enhancing Oopsies 196
Wrong Number 197

9. Mindfulness and Embodiment 199
"I Spy" Mindfulness Exercise 202
Rainbow Walk 204
"In My Body" Drawing 206

Thank You Breath 208
Listening to My Body: Feelings and Sensations 209
I Am Peace: Fun with Music 211
Radar Senses 212
Breathing Power 215
Catching Thoughts 217
Special Stones 219

10. Bullying, Boundaries, and Kindness 221

Boundary Sandtray 223
Popsicle Stick Boundary Setting 224
Hula-Hoop Boundaries 226
Bullying and Perspective Taking 229
The Boy, the Mole, the Fox, the Horse, and the Sand Tray 231
Kindness Ripples 233
Smartie Pants Activity 237
Shubert's BIG Voice 239
Create Your Own Super Animal 240
Everyone Counts 241

Acknowledgments 243
List of Contributors 243
References 245
About the Author 251

Introduction

I have been a play therapist for children and families for over 20 years. Having been trained as a client-centered play therapist, the idea of using books therapeutically was never introduced to me. It was not until I attended my first Association for Play Therapy Conference that I met Dee Dee Gruenberg, the owner of The Self-Esteem Shop at the time. She would pick up books and read them to me with such enthusiasm and delight—sharing with me how powerful these books were to use in therapy—that it quickly opened my eyes to the magic of bibliotherapy. I was hooked! Dee Dee and I became fast and furious friends and, thanks in large part to her, I am forever grateful to have created my therapeutic library, which has healed so many children and families.

In contrast to talk therapies, books and play create a safe psychological distance from the problem, creating a deeper level of healing. They offer children a feeling of safety, grounding, connection, and mastery. Children are able to identify with the characters in the books, which normalizes their experiences, thoughts, and feelings in a developmentally appropriate way. Even the smallest of children are mesmerized by books, only wanting more! Whether you are seeing clients in person or providing telehealth, books are a beautiful way to connect and learn more about the children and families you work with. In this resource, I hope to introduce you to the wonderful opportunities that bibliotherapy has to offer even your littlest clients.

What Is Bibliotherapy?

Bibliotherapy refers to the use of literature to help clients deal with psychological, social, and emotional problems. It is a form of supportive psychotherapy in which the client is given a carefully selected, developmentally appropriate book to read. The goals of bibliotherapy are to help children:

- Identify and validate their feelings
- Elevate self-awareness and increase resiliency
- Recognize that other children have problems similar to their own
- Stimulate discussion and play
- Express thoughts and self-awareness
- Discover possible coping skills and solutions

Depending on your role, you may be practicing what is called *developmental bibliotherapy*, which deals with more everyday issues that do not require the support of a trained mental health professional. This form of bibliotherapy is used primarily by educators, but it is also great for parents to use. If you are a clinician, you likely practice *therapeutic bibliotherapy*, which refers to the use of books in a psychiatric or mental health model through intentional and planned interventions—like many of the activities described in these pages.

What Is in This Book

In this book, you'll find over 100 bibliotherapy interventions you can use whether you are a clinician, school counselor, teacher, parent, or any trusted adult working with children. There are so many books in the world, so this resource is not an exhaustive list! I have included my go-to books that children have really identified with and that I use most frequently in my office. Therapists and authors from around the globe have also contributed some of their favorite books and bibliotherapy interventions. I always love to learn about new books that inspire you and your kids, so feel free to email me at tammi@mainlineplaytherapy.com to let me know what books work for you in your playroom.

The chapters in this book are broken down into the following different categories, so it is easy to find an intervention that is most appropriate for your client:

1. Anger and other big emotions
2. Resilience and self-esteem
3. Diversity, equity, and inclusion
4. Psychoeducation on the neuroscience of behaviors
5. Neurodiversity
6. Trauma and attachment, including grief and loss as well as adoption, foster care, and kinship care
7. Separation, divorce, and sibling rivalry
8. Anxiety, fear, perfectionism, and OCD
9. Mindfulness and embodiment
10. Bullying, boundaries, and kindness

The interventions I've included often fit more than one category, so it is helpful to go through them all to find the best fit. Remember that every child is different and that there is no such thing as a one-size-fits-all intervention, so what may be a great option for one child may not be relevant or effective for another. In some of the activities, reproducible worksheets or handouts are included to bring clarity to the interventions. Some include adaptations for telehealth as well. Each chapter also provides a list of suggested books and materials (e.g., toys, art supplies) to add to your toolbox that may help your clients work through what is troubling them.

You'll notice that many of the interventions involve the use of a sand tray and small toys or objects called miniatures. Sandtray is the heart of my practice and has been a game changer for me both personally and professionally. Sandtray therapy is a powerful expressive therapy tool that connects the conscious mind with the unconscious mind, which are often in conflict. Although it may look like a box of sand and toys, it is so much more than that. As miniatures or images are placed in the sand, different emotions come to the surface and the child is able to make sense of their inner world. There are many types of sand therapy, but the interventions listed in this book are sandtray interventions in particular. I use the term *sandtray* because it is a more generic term that incorporates different theoretical orientations and both nondirective and directive prompts.

Finally, all of the interventions in this book are grounded within the theory of play. Play therapy and bibliotherapy complement each other beautifully—both offer that safe psychological distance from the child's problems, taking them on magical adventures through stories that hold significant symbolism and metaphors. Although there are many different play therapy theories, I was trained as a client-centered play therapist, meaning that I invite the child into the playroom and then follow the child's lead. I trust that the child will take me where they need to go and play out what is troubling them.

Regardless of the play therapy to which you subscribe, it is important to remember that play therapy is the most developmentally appropriate treatment for children because children speak the language of play and their toys are their words. In play therapy, the play itself is the source of change, not the medium or the facilitator by which change occurs. Drs. Charles Schaefer and Athena Drewes (2013) highlight the importance of play in their book *The Therapeutic Powers of Play*, where they describe the four powers that play offers: It facilitates communication and self-expression, fosters emotional wellness, enhances social relationships, and increases personal strengths. You will see these different powers addressed in the interventions provided in this book.

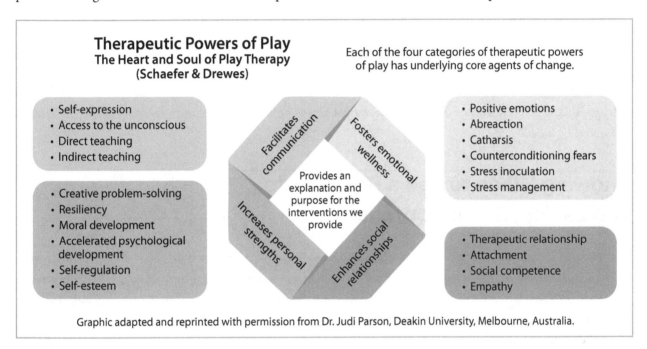

Graphic adapted and reprinted with permission from Dr. Judi Parson, Deakin University, Melbourne, Australia.

How to Use This Book

Most of the books listed in this resource are for children ages 4 to 10, but they can be read at any age. If the book is too long, summarize and improvise! If the book is too short, I have often made up a "part 2" of the story, created a new ending, or asked the child to create their own ending to expand on the themes even more. If introducing books to children is new to you, here are some suggestions to make the process easier:

- Select a book to read with the child and their parent or guardian, making sure it is developmentally appropriate.
- Depending on the age of the child, you can ask the child whom they would like to read the book.
- Be aware of the length of the book and the length of the session—summarize and adjust if necessary.
- Expand the metaphors and themes within the book through nondirective or directive play therapy. You can use art, clay, a sand tray, dollhouses, puppets, LEGO®, music—whatever the child leads you to!
- Expand the story through prompts or questions, such as:
  - What was your favorite part of the book?
  - Who was your favorite character?

- Did you and the character have things in common?
- What would you have done if you were the character in the book?
- How was the main character feeling in the story?
- Are there times you feel that way?
- If you could be one of the characters, who would you be?
- How might this book help you in the future?

When reading to a child who needs sensory input, I often recommend using a weighted cushion or stuffed animal—or a therapy dog if you have one! Cuddling with a parent or caregiver also provides that sensory feedback and nurturing touch. You can also read books outdoors, perhaps while sitting under a tree, to bring in all the senses of nature. I am fortunate to have an outdoor space, and I have several big blankets and pillows that I bring out. (Though I once asked a child if she wanted a pillow and her response was "Grass is nature's pillow.") If you love to incorporate nature into your work with children, check out Dr. Janet Courtney and colleagues' (2022) book *Nature-Based Play and Expressive Therapies: Interventions for Working with Children, Teens, and Families*.

Knowing When to Use a Bottom-Up Versus Top-Down Approach

Talk therapies, like cognitive behavioral therapy, use a top-down approach in that they primarily work through issues at the cognitive level in order to create change. However, in sandtray, play, and other expressive therapies, we often use a bottom-up approach, meaning that we work from the body up—starting with the brain stem, which is responsible for our breathing, heart rate, impulses, and fight-or-flight response. Then we move up to the limbic system, which governs our emotions and feelings, and then to the prefrontal cortex, which is our thinking brain where we can best make decisions, problem-solve, show empathy, and develop self-awareness. I love how Dr. Mona Delahooke (2019) refers to the bottom-up approach as a "body-up" approach for this reason.

Dr. Bruce Perry (Perry & Dobson, 2013) describes the bottom-up approach best with his three R's: regulate, relate, and reason. In order to help a child who is upset or dysregulated, we need to move through the three R's in sequential order: We must start by helping the child *regulate* and calm their nervous system; then *relate* to and connect with them, helping them feel safe in the relationship; and only then can we move on to *reasoning* by working with them to problem-solve. These three R's apply to adults as well. How many of us can think rationally when we're upset? Think about a time when your alarm didn't go off in the morning or your computer decided to crash right before sending out an important email. Chances are this moment threw you off guard and sent you into a state of panic. This happened because your body felt a perceived threat, and your nervous system responded as if you were in true danger.

The same is true of a child who is coming to see you for the first time. They may have anxiety about going to therapy and have no idea what to expect—not to mention that they have not yet determined whether you are a safe person. For children who love books, bibliotherapy may be the perfect regulator to create that safety in the therapeutic relationship. In this situation, books can play a bottom-up role by allowing you to safely introduce play therapy and your role in helping the child.

However, bibliotherapy can often be a top-down approach, too, as books have specific messages for the child to cognitively process. If you are seeing a child who is dysregulated and not feeling safe in the relationship with you, they may reject bibliotherapy interventions because you have not set up the safety for the child to show vulnerability to do the work. Always make sure you can decipher what the child needs at this time. Check in with yourself and ask:

- Is this my agenda or theirs?
- Am I meeting the child where they are?
- Does the intervention or book feel forced? Am I trying too hard?
- Am I trying to prove something to myself or the parents I work with?

If the child does not want to read a book, you can still do the intervention, as many of these interventions can be done without the book. If the child does not want to do the intervention, move on. You want to *invite* children to read these books and do these interventions, but never push them. They will often accept your invitation once they have created an attuned trusting relationship with you.

At this point, you might be wondering, *But what do I do with a child who doesn't like books?* The answer may be as simple as "Don't use books." There are so many creative therapeutic interventions you can do based on these books without necessarily sitting and reading the book itself. You may just want to talk about the book and link it to the child's own story or highlight the book through puppets, art, or sandtray. There are no rules! You may find that certain interventions spark an idea from you or the child, and I encourage you to lean into that curiosity and creativity.

As you embark on this journey of bibliotherapy, please continue to find books that are a good fit for you and your clients. I encourage you to ask your clients what their favorite books are and if they would like to bring them in to share with you. Children often have the best ideas when it comes to creative interventions, yielding powerful messages and bonding experiences. They are our greatest teachers, so let's learn and grow alongside them!

CHAPTER 1

Expression of Anger and Other Big Feelings

Kids are often taught that they are not allowed to show their big feelings, especially when they're angry. The more children are denied this release of emotions, the more dysregulated they can become and the more power struggles with them can escalate. Oftentimes, these power struggles can involve not getting something they really want (whether that be a toy, dessert, or a playdate) or refusing to go to a scheduled activity (whether that be school, a dance class, or another extracurricular activity). Power struggles reflect a need for autonomy, and if transitions like leaving the house cause anxiety, a power struggle will likely occur.

The beauty of books and play therapy is that they allow children to embrace and befriend their anger or sadness while expressing these big feelings in a safe way. For example, a child who struggles with out-of-control feelings might read a book about another child or animal with big emotions, allowing them to connect with the characters and *finally* feel understood. When children identify with the characters, they feel less alone. The power of connection is a vital part of the healing process.

When I think of children who are displaying aggressive behaviors, I always refer back to my dear friend and mentor, Dr. David Crenshaw (2007), who talks about these children being "fawns in gorilla suits." Reacting to these children as gorillas causes their behaviors to escalate—but if we pause to unzip the child's gorilla suit, we see a deer in headlights that needs to be nurtured and loved. We should always be mindful of the need behind the emotions and behaviors. Oftentimes, we'll find that children who are angry or upset simply feel unseen, unheard, or unloved. These behaviors aren't driven by a child's desire for attention but rather by their need for connection.

In this chapter, you will find several interventions to help children better identify and express big emotions, including anger, shame, and sadness. There are also tools to enhance their conflict resolution skills and improve their ability to recognize the full spectrum of emotions they may experience on any given day.

Suggested Materials

- Expressive art supplies (e.g., stones, paint, clay)
- Sandtray figures (e.g., toy soldiers, army equipment, knights)
- Toy handcuffs and toy weapons (depending on your theoretical orientation and comfort)*
- Bobo/bop bag (this is used as a directive tool to titrate their physical intensity, such as counting together, decreasing movement from a punch to a one-finger tap, or scaling light to hard)

Suggested Books

Featured in This Chapter

- *The Rabbit Listened* by Cori Doerrfeld (2018)
- *I Am Human: A Book of Empathy* by Susan Verde, illustrated by Peter H. Reynolds (2018)
- *Anh's Anger* by Gail Silver, illustrated by Christiane Krömer (2009)
- *I See, I See* by Robert Henderson (2019)
- *Alexander and the Terrible, Horrible, No Good, Very Bad Day* by Judith Viorst, illustrated by Ray Cruz (1972)
- *My Zoo: A Book of Feelings* by David Griswold, illustrated by Eliza Reisfeld (2022)
- *I Am Octopus: Playful Projections to Strengthen One's Sense of Self* by Jackie Flynn, illustrated by Angel Flynn (2022b)
- *Be Mindful of Monsters: A Book for Helping Children Accept Their Emotions* by Lauren Stockly, illustrated by Ellen Surrey (2020)
- *The Magic Home: A Displaced Boy Finds a Way to Feel Better* by Isabella Cassina (2020)
- *The Color Monster: A Story About Emotions* by Anna Llenas (2018)
- *The Very Hungry Worry Monsters* by Rosie Greening, illustrated by Lara Ede (2020)
- *A Kids Book About Shame* by Jamie Letourneau (2019)

---

* It's important to remember that aggressive play without a safe space and boundaries, or without resiliency and strengthened regulation and self-esteem, can actually increase big feelings and outbursts. Titration and co-regulation are key!

The Rabbit Listened

Book
The Rabbit Listened by Cori Doerrfeld (2018)

Description
The Rabbit Listened is a must-have for everyone, everywhere! This book is so powerful that little intervention is needed. It is an important message of kindness, empathy, and the power of *being with* rather than *doing*. When the main character in the story, Taylor, struggles with big feelings, all the animals try to help Taylor feel better. They try to tell Taylor how to feel better, which only makes Taylor feel worse. The rabbit shows up at the end and just listens. I have given this book to parents to illustrate the importance of them listening to their child (and to others in their life). I have a large, soft toy rabbit that children often cuddle with as we read. I call this my "therapy bunny" and each child in my playroom gives it a special name so that they know that the bunny is always there to listen and hold space for them.

Treatment Goals
- Teach kindness and empathy
- Show the power of listening
- Identify how family members react (and how the child reacts to their reactions)
- Identify what children need and *don't* need when they have big feelings

Materials
- Stuffed animal bunny
- Paper and markers, sand tray and animal figures, or animal puppets (optional)

Directions
1. Introduce the stuffed "therapy bunny." Invite the client to name the rabbit and cuddle with it if they would like to.
2. Read the book with the client. As you get to each animal's reaction to Taylor being upset, pause and check in with the client by asking what they have experienced when they have been upset:
   - Who do you know who is like the chicken and wants to talk, talk, talk?
   - Who do you know who is like the bear and wants you to yell about it?
   - Who do you know who is like the hyena and wants to laugh about it?
   - Who do you know who is like the ostrich and wants to hide and pretend nothing happened?
3. You can further explore and reenact the different animals' reactions by drawing the animals on paper or in the sand tray, using figures or puppets, or inviting the child to act out the animals.

"I Am Human" Collage

Book
I Am Human: A Book of Empathy by Susan Verde, illustrated by Peter H. Reynolds (2018)

Description
I Am Human is a beautiful book about being human and imperfect. There are many things that make us human, and this story highlights the ability to show empathy. In this intervention, the client is invited to make an "I Am Human" collage, which is a combination of a vision board and an "All About Me" poster where they can explore, celebrate, and learn from all that makes them human.

Treatment Goals
- Enhance empathy, kindness, and compassion
- Teach that we can learn from our mistakes

Materials
- Poster board
- Magazines
- Glue stick
- Scissors
- Markers
- Other arts and crafts materials as desired

Directions
1. Read the book with the child.
2. Invite the client to make a collage by finding images and adding them to the poster board. You can keep the prompt open-ended by simply saying, "Make a collage of what makes you human."
3. If your client would like more help getting started, you can follow up with questions like:
    - What are your big dreams?
    - What are you curious about?
    - What are some cool things that amaze you?
    - What are some things you are fearful of?
    - Is it hard to try new things?
    - What is a poor choice you made that became a better choice with thoughtfulness?
    - What do you do to show compassion and lend a helping hand to others?

Anger Stones

Book
Anh's Anger by Gail Silver, illustrated by Christiane Krömer (2009)

Description
This book tells the story of a little boy, Anh, who is building a block tower and does not want to stop what he is doing to eat dinner. He becomes angry as he cries, screams, and falls apart. Anh's grandfather tells him to go to his room and "sit with his anger." Anh wonders what this means, until his anger appears in the form of a red-haired monster who asks to be his friend. They sing, dance, and breathe in and out. As Anh plays with his anger, he becomes calmer; his anger grows smaller and then disappears. This intervention expands on the book by giving your client an opportunity to befriend and decorate a stone that symbolizes their angry feelings. Teaching children to externalize their anger in this way is a powerful therapeutic tool to help them gain control. It helps them understand that anger is a feeling inside of them, but it does not define who they are.

Treatment Goals
- Externalize feelings of anger
- Decrease lashing-out behaviors
- Enhance strategies to calm down

Materials
- Stones
- Permanent markers or paint
- Additional art supplies as desired

Directions
1. Read the book with the client.
2. Ask the client, "What does it mean for you to 'sit with your anger'?"
3. Invite the client to decorate a stone to represent their anger. They may use permanent markers, paint, or whatever materials they wish.
4. Invite the client to give their anger stone a name, sit with their stone, make friends with their stone, dance with their stone, and play with their stone.
5. The child can keep the stone in their pocket or in a special place to help them ground themselves. It will serve as a reminder that their anger is not their enemy.
6. Let the child know that they need to take good care of their anger stone. It is not for throwing and it is not for hurting themselves or others; it is a stone to remind them to slow down and settle their busy thoughts. (If you have a client who you feel may be unsafe with their anger stone, you may want to use model magic, paper, or another material that they cannot use to hurt themselves or others.)

I See, I See*

Book
I See, I See by Robert Henderson (2019)

Description
This vibrant children's picture book is a fun way to teach kids of all ages about differing perspectives. The book uses rhyming, opposite viewpoints, and images to help readers literally see two differing points of view. The book is designed to be read by two people sitting across from each other, allowing each reader to experience a new perspective on each page. For example, a thumbs-up can also be seen as a thumbs-down when the book is turned upside down. By inverting the page and viewing the same image from a new perspective, readers realize that there can be more than one way to view things. This intervention uses scenario cards to help your client explore different situations and viewpoints. A second option is to have the client create something with air-dry clay that can be viewed from multiple perspectives. You can do this intervention in an individual session with the child, in a family session, or even in a group setting.

Treatment Goals
- Identify and normalize different thoughts and feelings
- Build empathy and communication skills
- Increase understanding of differing points of view to increase conflict resolution skills
- Expand flexible thinking to enhance problem-solving abilities

Materials
- Picture or scenario cards (provided at the end of this intervention)
- People miniatures (optional)
- Air-dry clay (and, optionally, markers or acrylic paint markers)

Directions
1. Read the book *I See, I See* while sitting across from each other.
2. As you read, discuss and explore the different perspectives shown in the book.
3. Explore how different viewpoints—such as parent and child, teacher and student, or two peers—can occur in daily life.

---

* Intervention by Lisa Remey, LPC-S, RPT-S

4. Utilize scenario cards to identify different perspectives, thoughts, and feelings, identifying how each is correct with multiple ways to experience a situation. For example:

    Scenario: The teacher asks a student to be quiet in class.

    Perspectives: The student may think the teacher does not like them.

    The teacher may have a headache and need a quiet classroom.

5. Alternatively, invite the client to create an individual item from air-dry clay that can be viewed in multiple ways. This may take some time as the client explores ideas. An example may be a clay creation that could be viewed as a bowl or as a hat, or even an item that is different when looked at from the front versus the back. The addition of the clay activity provides an opportunity for the client to have a tangible reminder during the week of the skills they learned in session.

Scenario Cards

Felix does not want to play with Sam at recess.	The teacher sounds angry when giving instructions.
Eva is not invited to join a game.	Jordan's parent yells at him for not doing his homework.
Gabrielle is not allowed to have a sleepover.	Jayden was looking forward to weekend plans, which were suddenly canceled.
Brianna is not invited to George's birthday party.	Isaiah's teacher corrects him in front of the class.
The class field trip is canceled.	Julia's friend does not want to play her favorite game.

"Terrible, Horrible, No Good, Very Bad Day" Drawing*

Book
Alexander and the Terrible, Horrible, No Good, Very Bad Day by Judith Viorst, illustrated by Ray Cruz (1972)

Description
This classic children's book tells the story of a boy named Alexander, who wakes up in the morning with gum in his hair and decides that it is going to be a terrible, horrible, no good, very bad day. Throughout the rest of his day, Alexander encounters various scenarios that go awry, adding to his frustration. He soon realizes that everyone has bad days sometimes and that everyone gets angry. This intervention is best used in a group setting when you know each group member and have established rapport with them. However, it can also be used in an individual session.

Treatment Goals
- Identify factors contributing to anger as well as warning signs that the child may have
- Express and communicate feelings of anger and frustration in an appropriate manner

Materials
- Paper
- Coloring utensils

Directions
1. Read the book out loud to the group. You can interchange some of the names in the book and situations to reflect group members and their current frustrations. This helps normalize the experience of anger—reminding children that everyone gets angry sometimes—and it also helps the book be more personal and meaningful for each child.

2. Have each group member draw a picture to represent a "terrible, horrible, no good, very bad day" they recently experienced.

3. Process the drawings with the group and invite each child to share their drawing if desired. Continue to facilitate conversation regarding anger and frustration by asking questions like:
    - What was easy (or difficult) about this activity?
    - What did you enjoy?
    - What did you learn about yourself?
    - What will you be able to do the next time you get angry?

---

* Intervention by Christine Wheeler-Case Jones, MA, LPC

Mixed-Up Animals*

Book
My Zoo: A Book of Feelings by David Griswold, illustrated by Eliza Reisfeld (2022)

Description
My Zoo is a book about feelings, including how to identify them and how it's possible to feel a few different emotions—or even all of them!—at the same time. It uses animals to represent different feelings (like an angry lion, a calm sloth, and a happy puppy) and invites children to look inside themselves so they can get to know, accept, and become a "zookeeper" of all their feelings. This intervention builds on the psychoeducation provided in the book by inviting the client to explore their many overlapping feelings via an art activity.

Treatment Goals
- Identify and explore feelings through creative expression
- Understand what emotions physically feel like and what they may look like

Materials
- Paper
- Coloring utensils

Directions
1. Read the book with the client.
2. Discuss the different feelings that go with each animal.
3. Ask the child to choose three feelings they sometimes experience and to combine these into a new animal that features different parts of each one. They can then name their new feelings animal. For example, if the client expresses that they often feel embarrassed (turtle), scared (lemur), and happy (puppy), they might draw an animal with the shell of a turtle, the eyes of a lemur, and the tail of a puppy—they might decide to call this creature a "leturpy!"

Variation
- This intervention can also be done using *I Am Octopus: Playful Projections to Strengthen One's Sense of Self* by Jackie Flynn, illustrated by Angel Flynn (2022b). This book, which is an application of the Oaklander model of play therapy, uses animal analogies and projection questions to help children explore their strengths, struggles, choices, felt sensation of emotions, and options to regulate their autonomic nervous system.

---

* Intervention by Kelly Pullen, MA, LPC-S, RPT

Shrink Your Monsters*

Book
Be Mindful of Monsters: A Book for Helping Children Accept Their Emotions by Lauren Stockly, illustrated by Ellen Surrey (2020)

Description
This book illustrates the power of mindfulness, self-compassion, empathy, and acceptance in navigating and embracing our emotions. Through the main character, Ezzy, children learn that just like the monsters in the story, emotions can seem overwhelming at times, but by acknowledging and understanding them, they can be tamed and transformed into allies.

Treatment Goals
- Teach the importance of accepting and befriending all our emotions

Materials
- Shrinky Dinks® sheets
- Markers
- Scissors
- Shrinky Dinks oven, toaster oven, or standard oven
- Sand tray, shoebox, or other container
- Sandtray miniatures, stones, or other small objects

Directions
1. Read the book with the child.
2. Explain to the child that our emotions all serve a purpose and that it is okay to experience them—avoiding them only makes them larger and stronger. When we start to see our "worry monster," for example, as trying to protect us in some ways, we can learn to befriend it. And when we face our monsters, they shrink! They're not so powerful anymore.
3. Invite the child to use the Shrinky Dinks sheet to draw a representation of their anger monster, depression monster, worry monster, fear monster, or any other big emotion they have a difficult time experiencing. When they have finished, cut around the monster to trim any excess material from the edges.
4. Invite the child to create a "trap" for their monster using the container. In the trap, the child can place miniatures, stones, or other objects to represent their strengths and resources.

---

* Intervention by Sophia Ansari, LPCC, RPT

5. Explain that the child will leave their monster in the trap and that during their next visit, the child will be able to check on their monster. You may also choose to assign the child a task before the next session to use one of their strengths in a new way every day during the week.

6. In between sessions, shrink the child's monster in an oven. When the child returns for the following session, they will see their monster has shrunk! Or you can use a Shrinky Dinks oven during the session, helping the child verbalize their strengths and reframe their negative thoughts while their monster shrinks: "It's okay, worry monster! I've got this!"

The Magic Home*

Book
The Magic Home: A Displaced Boy Finds a Way to Feel Better by Isabella Cassina (2020)

Description
The Magic Home offers support for children who have faced disruptions or difficult changes in their lives, resulting in feelings of sadness, loss, and displacement. The story is about a little boy who lives with his family; plays happily in the courtyard with his brother and sister, a brown dog, and a fluffy white rabbit; and cannot wait to start school. Suddenly, he has to leave for an unpredictable journey. He faces many uncertainties in his new life until he meets Ina, a schoolteacher who shares a secret that helps him feel less lonely, gives him a sense of control over the circumstances, and gives him hope for a brighter future. The secret is that we all have a "magic home" and all our fondest memories will always be there with us, as they live in our hearts and will remain there for as long as we want them to. At the end of the story, a series of activities related to this metaphor are described to tap into the child's resilience using the healing power of play and expressive arts. In addition, it includes photocopiable pictures of the main characters that the child can complete to facilitate the processing and recognition of feelings.

Treatment Goals
- Help the child identify big feelings
- Support the child in having a sense of control over the context
- Foster the child's resilience

Materials
- Paper and coloring utensils
- Clay, LEGO® bricks, or miniatures (optional)
- Puppets or disguises (optional)

Directions
1. Read the book with the child.
2. Start the conversation with a simple open-ended question that makes sure to address specific parts of the story, such as:
    - What are the main changes in the boy's life?
    - How does he feel at the beginning of the story (including symptoms in his body)? How does he feel at the end of the story?

---
* Intervention by Isabella Cassina, MA, TPS, CAGS, PhD candidate

- What happens to you and your body when there's a change in your life that you don't like or want?
- What does the boy do in difficult times to find relief?

3. Invite the child to build their own "magic home" and its contents (people, pets, and belongings) using an expressive modality of their choice (e.g., clay, LEGO bricks, or miniatures). They can also draw their magic home and its contents on paper. In this case, suggest that the child draw a large heart and place all the elements inside it.

4. If expanding the sequence of activities would be appropriate, invite the child to dramatize the story using puppets or disguises. You can suggest that they change the ending of the story to their liking. It is advisable to end each activity by offering a brief moment of verbal sharing related to the emotions the child felt during and after the activity. For older children who wish, you can also offer the option of sharing their emotions through writing.

Monster Simon Says*

Book
The Color Monster: A Story About Emotions by Anna Llenas (2018)

Description
In this story, a monster who is experiencing many feelings all at once learns how to identify and sort these emotions by associating each one with a different color, which helps him gain peace and self-awareness. This intervention invites the client to help the color monster figure out his feelings through a simple game that is analogous to Simon Says (i.e., you name the emotion the monster is feeling, and the child acts out the emotion). It is also a great activity for caregivers to participate in during the session.

Treatment Goals
- Identify and explore feelings through kinesthetic play
- Encourage emotional intelligence through identification and expression of feelings
- Strengthen impulse control and listening skills
- Build rapport through games of reciprocity and kinesthetic play

Materials
- None needed

Directions
1. Read the book with the client.
2. Say, "Let's help the color monster figure out what he is feeling! When I say an emotion, you show the color monster what that emotion looks like. So when I say, 'The color monster feels . . . angry,' you act out feeling angry, like by growling and stomping around."
3. Similar to Simon Says, the child should only act out feelings that begin with the prompt "The color monster feels . . ." Otherwise, the child should remain in place and wait for the next cue. You can playfully point out to the child when they accidentally act out a feeling that did not begin with the prompt (e.g., "Whoops, that sure is what anger looks like, but the color monster didn't feel that!").
4. Give the client some time to practice responding to your prompts, then give them the opportunity to be the one in control while you act out the emotions. Here are some more suggestions for feelings and responses you can use, though you want to allow the child to decide what each feeling looks like:
    - *Happy:* Jump and clap your hands
    - *Sad:* Cry and rub your eyes
    - *Afraid:* Hide behind your hands
    - *Calm:* Close your eyes and breathe deeply
    - *In love:* Hug yourself and say, "I love you"

---
* Intervention by Kelly Pullen, MA, LPC-S, RPT

Monster Puppet Play*

Book
The Color Monster: A Story About Emotions by Anna Llenas (2018)

Description
In this story, a monster who is experiencing many feelings all at once learns how to identify and sort these emotions by associating each one with a different color, which helps him gain peace and self-awareness. In this accompanying intervention, children will have an opportunity to personify many different color monsters through the use of finger puppets, allowing them to explore a variety of different emotions.

Treatment Goals
- Identify and explore feelings through artistic creation and puppet play

Materials
- Six toilet paper rolls
- Thick craft paper in red, yellow, green, blue, black, and pink
- Markers
- Scissors
- Glue stick
- Googly eyes or other additional art supplies (optional)

Directions
1. Read the book with the client.
2. Invite the client to make monster finger puppets out of toilet paper rolls. Encourage the client to take a toilet paper roll, wrap it in colored paper, and use the other materials to decorate it to look like a particular emotion, continuing until they have made a variety of feelings monsters.
3. Have the client retell the story from the book or make up their own story using their puppets. They can keep the puppets at your office if desired to make more feelings puppet shows in the future or take them home to use with their parents.

---

* Intervention by Kelly Pullen, MA, LPC-S, RPT

Monster Feelings Sandtray*

Book
The Color Monster: A Story About Emotions by Anna Llenas (2018)

Description
In this story, a monster who is experiencing many feelings all at once learns how to identify and sort these emotions by associating each one with a different color, which helps him gain peace and self-awareness. This intervention expands on the story by allowing children to use sandtray miniatures to personify the six different emotions that the color monster experienced: anger, happiness, sadness, fear, calm, and love. Children are invited to dedicate as much space as they want to each emotion in the sand tray, which gives insight into their emotional world.

Treatment Goals
- Explore feelings with psychological distance and creativity

Materials
- Sand tray and a variety of miniatures

Directions
1. Read the book with the client.
2. Introduce the sand tray and explain that there will be six sections in the tray today, one to represent each feeling the color monster had (angry, happy, sad, afraid, calm, and in love).
3. Invite them to choose as many miniatures as they like to represent the feelings. The client can also divide the tray however they wish—for example, they may decide that "happy" gets a larger portion than "love." While the client is working, sit back and take note of the process.
4. After the client is finished, process the tray together. Some processing questions could be:
    - Can you tell me about your tray?
    - If you could name this tray, what would it be?
    - Can you tell me about this section (or this miniature)?
    - If you could name this section, what would it be?
    - Is there a section (or miniature) that speaks to you the most?
    - Which section has the most energy?
    - If that miniature could speak to you, what would it say?

---

* Intervention by Kelly Pullen, MA, LPC-S, RPT

Color Monster Creation*

Book
The Color Monster: A Story About Emotions by Anna Llenas (2018)

Description
In this story, a monster who is experiencing many feelings all at once learns how to identify and sort these emotions by associating each one with a different color, which helps him gain peace and self-awareness. Similar to the *Monster Puppet Play* intervention (p. 16), this activity invites children to personify their own color monsters but also gives them the freedom to use whatever artistic medium they would like, which opens the door to explore their emotions from a safe psychological distance.

Treatment Goals
- Identify and explore feelings though artistic and creative expression

Materials
- Paper
- Coloring utensils
- Additional art supplies (e.g., scissors, glue, pipe cleaners, stickers, glitter, gems, feathers, paint)

Directions
1. Read the book with the client.
2. Invite the client to make their own color monster using the materials provided. They can simply draw their monster using the coloring utensils or create a more intricate collage that includes three-dimensional elements such as feathers, pipe cleaners, and so on. The choice is theirs!
3. When the client is done with their creation, discuss how their monster is feeling today. You might use some of the following prompts or create your own:
    - I wonder how your monster is feeling today.
    - I wonder what caused your monster to feel this way.
    - I wonder if your monster has many feelings.
    - I wonder if there is anything your monster needs to say.
    - I wonder if there is anything your monster needs to hear.
    - I wonder if there is anything you would like to say to your monster.
    - I wonder if there is anything your monster needs today. (If the client says yes, and it is a tangible object, such as a blanket, you can follow up with: Would you like to make a blanket for your monster?)

---
* Intervention by Kelly Pullen, MA, LPC-S, RPT

The Very Hungry Worry Monsters*

Book
The Very Hungry Worry Monsters by Rosie Greening, illustrated by Lara Ede (2020)

Description
The Very Hungry Worry Monsters is a fun way for children to take a look at their anxiety, fears, and worries as something separate from them. In this activity, you'll invite the child to create their own worry monster, which they can keep in a safe place for whenever it is needed. They can then give away and "feed" their worries to the monster to find relief from their big feelings. This intervention can be done at any phase of treatment and is an opportunity to involve the caregiver as well.

Treatment Goals
- Reduce anxiety and facilitate expression of emotions
- Boost self-confidence (the child is in control of their worry thoughts!)

Materials
- Empty tissue box
- Construction paper
- Scissors
- Glue
- Additional art supplies (e.g., googly eyes, cotton balls, stickers, stamps)

Directions
1. Read the book with the client.
2. Invite the client to create their own worry monster! Use the tissue box opening as the mouth of the hungry worry monster. Encourage the client to decorate their monster with the supplies of their choice.
3. Invite the child to write down or draw their worries or fears on slips of paper. They can then crumple or tear the paper up (or both!), "feed" it to their monster through the tissue box opening, and take a few deep belly breaths. Allow the client to repeat this process as needed.
4. They can take their worry monster home and keep it in a safe place for whenever it is needed.

Adaptation for Telehealth
- This can be done virtually as long as the child has the supplies needed. Who doesn't always have empty tissue boxes? ☺

---
* Intervention by Rachael Scott, MA, LPC, RPT

Shame Monster*

Book
A Kids Book About Shame by Jamie Letourneau (2019)

Description
Shame can be an overwhelming feeling that is not often labeled or discussed. Unacknowledged shame can lead to both internalizing and externalizing behaviors in children and is especially detrimental to those who have experienced trauma. This intervention allows your client to safely explore and express their own feelings of shame by creating a metaphorical visual of their shame monster.

Treatment Goals
- Identify what shame feels like
- Increase understanding that shame is a difficult and normal human emotion
- Identify triggers that elicit shame
- Develop strategies to identify, express, and work through shame

Materials
- Paper
- Additional ripped pieces of paper big enough to write on
- Glue
- Coloring utensils
- Sand tray (optional)

Directions
1. While reading the book with the client, encourage them to share any experiences when they (or someone close to them) may have experienced shame. Encourage the child to discuss where in their body they felt this emotion and what it felt like to them.
2. Once you finish reading the book, invite the client to make their own shame monster. They can use pieces of ripped paper to design what they believe their shame monster might look like. You can also encourage them to draw their shame monster or construct a shame monster within the sand tray.
3. If your client needs help getting started, you may wonder aloud about different attributes a shame monster may have, such as how it feels; its size, color, or shape; and so forth.
4. Once the client has completed their shame monster, encourage them to name it.

---
* Intervention by Margot Burke, PsyD

5. Next, encourage the client to write down various triggers that elicit feelings of shame within them. You can normalize these feelings and discuss that it is a difficult human emotion.

6. Brainstorm with the client how they can talk back to their shame monster. Encourage the client to think of one or two statements to boss back their shame monster and have them add this to their shame monster paper. Encourage them to talk back to their shame monster using one of these statements over the next week or to share their shame monster art with a trusted adult.

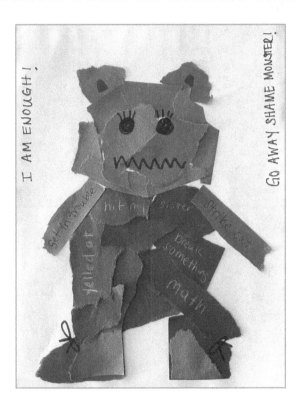

CHAPTER 2

Resilience and Self-Esteem

Resilience is a big topic in my playroom, as many children can be so hard on themselves that they quickly crumble under pressure. Some children even see themselves as failures and spiral into negative thinking. You may be wondering what makes some children more resilient than others. The reality is that kids are all wired differently. Some have more vulnerable nervous systems, sensory sensitivities, or learning difficulties that erode their self-esteem. They see everyone else's life as better than theirs. We also need to recognize how hard it can be to be a kid. So often, kids receive negative messages at home and at school—about their capability, their intelligence, and their overall worth—that can affect their behavior and their performance.

As therapists, it is important that we do not just put a label of "low self-esteem" on the child and create a treatment plan to "build resilience"; instead, we must delve deeper. We must connect to the child's hurts and celebrate the strengths they have to offer to the world. So much energy and attention go into negativity, but we need to shift and energize what is going well. We have to point out all the good that we see in each child and coach their parents to do the same. When we are able to help children see their amazing strengths and fill their love tanks, they can begin to feel it internally. I often use metaphors and analogies to teach resilience and inner beauty in the playroom. One metaphor that I love to use is the example of geodes, which are rocks that look ordinary on the outside, but inside they are each unique, filled with extraordinary beauty. Like geodes, children need to know of their self-worth and inner beauty so they can grow into successful and resilient humans.

Similarly, I often use an oak tree and palm tree analogy that was introduced to me by my colleague Michael Fogel to represent the concepts of resiliency and flexible thinking. The oak tree may look strong and sturdy, but in the midst of a storm, its branches just snap (which is why I call it the "no" tree). Although the palm tree does not look as strong, it always bounces back and can endure the toughest of storms (making it a "yes" tree!). To reinforce these concepts, I will often ask children to share with me their "palm tree moments" for the week. These are moments where they showed flexibility when they may have been more rigid in the past. When children show wins like being flexible in situations where they used to be stuck, we can celebrate their progress and build their resiliency.

The interventions in this chapter will help your clients build resiliency and enhance their self-esteem—turning them from "I can't" kids into "I can" kids.

Suggested Materials

- Superhero capes (have the child make their own!)
- Greatness sticks* or popsicle sticks
- Sandtray miniatures with different body shapes and sizes, traps and fences, superheroes and villains, scales, food
- Gems, stones, and geodes
- Play food and cash register
- Expressive art supplies (e.g., paint, markers, paper, clay)

Suggested Books

Featured in This Chapter

- *Three Little Words* by Amy Novesky, illustrated by Grace Lee (2016)
- *What Do You Do with an Idea?* by Kobi Yamada, illustrated by Mae Besom (2014)
- *What Do You Do with a Problem?* by Kobi Yamada, illustrated by Mae Besom (2016)
- *What Do You Do with a Chance?* by Kobi Yamada, illustrated by Mae Besom (2018)
- *I Can Do Hard Things: Mindful Affirmations for Kids* by Gabi Garcia, illustrated by Charity Russell (2018)
- *Everyone Poops* by Tarō Gomi (1977/2020)
- *I've Got This! A Child's Guide to Lifting Yourself Up When You're Feeling Down* by Lisa Shadburn, illustrated by Robert Noonan (2022)
- *Bloom* by Ruth Forman, illustrated by Talia Skyles (2022)
- *Happiness Doesn't Come from Headstands* by Tamara Levitt (2017)
- *Because* by Mo Willems (2019)
- *The Reflection in Me* by Marc Colagiovanni, illustrated by Peter H. Reynolds (2017)
- *I Am Octopus: Playful Projections to Strengthen One's Sense of Self* by Jackie Flynn, illustrated by Angel Flynn (2022b)
- *Casey's Greatness Wings: Teaching Mindfulness, Connection & Courage to Children* by Tammi Van Hollander, illustrated by Annie Wilkinson (2018a)
- *I Love You the Purplest* by Barbara M. Joosse, illustrated by Mary Whyte (1996)

Also Recommended

- *The Greatness Chair* by Kathleen Friend (2018)
- *The Nose That Didn't Fit* by Andi Green (2008)
- *I Like Me!* by Nancy Carlson (1988)
- *Oh, the Places You'll Go!* by Dr. Seuss (1990)
- *I Am Enough* by Grace Byers, illustrated by Keturah A. Bobo (2018)
- *Maybe* by Kobi Yamada, illustrated by Gabriella Barouch (2019)

---

* Premade *Greatness Sticks*™ and *Greatness Cards* are available for purchase at https://www.mainlineplaytherapy.com/shop-1.

The "Never Give Up" Tank

Book
Three Little Words by Amy Novesky, illustrated by Grace Lee (2016)

Description
I love this inspirational book of perseverance, which is based on Pixar's movie *Finding Dory*. In the story, the author explains that no matter how hard things can feel, we just need to remember these three words: *just keep swimming*. Similar to the book, this intervention invites children to make a "never give up" tank that encourages them to persevere in the face of difficulties.

Treatment Goals
- Teach flexibility
- Build perseverance and resilience

Materials
- A bowl, box, or other container
- Small colorful pom-poms
- Additional art supplies to decorate the container (e.g., glitter, stickers, markers)

Directions
1. Read the book with the child.
2. Explain to the child that our brains can sometimes get stuck when we are asked to do hard things. In these moments, we may just want to give up or quit. Ask the child what they think would have happened if Dory gave up. Then ask them to identify all the times they were like Dory and *just kept on swimming*.
3. Invite the child to create a "never give up" tank and to decorate it with whatever materials they choose. Then have the child fill their tank with colorful pom-poms to represent all the times they showed flexibility in the face of difficulty. If the child cannot think of anything, offer them pom-poms to recognize the times you've seen them being flexible, even if it was just in the moment: "You just showed flexibility by doing this project with me. You could have chosen to do something else with our time together, but you trusted that this would be fun."
4. You can keep the tank in your office and revisit it each week, adding pom-poms as the child or caregiver is able to identify these flexible moments that help build resiliency. Or you can encourage the child and caregiver to take it home, add pom-poms together, and bring it in each week to show you the child's progress.

Create Your Opportunity

Books
- *What Do You Do with an Idea?* by Kobi Yamada, illustrated by Mae Besom (2014)
- *What Do You Do with a Problem?* by Kobi Yamada, illustrated by Mae Besom (2016)
- *What Do You Do with a Chance?* by Kobi Yamada, illustrated by Mae Besom (2018)

Description

The *What Do You Do?* books integrate seamlessly with projection techniques from the Oaklander model (Oaklander, 1978, 2006; Fried & McKenna, 2020), which helps children to externalize any problems or ideas. It offers endless possibilities of creativity and wonder to deepen curiosity and build resilience. No idea is too big, no chance is too small, and every problem is an opportunity to grow and learn. In this intervention, you will ask your client to identify an idea they have, a problem they are facing, or a chance they've been given, and then invite them to create it. Having children create opportunities from their idea, problem, or chance is incredibly powerful!

Treatment Goals
- Teach the child to creatively problem-solve
- Enhance flexibility and creativity
- Build resiliency

Materials
- Paper and coloring utensils, clay, or sand tray and miniatures

Directions

1. Read a quote from one of these books aloud. It is helpful to choose quotes that focus on the child's individual needs or their favorite quote in the book. For example: "My problem held an opportunity. It was an opportunity for me to learn and to grow. To be brave. To do something." The child can read the quote or write it if they choose.

2. Invite the client to draw, use clay, or create a sandtray to represent the idea, problem, or chance in their life. For example, they might create an angry dragon to represent the problem of being bullied at school.

3. Invite the child to share what they have made.

4. Ask the child to speak as the idea, problem, or chance and to give it a voice as you ask it questions like:
    - What is the hardest thing about being you?
    - How do people see you?

- What makes you important?
- What do people learn from you?

5. Invite the client to draw, use clay, or do a sandtray to represent an opportunity that might come from this idea, problem, or chance. Then ask similar processing questions, following the child's lead.

6. At the end of the session, the child can take a picture of the opportunity to carry with them.

Doing Hard Things*

Book

I Can Do Hard Things: Mindful Affirmations for Kids by Gabi Garcia, illustrated by Charity Russell (2018)**

Description

I Can Do Hard Things is a beautiful and empowering book that includes important messages about strength, resilience, and diversity. It contains several mindful affirmations to provide kids with words of encouragement when they need it most. As the book says, "Hard things can be about the things we think, feel, say or do. What's hard for me may not be hard for you. You are you, and I am me. We walk through the world differently." This intervention expands on the book by inviting clients to create their own mindful affirmations through a combination of bibliotherapy and Virtual Sandtray® therapy. While this intervention can be used at any time during the course of treatment, it is best used when solid rapport has been established, as this allows you to more deeply explore hard things from the perspective of the child.

Treatment Goals

- Build resilience and empowerment
- Provide encouragement with mindful affirmations
- Facilitate self-expression, self-exploration, and self-identification

Materials

- Virtual Sandtray app on an iPad or iPhone***

Directions

1. Read the book with the client.
2. Open the client's account within the Virtual Sandtray app and begin a fresh, new tray creation.
3. Invite the client to create a tray that depicts a "hard thing." Start with one theme: a known task, interaction, experience, or similar situation. When they have finished, save the tray and name it accordingly. This step is a bit of a warm-up and can be repeated as appropriate.
4. When the client is ready to broaden, create a new tray and divide it into halves (or quarters). Build upon the previous successes by asking the client to identify two (or four) times they were able to do hard things. Save this tray before moving on.
5. Create another tray and ask the client to identify two (or four) times they were not able to do hard things; save this tray as well.

---

* Intervention by Jessica Stone, PhD, RPT-S
** A Spanish edition of this book is also available: *Yo Puedo Hacer Cosas Difíciles: Afirmaciones Conscientes Para Niños*.
*** The Virtual Sandtray app is available for download at https://jessicastonephd.com/virtual-sandtray-app. You can also use a physical sand tray.

6. These steps can be repeated as desired.

7. Throughout this process, witness and honor the client's creations. You may also intervene, discuss, reinforce, or problem-solve at each step of the intervention according to your play therapy or sand therapy theoretical foundation. You can review saved trays and pictures of the trays together with the caregivers or on your own alone for depictions, themes, progression, regression, and more.

8. If it aligns with your theoretical approach to sandtray work, you may ask the client to identify or write down any mindful affirmations based on what they've created in their trays. To integrate these affirmations in their day-to-day interactions, remind the client to use the affirmations on their list when faced with a hard time during the week. As appropriate, these can also be shared with caregivers or teachers for further support.

Adaptation for Telehealth

- Conduct the session and read the book through a HIPAA compliant telehealth platform, and connect virtually through the Virtual Sandtray app.

Everyone Poops*

Book
Everyone Poops by Tarō Gomi (1977/2020)

Description
On the surface, this book is about how the body functions. It is simple and direct, and has a degree of silliness because of its focus. However, because of its focus on "poop," it also provides you with an opportunity to deepen its underlying meaning and talk about imperfections, mistakes, and the ungraceful aspects of life that we all experience as we navigate the world. Indeed, although we all look different on the surface, we still have shared basic experiences. Ultimately, this book highlights how we have a say in our self-esteem and body image, normalizes our bodies and our bodily functions, and promotes acceptance of self and others.

Treatment Goals
- Normalize curiosity and discussion about bodies and bodily functions
- Model language that creates an accepting relationship with the self, including the body
- Help children flip the switch from inner critic to inner coach

Materials
- Miniatures (or other materials that can be used for figures, such as clay for sculpting or paper and stickers or pictures from magazines)

Directions
1. Read the book with the child.
2. Invite the child to choose a figure to represent the self. Instead of choosing a figure, you can also supply materials for creating a drawing or a three-dimensional version of the self.
3. Explain that the self is made up of what you think, feel, and do; it's what happens in your brain, heart, and body.
4. Invite the child to share or create a story about their self that is fascinating, cool, or surprising.
5. Then invite the child to share or create a story about their self that bothers, annoys, or upsets them or that they just do not like. Allow the child to choose whether to use additional miniatures to represent this part of their self.
6. Next, have them flip the switch in the spirit of *Everyone Poops*: How can this part that bothers them be viewed in another way? Depending on the child's answer, you might offer an alternative perspective that normalizes the utility of this part of themselves.

---

* Intervention by Jodi Ann Mullen, PhD, LMHC, RPT-S

7. Now is an opportunity to illuminate the child's connections to others. Allow the child to choose additional miniatures to help them honor something about others that is fascinating, cool, or surprising.

8. Give the child the option of taking a photo of what they created and giving it a title. This gives both the therapist and the child an opportunity to revisit what emerged from this intervention in the future. Additionally, the child can come up with a title that may speak to the bigger picture, or theme, of how the child sees themselves, others, and the world.

I've Got This*

Book
I've Got This! A Child's Guide to Lifting Yourself Up When You're Feeling Down by Lisa Shadburn, illustrated by Robert Noonan (2022)

Description
This intervention uses the book *I've Got This!* to help children cope with stressful situations through the use of self-encouragement and self-compassion. All children have worries and fears, but they often don't realize that the things they say to themselves can sometimes make things even harder. With this intervention, you'll help your client identify helpful, encouraging words they can use to replace worried or discouraging thoughts. If your client has difficulty thinking of something encouraging to say to themselves, ask them to think of something they could say to support a friend in the same situation.

Treatment Goals
- Increase positive self-talk and decrease negative self-talk
- Enhance clients' ability to using coping skills in the face of difficulty, frustration, or worry
- Improve self-confidence and self-efficacy

Materials
- Paper
- Colored pencils or pens
- Sticky notes

Directions
1. Read the book with the client. As you read the book together, ask the child if they can think of a time when they felt the same way as the characters in the book.
2. Help the client think of phrases the characters could have said to encourage themselves and create more positive self-talk while overcoming their negative thinking.
3. Next, ask the client to think of encouraging phrases they can say to themselves when they are feeling discouraged. If needed, you can share the following examples to illustrate discouraging thoughts and identify encouraging words that someone might think or say to themselves instead.

---
* Intervention by Lisa Shadburn, PsyD, RPT-S

Discouraging Thought	Encouraging Words
This is too hard. I'll never get it! →	This is hard, but nobody is perfect the first time. If I keep trying, I know I can do this!
I'm terrible at this. →	I have the ability to get better at this if I practice. The more I practice, the better I'll get!
Everyone is going to hate me. →	I'm a good person. I will be as kind and helpful as I can, and people will notice.

4. After you've finished making a list of positive self-statements, invite the client to pick a few encouraging phrases that resonate with them and choose a color to write each statement on a sticky note. Invite them to take the notes home and post them somewhere in their home where they can see them. You can also decorate the list of encouraging phrases to send home with them as well. Discuss how they can use these phrases to practice self-encouragement at home, school, and elsewhere.

5. To encourage caregivers to continue helping children learn and practice self-encouragement, ask them to do the following between sessions:

    - If they are in a frustrating situation, they can acknowledge their frustration and model saying positive, encouraging things to themselves. For example: "Oh, this is so frustrating, but I'm not going to give up. I know I can do it!" or "Well, that didn't go the way I'd hoped, but that's okay. I know I can do it if I keep trying!"
    - Practice self-compassion by being accepting and kind to themselves.
    - Use encouraging words as often as possible when talking to their child and others, and help their child find opportunities to say encouraging things to others.
    - Look for situations where people are encouraging each other (in life, in books, on television, etc.) and point them out to their child.

The Rosebush Drawing*

Book
Bloom by Ruth Forman, illustrated by Talia Skyles (2022)

Description

Bloom is a wonderful book that uses the metaphor of a lovely garden to celebrate the beauty of Black girls. This intervention expands the book's concept of identity and appreciation of the self with the rosebush drawing. Oaklander (1978) has explained that guided drawing promotes powerful tools of fantasy and imagery that allow children to express their feelings and thoughts in a safe, nonintrusive, and client-led way, which is easier than verbal communication. By inviting children to draw a fantasy metaphor of their lives, which bridges creativity and inner thoughts and feelings, they can better articulate and become aware of any issues they are facing. With the therapist's prompting, clients can examine and explore the image they create and, when ready, "own" or acknowledge aspects of it that support and strengthen their sense of self.

Treatment Goals

- Strengthen the child's sense of self by allowing them to create their experience and make choices (e.g., regarding the appearance, size, health, etc. of the rose bush)
- Encourage the child's expression of their own ideas and preferences
- Improve the child's self-nurturing via the book's messages of self-acceptance and social belonging

Materials

- Paper and coloring utensils
- Bell or chime

Directions

1. Read the book with the child.

2. Then ask the client to relax their gaze or close their eyes (if they are comfortable doing so) as you read the following script.

    ○ I'd like you to just get as relaxed as you can. Just go inside yourself and see how you're feeling in there. See how your head feels, how your shoulders feel, and how your arms, stomach, chest, and back feel. [*Pause for 5 seconds.*] Wiggle your toes too—sometimes we forget that we go all the way down to our toes. Then take a deep breath, hold it, and let it out. Let's do that a couple more times. [*Pause for 20 seconds.*]

    ○ Now I'm going to make a sound, and just listen to the sound as long as you can. [*Ring a bell or chime three times; continue when the chime stops sounding.*]

---

* Intervention by Karen Fried, PsyD, MFT. Adapted from *Healing Through Play Using the Oaklander Model* (Fried & McKenna, 2020).

- When you're ready, I'd like you to imagine that you're a rosebush, or any flower bush that we will call a rosebush. What kind of rosebush are you? Are you small? Are you large? Are you wide? Are you tall? Do you have flowers? If so, what kind? (They don't have to be roses.) What color are your flowers? Do you have many or just a few? Are you in full bloom or do you only have buds? Do you have leaves? What kind? Do you have thorns? If so, what do they look like? What are your stems and branches like? What are your roots like? Or maybe you don't have any. If you do, where are they? Are they long and straight? Are they twisted? Deep?

- Where are you? You can be anywhere—on the moon, in the middle of the ocean, in a yard, in a pot—anywhere. Are you in a park? The desert? In the city? In the country? Are you growing in the ground or through cement, or even inside somewhere?

- What's around you? Are there other bushes or trees? Animals? Birds? A fence? Or are you alone?

- What's it like to be a rosebush? How do you survive? Does someone take care of you? What's the weather like for you right now?

- When you're ready, open your eyes and draw your rosebush and whatever else is in your mind's picture. Don't worry about the drawing; you will be able to explain it to me.

3. Invite the client to create their own rosebush drawing with the materials provided.

4. Help the client explore and express the created image. Prompt the child to explain the drawing to you in the present tense ("The rosebush is . . ."). As the child describes the drawing, write down the description for follow-up prompts and statements. You might pursue qualities of the rosebush such as its size, health, location, isolation, or community. You may also explore the earlier prompt "Who takes care of you?" which may yield considerable information and feelings.

5. After the child gives the description and you have prompted further exploration, you can read what the child said back, and then ask if what they said about being this rosebush fits for them in their life.

6. Follow up on the ways the drawn rosebush fits, or does not fit, the child's life.

7. Provide a chance to alter the drawing to make it fit the child's life better.

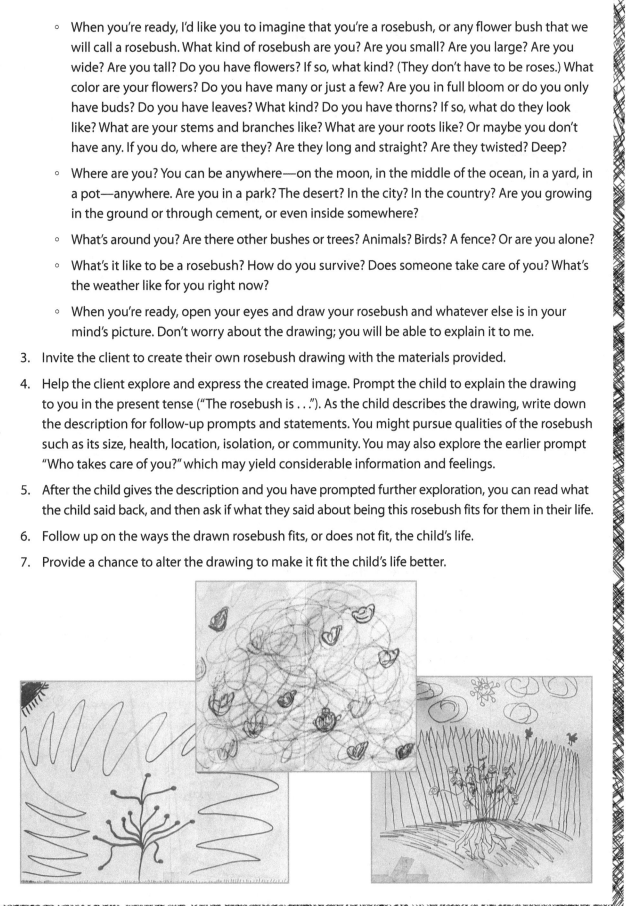

Happiness Doesn't Come from Headstands

Book
Happiness Doesn't Come from Headstands by Tamara Levitt (2017)

Description
Happiness Doesn't Come from Headstands is a story about a little girl who tries as hard as she can to do a headstand but can't. In contrast to the classic children's book *The Little Engine That Could,* which teaches the lesson that if you try hard enough, you can do anything, this book speaks to the reality that we may excel at some things but struggle with others. The little girl may never be able to do a headstand, but she can do many things that other kids can't do. This intervention is helpful for kids with perfectionism who can be hard on themselves. If you can't change the outcome of what you are not good at, you can change how you think and feel about it.

Treatment Goals
- Teach flexibility and combat perfectionism
- Identify the child's strengths
- Practice positive self-talk

Materials
- Paper
- Coloring utensils

Directions
1. After reading the book with the child, ask them if there has ever been something they worked really hard at but still thought the outcome wasn't good enough. Have them write this activity on the paper and circle it in red.
2. Ask the child to identify how good they think they are at this activity on a scale from 1 to 5 (with 1 being "not very good at all" and 5 being "very good"). Have them write this number in the red circle.
3. Next, ask the child how much time they spent worrying about the activity they feel they are not good at. With a blue marker (or a color different from red), rate how big the worry is on a scale from 1 to 5 (with 1 being "not big at all" and 5 being "the biggest worry ever").
4. Then invite the child to draw an image of themselves doing that activity, or at least trying to!
5. When the child is done with this first drawing, ask them to identify something they worked really hard on and were proud of their improvement. Have them write this activity on the paper and circle it in a different color.

6. Ask the child to identify how good they think they are at this activity on a scale from 1 to 5 (with 1 being "not very good at all" and 5 being "very good"). Have them write this number in the circle.

7. Next, ask the child how much time they spent worrying about this activity. With a blue marker, rate how big the worry was on a scale from 1 to 5 (with 1 being "not big at all" and 5 being "the biggest worry ever").

8. Then invite them to draw a second image of themselves doing that activity.

9. Finally, ask the child to identify something they will probably never be able to do—and that is okay. Have them write or draw this activity in the corner of the paper and write "That's okay" next to it.

10. End the activity by having the child draw a picture of something they are good at and adding positive "I am . . ." statements or words of encouragement next to the picture.

There's More to This Story: Telling the Tale of Resiliency and Growth*

Book
Because by Mo Willems (2019)

Description
Mo Willems's book *Because* gives children a template to create meaningful narratives about their lives and helps explain how people in the world are interconnected. It provides an opportunity to discuss how things that are distressing for one person can actually offer an opportunity for another person. In this intervention, children will create a "because story" based on an event in their life, either positive or negative. For children with a history of traumatic or distressing events, use caution to not gloss over the trauma or offer this intervention too early in the treatment process. In this case, the intervention is best used toward the end of treatment when the child has completed trauma processing and is now in a stage of creating a narrative about the growth that occurred as a result of the traumatic experience. This process can be used as a resource to identify and promote resiliency and also as a springboard for identifying posttraumatic growth.

Treatment Goals
- Identify and express gratitude for helpers or resources in a child's life
- Normalize the presence of conflicting emotions (or parts of the self) in positive or negative experiences
- Identify patterns of success that inform future goal planning
- Create a meaningful narrative about a life experience that can be used to build self-esteem

Materials
- Paper
- Writing utensil

Directions
1. Read the book with the child.
2. With the child, decide what life event they'd like to tell a story about. The event might be a happy one or a distressing one (or a little bit of both).

---
* Intervention by Jennifer Taylor, LCSW-C, RPT-S

3. Work backward with the child's chosen event to identify the key factors that are part of the story. Some questions to consider include:
   - What is the ending that you want to celebrate or learn from?
   - What are ten things that happened *before* that event?
   - What people caused the event to happen or made it more likely to occur?
   - Was there anyone who experienced anything sad, distressing, or disappointing during this process? What was that like for them?
   - When you think back about this experience, what seems to be the best place to start?
4. Now that you have a series of events, you can begin to link them together using the following template:
   - Because [*this happened*] . . . then [*this also happened*].
   - Because [*this happened*] . . . then [*this happened next*].
   - Because [*this person did this*] . . . then [*this also happened*].
   - Because [*of all of these things*] . . . I was able to [*experience*].
   - Because I have this experience, I am now able to [*do something*] for others.
5. After reading this story, discuss who might be helped in the future based on the child's experience.

The Reflection in Me*

Book

The Reflection in Me by Marc Colagiovanni, illustrated by Peter H. Reynolds (2017)

Description

The Reflection in Me is an animated story of a young girl looking at her reflection in a mirror. The girl's reflection shares with the girl all the things she loves about herself that make her special. It's a wonderful representation of self-love. In this intervention, the client will take a few minutes looking at their own reflection and then identify different things they love about themselves that they wish to tell their reflection. This may be challenging for some clients, so if they are struggling with coming up with ideas, you can provide prompts or use visuals, such as the illustrated *Greatness Cards*.** Your client can then decorate strips of cardstock paper or popsicle sticks with each affirmation or positive thing they identified.

Treatment Goals

- Identify attributes the child loves about themselves
- Create positive affirmations
- Practice positive self-talk

Materials

- Handheld mirror
- Popsicle sticks or strips of cardstock paper
- Hot glue or Velcro®

Directions

1. Watch the animated story together, available at https://www.fablevisionstudios.com/reflection.
2. After watching the story, lead the client in a discussion regarding self-love and positive self-talk as they look at their own reflection in the mirror. If talking about themselves is hard, you can put a stuffed animal in front of a mirror and ask the same questions about the stuffed animal.
   - What was something the reflection shared that they liked about being themselves?
   - If your reflection could speak to you, what would it say?
   - What would you like it to say?
   - What does your reflection think?
3. On each stick, invite the client to write different things they love about themselves. Encourage the client to identify attributes that are beyond the physical.

---

* Intervention by Sarah Wintman, RPT, LICSW
** Premade *Greatness Cards* are available for purchase at https://www.mainlineplaytherapy.com/product-page/greatness-cards.

4. Using hot glue or Velcro, help the client attach each stick to the mirror.
5. Using the completed mirror, encourage the client to practice saying loving things to their reflection. Depending on your budget and the safety of the child, the child can take the mirror home with them.

Adaptation for Telehealth

- The child can use paper or sticky notes to attach positive affirmations to a mirror at home. The caregiver can also help the child create a positive affirmation ritual.

Sense of Self with Animal Projections in the Sand Tray*

Book

I Am Octopus: Playful Projections to Strengthen One's Sense of Self by Jackie Flynn, illustrated by Angel Flynn (2022b)

Description

I Am Octopus presents a wide selection of animal imagery to help children explore their own strengths and struggles that align with those of the animals. As the animals introduce themselves in the book ("Hi, I am Shark. I am alone most of the time. Making friends is hard for me"), children gain a sense of normalcy from these descriptive characteristics. The book introduces characteristics such as confidence, playfulness, creativity, impulsiveness, sadness, worry, and more to support children's openness and awareness about themselves. Some children may relate to one or more animals in the book. The following projective intervention, which is an application of the Oaklander model, draws from the book by having children explore their sense of self, including their values, likes, dislikes, strengths, and struggles.

Treatment Goals

- Gain insight about the child's values and purpose
- Enhance the child's ability to communicate about the self
- Increase awareness of personal strengths

Materials

- Sand tray with a selection of miniature animals (does not need to be the same animals as in the book)

Directions

1. Read the book with the child.
2. Invite the child to pick a few miniature animals for the activity, based on attraction or aversion. Each choice may hold subconscious significance.
3. Invite the child to embody the animal through body movement, sounds, facial expressions, and so forth.

---

* Intervention by Jackie Flynn, EdS, LMHC-S, RPT

4. Ask the child to a give first-person voice to the animals as you ask questions to support the client in self-exploration. For example, if the child is pretending to be a dolphin, you might ask:
    - Hi, Dolphin, how is it to be you?
    - What are some words or phrases to describe you, Dolphin?
    - What is something you do well?
    - What is something you struggle with?
    - Is there anything you want or need, Dolphin? [*If yes*] What is it?

5. Then invite the child to engage with the other miniatures in dialogue. For example, you might ask the child, "Dolphin, what is some advice you'd give to Mole?" This technique is great for letting the child lead. If you want more direction, simply ask them to talk more about each miniature and their interactions. Once done, check if they noticed any patterns or connections, and chat about their thoughts.

Variation

- This intervention is not limited to animal metaphors. Any object (e.g., table, stone, food) can be used for this intervention.

Greatness Sticks

Book

Casey's Greatness Wings: Teaching Mindfulness, Connection & Courage to Children by Tammi Van Hollander, illustrated by Annie Wilkinson (2018a)

Description

Casey's Greatness Wings is a playful, interactive story that can be told on the child's back using hand motions. It is a story about a caterpillar who feels different from the others and who worries that he is not good enough. His worries are as big as a giant elephant, and he does not know how to get the elephant off his back. It's not until the wise Grandmother Butterfly magically appears and cocoons Casey in her loving embrace that Casey can find a way to escape the elephant and see the beauty that has always lived inside of him.

Although the book offers worksheets and activities, a wonderful complement to those activities is the use of greatness sticks (Van Hollander, 2018b), which are popsicle sticks with positive qualities written on them. This is a great activity to do as an initial session, as a closing session, or throughout the therapeutic process to counter clients' tendency to focus on what is going wrong rather than what is going right. It is a wonderful activity to involve the caregiver in as well. I like to keep a cup of greatness sticks in my office since they can be used in so many ways. Make sure you have empty sticks available so that others can add to the collection!

Treatment Goals

- Decrease worries and quiet the mind
- Encourage empathy and kindness
- Increase self-esteem, confidence, and resiliency
- Strengthen positive communication within the family

Materials

- Thick popsicle sticks (colorful popsicle sticks are a bonus)
- Markers
- Copy of the *Greatness Words* handout (included at the end of this intervention)
- Sand tray and miniatures (optional)

Directions

1. Read the book with the client and talk about the positive qualities Grandmother Butterfly saw in Casey.
2. Show the child the *Greatness Words* list and ask them to identify which of these positive qualities they see in themselves.

3. Ask the child to circle these positive qualities in one color and to then pick a second color to circle what qualities they wish they had more of. Write down all these qualities on popsicle sticks. Then invite the client to give examples of all the positive qualities they possess.

4. If you are using a sand tray, invite the client to choose a miniature that represents themselves, as well as some to represent their family members, and to place them in the sand. Then place the greatness sticks in the sand tray next to each miniature and ask the client what qualities each family member has.

5. If at any point during the activity the parent asks to talk about the child's negative qualities, tantrums, disrespect, or negative behaviors, you should reply, "There are no negative qualities in this activity. It is about the strengths your child has, not the weaknesses."

6. At the end of the activity, place all the qualities that the child wishes they had more of on one side of the tray. You or the caregiver will then give examples of times the child has demonstrated these qualities since they do not see it in themselves.

7. Encourage the child to create their own set of greatness sticks to use at home. These can also serve as a wonderful gift to give to friends and family to acknowledge their greatnesses, whether on holidays, birthdays, Mother's Day, Father's Day, or World Kindness Day. I once had a six-year-old client create his greatness sticks and tie them in a big bow so he could give them to himself for his birthday! They are guaranteed to touch the heart and fill that love tank.

Greatness Words

Accepting	Affirming	Artsy	Bold
Brave	Calm	Caring	Clever
Comforting	Confident	Cooperative	Courageous
Creative	Curious	Energetic	Extroverted
Flexible	Focused	Forgiving	Friendly
Generous	Grateful	Helpful	Honest
Humble	Humorous	Imaginative	Important
Inspiring	Joyful	Kind	Kind-hearted
Leader	Loving	Magical	Mindful
Motivated	Observant	Optimistic	Passionate
Peaceful	Problem-solver	Relaxed	Resilient
Responsible	Safe	Sentimental	Smart
Strong	Strong-willed	Talented	Thoughtful
Trustworthy	Warm	Wise	Witty

I Love You the Purplest*

Book
I Love You the Purplest by Barbara M. Joosse, illustrated by Mary Whyte (1996)

Description
In this book, a mom spends quality time with her two children, who repeatedly ask her which child's performance or behaviors she prefers. Throughout the outing, the mother finds positive words to describe each child and avoids choosing who's "best" each time—because in the end, we all have positive attributes that we bring to the world and to our families. This intervention will coach parents to notice the language they use with their children so that it recognizes strengths that others may not notice.

Treatment Goals
- Develop a positive-focused mental attitude
- Build the child's sense of self
- Allow children with diverse strengths to feel valued
- Teach parents to use more diversity-inclusive language with children
- Support the self-esteem of both neurodiverse and neurotypical children

Materials
- None needed

Directions
1. Have the parent read the book with the child (or children, if multiple are participating).
2. Ask the child whether the mom in the story ever chose one child over the other. What words did she choose instead of saying one child was "better" than the other? Some examples include:
   - Caught the liveliest worms (versus caught the juiciest worms)
   - Rowed with the deepest strokes (versus rowed with the fastest strokes)
   - Bountiful fisherman (versus cleverest fisherman)

---
* Intervention by Sandra Holloway, LPC, RDMT, LBS

3. Ask the child to think of some negative things they have heard people say about them, or about another child. Is there a positive-focused way to say the same thing? For example, stubborn can be determined, clingy can be cuddly, aggressive can be energetic, and bossy can be powerful. Have the parent work with the child to write down positive words that can be used to reframe the child's qualities. Use the links below to help if needed:

    - *Adjectives:* https://byjus.com/english/adjectives-for-children
    - *Values words:* https://www.berkeleywellbeing.com/list-of-values.html
    - *Positive behaviors:* https://www.gov.nl.ca/education/files/k12_safeandcaring_teachers_pbs_behaviouralexpectations.pdf

4. When you're done writing down these words, choose an activity for the child to do—it can be anything! Examples include dancing to music, playing a game (e.g., tic-tac-toe, I spy, charades), a sport (e.g., ball catch), or a chore. If desired, the parent can include something the child is good at, something the child struggles with, or something the child will not do.

5. As the child does the activity, have the parent use a positive-focused mental attitude to bring attention to anything good they see the child do (by naming it out loud). If multiple children are engaged, make sure the parent gives an equal number of praises to each child.

6. Enjoy watching the child feel good about themselves!

CHAPTER 3

Diversity, Equity, and Inclusion

Teaching children about diversity, equity, and inclusion is an important part of raising kind, accepting, and tolerant humans in a world where there is racism, sizeism, homophobia, ableism, sexism, classism, and other forms of discrimination. We need to teach children to empathize with people who are different from them, to understand various subjects from multiple points of view, and to celebrate the differences within all of us. But how do we do this? How can we help children understand that the stereotypes they may hear in the media (or maybe even at home) are not true? How can we raise curious, responsible children who want to learn the beauty of differences and celebrate each person's unique identity? How can we raise children to be anti-racist, gender affirming, and accepting of those with different abilities? How can we teach that love wins and there is no place for hate?

Well, books are a good start to teaching these values when children are young. Starting at an early age, it is incredibly important to expose children to different races, gender identities, abilities, and more. If we are only showing children books with white, abled, cisgender characters, how are they supposed to learn about differences? In order to work therapeutically with children and to create safe spaces where *all* are welcome, we need to:

- Celebrate diversity rather than teaching color-blindness
- Have diverse books and toys that are representative of different ages, religions, races, cultures, identities, and abilities
- Emphasize values that create equity over competition
- Try not to make any one difference better or worse—instead honoring differences at all times
- Teach about white privilege and encourage children to use their voice to speak up about inclusion, identity, equity, and diversity

In this chapter, you'll find a variety of books and accompanying interventions that will help you do just that. As part of this process, it is important that you also create an inclusive playroom. Play is universal, so you want to make your playroom one that is universally welcoming to children from different social and cultural locations. Have you ever tried to find a dollhouse-sized courtroom? Anatomically correct dolls? Multicultural toys that are not stereotypical? Figures that may have adaptive abilities? Unfortunately, the toy industry still has a lot of work to do when it comes to finding toys that are inclusive and representative of the diverse populations you may work with. They exist, but you may need to look deeper!

Suggested Materials

- Gender-neutral dollhouses (I recommend wooden dollhouses—although they are more expensive than plastic, they are more durable)
- Toys in gender-neutral or non-gender-conforming colors (e.g., pink trucks, male baby dolls)
- Sandtray miniatures:
    - Rainbows, flags, bridges
    - Figures to form different kinds of families (e.g., two moms/two dads, multicultural families)
    - Figures with disabilities (e.g., figures in wheelchairs, with canes)
- Diverse puppets and dolls featuring different races, genders, cultures, ages, religions, abilities, and so forth
- Variety of dress-up clothes and jewelry
- Crayola® Colors of the World skin tone crayons
- Everyone Is Awesome LEGO® set
- Wooden toys and peg people
- Learning Resources® All About Me Family Counters™ (set of 72)
- Get Ready Kids Friends with Disabilities Play Figures
- Creatable World™ Deluxe Character Kit

Suggested Books

Featured in This Chapter

- *Red: A Crayon's Story* by Michael Hall (2015)
- *My Shadow Is Pink* by Scott Stuart (2021)
- *Her Body Can* by Katie Crenshaw and Ady Meschke, illustrated by Li Liu (2020)
- *His Body Can* by Katie Crenshaw and Ady Meschke, illustrated by Li Liu (2021)
- *Bodies Are Cool* by Tyler Feder (2021)
- *The Skin You Live In* by Michael Tyler, illustrated by David Lee Csicsko (2005)
- *Sulwe* by Lupita Nyong'o, illustrated by Vashti Harrison (2019)
- *Hair Love* by Matthew A. Cherry, illustrated by Vashti Harrison (2019)
- *Chocolate Me!* by Taye Diggs, illustrated by Shane W. Evans (2011)

Also Recommended

- *I Am an Amazing Asian Girl: A Positive Affirmation Book for Asian Girls* by Yobe Qiu, illustrated by Jade Le (2022)
- *We're Different, We're the Same* by Bobbi Kates, illustrated by Joe Mathieu (1992)
- *Morris Micklewhite and the Tangerine Dress* by Christina Baldacchino, illustrated by Isabelle Malenfant (2014)
- *Let's Talk About Race* by Julius Lester, illustrated by Karen Barbour (2005)
- *The Small and Tall Ball* by Frank Sileo, illustrated by Katie Dwyer (2023)
- *Curls* by Ruth Forman, illustrated by Geneva Bowers (2020)
- *Glow* by Ruth Forman, illustrated by Geneva Bowers (2021)

- *Bloom* by Ruth Forman, illustrated by Talia Skyles (2022)
- *Be Who You Are* by Todd Parr (2016)
- *It's Okay to Be Different* by Todd Parr (2001)
- *Be Who You Are* by Jennifer Carr, illustrated by Ben Rumback (2010)
- *I Am Jazz* by Jessica Herthel and Jazz Jenkins, illustrated by Shelagh McNicholas (2014)
- *Where Oliver Fits* by Cale Atkinson (2017)
- *I Am Enough* by Grace Byers, illustrated by Keturah A. Bobo (2018)
- *A Tale of Two Mommies* by Vanita Oelschlager, illustrated by Mike Blanc (2011)
- *A Tale of Two Daddies* by Vanita Oelschlager, illustrated by Kristin Blackwood and Mike Blanc (2010)
- *101 Ways to Help Your Daughter Love Her Body* by Brenda Lane Richardson and Elane Rehr (2001)

For resources about the important standards of care for transgender and gender-nonconforming individuals, check out the World Professional Association for Transgender Health at www.wpath.org.

Red Crayon I*

Book
Red: A Crayon's Story by Michael Hall (2015)

Description

This book is about a crayon named Red, who is a blue crayon with a red wrapper. All his life, this crayon has tried and tried to be red, but he just isn't. He tries to draw strawberries and firetrucks, but to no avail, leaving the other crayons often frustrated with him for not being red. One day, though, a new friend asks Red if he can draw an ocean for them. Although Red is afraid to fail again, with encouragement, he makes a beautiful ocean and finally feels recognized for who he truly is. Similar to the book, this intervention will help your client examine what it feels like to be in the "wrong crayon wrapper" and to be labeled differently than what they feel on the inside. You can do this intervention in the playroom with just the child or with the whole family.

Treatment Goals

- Promote inclusion and equality
- Identify what might be going on inside of the child that they might not have the words to express
- Help clients understand what being in the wrong "crayon wrapper" might feel like

Materials

- Masks or pieces of paper with a face outline on both sides
- Coloring utensils
- Additional art supplies, such as magazine clippings and glue (optional)

Directions

1. Read the book with the child.
2. Ask the child to identify all the feelings they felt for Red throughout the story.
3. Discuss how sometimes people show one thing on the outside, while on the inside, it is something completely different. For example, if someone asks you how you're doing and you outwardly smile and say, "I'm fine," while on the inside, your heart is beating fast after someone made a derogatory comment about your new haircut and you're now feeling like you aren't worth anything. Another example could be that on the outside you are getting good grades, conversing with friends, and interacting well with your family, while on the inside you are feeling hopeless, frustrated, and like you never do anything right.

---
* Intervention by Erika Walker, LSCSW, LCSW, LICSW, RPT

4. Invite the child to use the mask to show similarities and differences in what they show to the world and what they feel inside. If they need more than one mask because they hide different parts of themselves with certain people or in certain environments, allow them to create several masks as supplies warrant.

5. As appropriate, work with the client and family to safely bring these hidden parts of the client out so that others can see who they really are. Some clients, for a multitude of different reasons, feel that they need to keep their inner selves hidden. This could be for safety reasons, as they fear that if they were to reveal their inner selves to their families, they would be disowned or kicked out of their home. It could also be that they are unsure if their family will be able to accept their identity, even if they've been told time and time again that they will be loved and cared for no matter what. Whatever the situation may be, this is a conversation that should be handled delicately so as to not do harm to the client.

Red Crayon II

Book
Red: A Crayon's Story by Michael Hall (2015)

Description
This intervention builds on the previous activity by continuing to follow Red's story. At the end of the book, Red makes an important discovery about himself when he draws a blue ocean: He realizes that he's happier when he just embraces the blue that he truly is within. In this intervention, your client will also learn what it means to love themselves as they are and celebrate what is on the inside. This intervention is a wonderful opportunity to involve the caregiver as well.

Treatment Goals
- Help the child be true to themselves and embrace who they are on the inside
- Demonstrate the negative effects that labeling can have on people
- Increase self-esteem

Materials
- Crayons or other coloring utensils
- Paper
- Small labels

Directions
1. Read the book with the child and the caregiver.
2. Provide the child with an assortment of crayons and give another set to the caregiver. Invite them to put mismatched labels on their crayons—for example, they might put a blue label on a red crayon or a purple label on a yellow crayon.
3. Invite the child and caregiver to each draw a picture of themselves or a family portrait. Each person should request a color they'd like to use, and the other person should give them the crayon with that label, rather than that actual color, so their pictures turn out very different from what they'd had in mind (e.g., their golden retriever may end up with purple fur!).
4. Encourage the client and caregiver to reflect on what the experience was like (silly, confusing, frustrating, etc.).
5. At the end, invite everyone to scribble together to create their own unique color. Give it a unique name to celebrate the uniqueness in all of us. Highlight that every color is important and adds to the beauty of the picture.

What Color Is Your Shadow?

Book
My Shadow Is Pink by Scott Stuart (2021)

Description
My Shadow Is Pink is a sweet story that explores gender identity and helps dispel common gender stereotypes. The author's son inspired him to write this book. In the story, the main character learns that everyone has a shadow that they sometimes feel they need to hide. In the little boy's case, he has a pink shadow that loves princesses, ponies, dresses, and other things "not for boys." This is a powerful book that illustrates the importance of unconditional love, respect, acceptance, and positive parenting for LGBTQ+ and gender-nonconforming children, and it helps other children to understand and accept differences. In this intervention, you will help your client explore their own shadow with the help of their caregiver.

Treatment Goals
- Encourage self-love and acceptance
- Promote diversity, equality, and inclusion
- Explore issues related to gender identity

Materials
- Large roll of paper to trace a body (or regular paper)
- Coloring utensils
- Sidewalk chalk (optional)

Directions
1. Read the book with the child.
2. Create a life-size tracing of the child. Ask the child if they would like to be traced by you or their caregiver. Be aware that if there has been trauma or any sexual abuse, you may want to do this activity on regular-sized paper and use a gingerbread man template.
3. If the child would like to be traced, have them lie down on their back. I would encourage a caregiver to do the tracing as this can help create safety for the child. Check in that this does feel safe for the child.
4. Once the body is traced, ask the child, "What color is your shadow?" and have them color in the body with this color. Let the child know that their shadow can have as many colors as they want. There is no wrong way to color the shadow and no wrong color of a shadow.

5. When the child is done, have them introduce their shadow to you and the caregiver. To better understand their shadow, you can ask follow-up questions such as:
    - Does your shadow have a message for you?
    - Do you have a message for your shadow?
    - What do you think of your shadow?
    - What is your favorite part of your shadow?
    - Is there anything you wish you could change about your shadow?

Variation

- Creating shadow art outside with children is a fun way to expand on this activity since the book is about a shadow. Go outside in the daylight where the child can see their shadow, and have them strike a pose while you trace their shadow with whatever color the child chooses. Once the outline is complete, the child can color in the shadow (with help from you or their caregiver, if the child would like) and add nature elements for decoration. The following pictures are from my play therapy events—you can see that this is also a great activity for the beach!

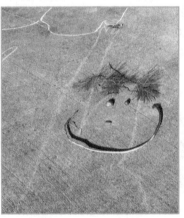

Your Body Can

Books
- *Her Body Can* by Katie Crenshaw and Ady Meschke, illustrated by Li Liu (2020)
- *His Body Can* by Katie Crenshaw and Ady Meschke, illustrated by Li Liu (2021)
- *Bodies Are Cool* by Tyler Feder (2021)

Description
Her Body Can is a beautiful book for young girls about practicing self-love and celebrating who they are. *His Body Can* is a companion book that empowers boys not to conform to societal gender roles of masculinity, which helps counter the stereotype of "boys will be boys." Finally, *Bodies Are Cool* talks about how all bodies are cool no matter someone's size, gender, skin color, or hair type. This is a great book for body image concerns, as it presents characters with a variety of body shapes, gender identities, abilities, and more. For this intervention, feel free to choose whatever book works best for your client. If you have another book you like on body image, feel free to use that as well—any book on self-love and body acceptance will work. The goal is to help your client befriend their body so they can feel more open and expressive.

Treatment Goals
- Empower the child to be who they are
- Enhance self-esteem and resilience
- Challenge societal norms of what is "pretty"

Materials
- Scissors
- Copy of the *"Your Body Can"* Cards (included at the end of this intervention)
- A container such as a bucket, hat, box, or bowl

Directions
1. Before the client arrives at the session, make a copy of the *Your Body Can* handout and cut out the individual cards.
2. In the session, read any of the listed books (or a book of your choosing on body acceptance).
3. When you're done reading, put the cards in the hat or container.
4. Take turns with the child picking out cards and answering the question on each card to demonstrate what the body can do! Have fun with it, and feel free to add silly questions.

"Your Body Can" Cards

YOUR BODY CAN	YOUR BODY CAN
What is the silliest thing your body can do?	What is the funniest noise your body can make?
SHOW ME	SHOW ME
YOUR BODY CAN	YOUR BODY CAN
Can you give a high five?	Can you roar like a lion?
SHOW ME	SHOW ME
YOUR BODY CAN	YOUR BODY CAN
Can you squeak like a mouse?	Can you take three deep breaths?
SHOW ME	SHOW ME

YOUR BODY CAN	YOUR BODY CAN
Can your body reach for the sky?	Can your body dance?
SHOW ME	SHOW ME
YOUR BODY CAN	YOUR BODY CAN
Can you touch your toes?	Can you run in place fast?
SHOW ME	SHOW ME
YOUR BODY CAN	YOUR BODY CAN
Can you crawl?	Can you blink your eyes three times?
SHOW ME	SHOW ME

YOUR BODY CAN	YOUR BODY CAN
Can you slither like a snake?	Can you stand like a superhero?
SHOW ME	SHOW ME
YOUR BODY CAN	YOUR BODY CAN
Can you move real slow?	What is something cool your body can do?
SHOW ME	SHOW ME
YOUR BODY CAN	YOUR BODY CAN
Can you stand on one foot?	What is your favorite part of your body?
SHOW ME	SHOW ME

YOUR BODY CAN	YOUR BODY CAN
What can your legs do?	What can your eyes do?
SHOW ME	SHOW ME
YOUR BODY CAN	YOUR BODY CAN
What can your nose do?	What is something cool that your body learned to do?
SHOW ME	SHOW ME
YOUR BODY CAN	YOUR BODY CAN
What is something you wish your body could do?	Can your body jump up and down?
SHOW ME	SHOW ME

My Unique Body*

Book
The Skin You Live In by Michael Tyler, illustrated by David Lee Csicsko (2005)

Description
The Skin You Live In helps children appreciate the many different shades of skin that they may see in the world. Through its whimsical rhymes, it provides several poetic descriptions of skin colors—from pumpkin pie slice skin to butterscotch gold skin—that promote acceptance of different races and ethnicities. This intervention expands on the book by helping children recognize and appreciate the uniqueness of their body while also pointing out its similarities with others. This is a wonderful intervention to do at any phase of treatment.

Treatment Goals
- Foster appreciation of the child's unique skin, hair, and eye color
- Help the child feel connected with others by noticing their physical similarities
- Increase self-esteem

Materials
- Paper and coloring utensils
- Sandtray miniatures (optional)

Directions
1. Read the book with the child and have the child identify pictures of children in the book that have similar skin, hair, and eye color as them.
2. Ask the child to draw a picture of themselves and to color in their skin, hair, and eyes.
3. Then ask the child to draw a picture of other people they know or see in movies, TV shows, or media who have similar skin, hair, and eye color as them. These people may or may not be related to them.
4. While the child is drawing, ask them the following questions:
    - What are you able to do with the skin you live in? (There are many examples in the book, such as laugh, cry, and run.)
    - If your skin were a type of food, what kind would it be? (There are also many examples in the book, such as candy corn, pumpkin pie, toffee, and lemon tart.)
    - What things in nature come in a variety of colors? (This can include flowers, animals, tree leaves, and so forth.)
5. If they like, the child can choose sandtray miniatures to represent their answers to these questions.

---

* Intervention by Jodi Crane, PhD, NCC, LPCC-S, RPT-S

The Beauty Within

Book
Sulwe by Lupita Nyong'o, illustrated by Vashti Harrison (2019)

Description
Sulwe is one of those books that everyone should have. Written by Academy Award–winning actress Lupita Nyong'o, this powerful, touching book is about colorism, self-esteem, and learning that true beauty comes from within. The main character in the book, Sulwe, has skin the color of midnight. She is darker than everyone in her family and everyone at school. Sulwe just wants to be beautiful and bright, like her mother and sister. Then a magical journey in the night sky opens her eyes and changes everything.

In this intervention, children will use an invisible UV pen to help them see the beauty within themselves. Many children have a hard time appreciating their own worth, and this activity gives them an opportunity to internalize positive beliefs about themselves and hold these beliefs in their hearts. By using an invisible UV pen, the client can also shine a light on whatever messages about themselves they feel ready to share with the world. When the caregiver is included in this intervention, it can also be a fun attachment-based activity.

Treatment Goals
- Increase self-esteem
- Celebrate the beauty of diversity

Materials
- Paper
- Coloring utensils
- Invisible "spy" pens with UV black light*

Directions
1. Read the book with the child.
2. At the end of the story, read aloud this quote from Sulwe's mother: "Real beauty comes from your mind and your heart. It begins with how you see yourself, not how others see you."
3. Then ask the child to draw a heart on a piece of paper. Inside the heart, have them draw how they see themselves; outside of the heart, have them draw how they think other people see them.
4. Ask the child to make another heart on a separate piece of paper. Inside the heart, have them use a UV pen to draw how they want to see themselves *and* how they want other people to see them. These can be affirmations or positive words such as "I shine like the brightest star" or "I am good enough just as I am." Since these UV pens are nontoxic, you can also ask the child to write

---
* Some options include DirectGlow or SCStyle UV pens and lights.

these answers on their arm or body. (Although the ink is invisible, always ask the caregiver if this is okay.) Remind the child that no one else can see these messages except when they shine the light on them.

5. When they're done writing, ask them to shine the UV light on their paper heart (or on their body) and have them share what they wrote. Let them know that there is always light that shines through the darkness.

6. If the child is comfortable sharing, invite the caregiver to join in on the activity. You can ask the caregiver to use the invisible pen to add to the child's heart (or to the child's body, if they are comfortable) what they love about them. Then have the child find the message with the UV light.

7. To enhance this attachment-based activity, you can also have the child write a special message on their caregiver's arm and have the caregiver find the message with the UV light and read it aloud.

Hair Love

Book
Hair Love by Matthew A. Cherry, illustrated by Vashti Harrison (2019)

Description
Hair Love is a sweet story of the relationship between a Black father and his daughter, Zuri. In the book, the father tries to help Zuri with her hair for a special occasion and does everything he can to make her hair look beautiful. Styling his daughter's hair proves to be quite the challenge, as Zuri's hair has a mind of its own. The tender relationship between the two of them shines through as they try to figure out a way to style her hair. When Zuri's mother comes home, they all style her hair together. Similar to the book, this intervention will also help children learn to appreciate and love their natural hair—all while putting a fun, silly twist on it. It is also a great way to include caregivers in the session.

Treatment Goals
- Build secure family attachments
- Enhance the child's self-confidence about their appearance
- Celebrate diversity and beauty

Materials
- Hairbrush
- Hair ties, barrettes, bows, and other hair supplies (I am a big fan of making braided barrettes. If you grew up in the '80s, you know what I mean. Just make sure the barrettes are large for thick hair.)
- Mirror

Directions
1. Read the book with the child and caregiver. It does not need to be a father, but it is a sweet father-daughter activity for the playroom.
2. After reading the book, have the caregiver and child work together to style the child's hair. If two caregivers are present, have each person style one side of the child's hair. The sillier, the better! Make sure the caregiver is collaborating with the child and letting the child come up with how they want their hair styled. For example, you can have the parent ask the child, "Do you like it with this big barrette or a red bow?"
3. When the caregivers are done, the child can look in the mirror at the silly hairstyle that they created.
4. Ask the child to give their hairstyle a fun, silly name. If the family wishes, they can also take selfies together that feature the child's hair. (This would need to be done on the caregiver's device, not yours, due to HIPAA restrictions.)

Chocolate Me!

Book
Chocolate Me! by Taye Diggs, illustrated by Shane W. Evans (2011)

Description
Chocolate Me! is a book about how it feels to be teased for having darker skin and not looking like everyone else. The book celebrates how each of us is "sweet and lovely and delicious" on the inside, no matter how we look. I was always a fan of Taye Diggs, but I love him even more after reading this wonderful book. This intervention encourages children to proudly embrace what they look like on the outside, even in the face of unkind or hateful messages from others. It is also an intervention that offers a wonderful opportunity for caregivers to participate.

Treatment Goals
- Promote self-love and self-acceptance
- Celebrate diversity
- Build resilience

Materials
- Sticky notes and a writing utensil

Directions
1. Read the book with the child.
2. After reading the book, ask the following questions:
   - How do you think the boy in the book felt when kids said unkind things?
   - Did you ever want to hide when kids were unkind about how you look?
   - What would you have done if you were this little boy?
   - What do you wish you could change about yourself?
   - What do you love about yourself when you look in the mirror?
3. If a caregiver is there, ask them what they love about their child when they look at them. Have them write these positive qualities down on sticky notes. The parent can put all these sticky notes on the child, though always ask permission if it is okay to touch the child or stick anything on them. The child can also add things they like about themselves and stick these on their body too.
4. Next, ask the child if anyone has said unkind things to them about their appearance. If so, invite them to write these messages on a sticky note and then stomp on it while saying aloud one of the positive qualities about themselves (or stating, "That is not true!"). They can then rip up the negative message and throw it in the trash.

CHAPTER 4

Neuroscience for Kids 101

As we learn, our brains continually change. This represents the basis of neuroplasticity, which reflects the brain's amazing ability to change and adapt in response to every interaction and experience. And lucky for us, children are like sponges, always wanting to learn! Even your littlest clients can begin to learn about the brain's structure and function, which is vital to how they see, hear, feel, and act in the world.

One way to teach children about the neuroscience behind their emotions and behaviors is to help them understand the difference between the thinking brain versus the emotion brain. The "thinking brain" refers to the prefrontal cortex, which is a region of the brain responsible for higher-order cognitive functions and executive processes. In contrast, the "emotion brain," which includes the amygdala and other structures in the limbic system, is responsible for our emotions and immediate reactions. It's like an alarm system in our bodies. When we experience strong feelings like fear, anger, or excitement, it's our emotion brain that is online. Our emotion brain reacts quickly to protect us when there's a perceived threat—sending us into fight, flight, freeze, or shutdown mode—but sometimes the perceived threat is a false alarm, or faulty neuroception.

Dr. Dan Siegel's hand model of the brain is an excellent resource for teaching children about these concepts.* It provides a simple visual representation of the brain that kids can easily grasp. The hand model analogy can help children understand their emotional responses and why they occur, recognize when their thinking brain is offline (has "flipped its lid") and how to regain control, and develop strategies for managing strong emotions and stress. It's also a great tool for teaching kids about the importance of co-regulation when they perceive a threat or feel out of control.

The books in this chapter are also a wonderful way to help children understand how the brain works and what is happening in their autonomic nervous system when they are in a state of fight, flight, freeze, or shutdown. For more information on the neuroscience of children's behavior, I highly recommend that clinicians, parents, educators, and other professionals working with children read Dr. Mona Delahooke's books *Beyond Behaviors* (2019) and *Brain-Body Parenting* (2022), Dr. Dan Siegel and Tina Payne Bryson's *The Whole-Brain Child* (2011), and Dr. Robyn Gobbel's *Raising Kids with Big, Baffling Behaviors* (2023).

---

* You can watch Dr. Siegel explain his hand model on his website (https://drdansiegel.com/hand-model-of-the-brain) or on YouTube (https://www.youtube.com/watch?v=f-m2YcdMdFw&t=9s).

Suggested Materials

- Science toys that represent the brain—some examples include:
    - Learning Resources® cross-section brain model
    - Burrell Working Solutions handy brain model B-2 (large)
    - GIANTmicrobes deluxe brain with plush neurons and neurotransmitters
- Models or puzzles that show the parts of the brain
- Pipe cleaners and beads (to show how neurons communicate)
- Sensory toys (e.g., fidgets, stress balls, pop toys)
- Energy Sticks® or energy balls (to demonstrate how signals and impulses are sent)

Suggested Books

Featured in This Chapter

- *Some Days I Flip My Lid: Learning to Be a Calm, Cool Kid* by Kellie Doyle Bailey, illustrated by Hannah Bailey (2019)
- *Now Maps Jr.: Adventure Stories to Help Young Kids Navigate Everyday Challenges & Grow in Caring and Kind Ways* by Daniel J. Siegel (2022)
- *Your Fantastic Elastic Brain: A Growth Mindset Book for Kids to Stretch and Shape Their Brains* by JoAnn Deak, illustrated by Sarah Ackerley (2010)
- *Good Night to Your Fantastic Elastic Brain: A Growth Mindset Bedtime Book for Kids* by JoAnn Deak and Terrence Deak, illustrated by Neely Daggett (2022)
- *Neuro & the Ception Force Friends: A Special Team of Receptor Neurons That Help Your Body & Brain with Regulation* by Dora Henderson, illustrated by Heather Worley (2022)
- *The Fabulous Fight or Flight Stress System: Neuroscience & Polyvagal Theories Through Animal Metaphors* by Jennifer Lefebre (2021)
- *Seven Sensational Senses for Little Sprockets: Part of the Fabulous Fight or Flight Stress System Series* by Jennifer Lefebre (2023)

Also Recommended

- *Being Human: A Polyvagal Informed Story About the States of the Nervous System* by Jackie Flynn (2022a)
- *Hey Warrior: A Book for Kids About Anxiety* by Karen Young, illustrated by Norvile Dovidonyte (2017)
- *My Body Sends a Signal: Helping Kids Recognize Emotions and Express Feelings* by Natalia Maguire, illustrated by Anastasia Zababashkina (2020)

Flip Your Lid

Book

Some Days I Flip My Lid: Learning to Be a Calm, Cool Kid by Kellie Doyle Bailey, illustrated by Hannah Bailey (2019)

Description

Some Days I Flip My Lid is a great resource to help kids recognize their big feelings. The book follows a third grader named Max as he learns how to stop flipping his lid when he is scared, worried, sad, or upset at home or school. This intervention expands on the book by helping kids understand how the brain works when they lose their cool, have strong emotions, or feel stressed out. The intervention is broken down into three parts that can be done in one session or across several sessions: Part 1 begins with processing questions to help the child identify their fight, flight, and freeze responses. Part 2 is a fun and easy science project that demonstrates what "flipping your lid" looks like. Part 3 is a mindfulness activity and a reminder to "breathe on purpose" and ground themselves in times of stress.* For additional ideas, I also recommend you add Kellie and Hannah's other great books to your therapeutic library, including *Some Days I Breathe on Purpose* (2021) and *Some Days I Make Mistakes* (2022).

Treatment Goals

- Provide psychoeducation on the brain's fight, flight, and freeze responses
- Identify anger triggers
- Teach mindfulness and self-awareness

Materials

- Film canisters with lids (or similar small containers with fitted lids)
- Pitcher or bottle of water
- Alka-Seltzer® tablets
- Safety goggles
- Towel
- Outdoor space
- Art supplies (e.g., acrylic paints, permanent markers, glitter glue)

---

* For more information on this intervention, check out my YouTube video: https://www.youtube.com/watch?app=desktop&v=EWYUSKZfSas

Directions

Part 1: Reading

1. Read the book with the child.

2. Ask processing questions to identify their fight, flight, and freeze responses:

    - When do you flip your lid?

    - Do you ever want to push, punch, bite, kick, or hit someone or something when you don't get what you want? Have you ever been so angry that you threw something at someone or really wanted to? Have you ever been hit by a sibling or peer, and you immediately hit them back? What animal are you when this happens? A fire-breathing dragon? An angry gorilla? Show me what it looks like when you are that animal. What sound does the animal make? How does it feel in your body?

    - Do you ever want to just run away? When you want to run away, what animal are you? A tiger? Cheetah? Bird? Show me what it looks like when you are that animal. What sound does the animal make? How does it feel in your body?

    - Do you ever freeze up in certain situations? What are you like when you freeze? Are you like a snowman, a frozen mouse, or something else? Show me what it looks like, sounds like, and feels like in your body.

Part 2: Flipping Your Lid

1. This part of the activity should be done outside for safety—these canisters pop very fast and high! Ask the caregiver's permission to do this activity and to take their child outside. (I ask them to sign a release.) Then bring the client and the listed materials (except the art supplies) outside.

2. Explain to the child how the canister represents their brain and the Alka-Seltzer tablet represents a stressful situation that makes them want to flip their lid. Ask the child to identify a specific situation and have them visualize this scenario when doing the activity.

3. Let the child know that this activity could be unsafe, so you need to do everything possible to stay safe. This includes doing the activity outside and making sure everyone places their safety goggles on.

4. Make sure everyone's goggles are on, then add a small amount of water to a film canister and add an Alka-Seltzer tablet. Place the lid on the canister, turn it upside down, take several steps away from the table or ground, and get ready for it to pop. You can experiment by putting different amounts of Alka-Seltzer in the film canister to discover what changes about the reaction, illustrating how we can react differently to different amounts of stress.

5. Process the activity together. Some processing questions could be:

    - When it popped, was it loud? Scary? Unpredictable? Explosive? Messy?

    - How could you tell it was about to explode?

    - Would it still have exploded if we opened it up right when it started showing signs of bursting?

6. End this portion of the activity by explaining to the child that when they flip their lid, it is scary for them and others because it can be loud, unsafe, and unpredictable. It does not feel good to feel out of control. Today, everyone's safety goggles kept them safe, but when they flip their lid, they don't have their "safety goggles" on. How can they be safe when they flip their lid?

Part 3: Mindfulness Canister

1. Return to your office and explain to the child that the lid is now on safely because they have learned to control their big emotions.

2. Invite the client to decorate one of the canisters using the art supplies. Painting is often more relaxing, but the child can choose from the materials available.

3. While they are coloring the canister, check in with how they are feeling in their mind and body, and have them take three mindful breaths on purpose.

4. Explain that this canister can now serve as a reminder for the child to keep their cool and to "breathe on purpose" like in the book. Inside the canister, ask the child to place an object they can use to ground themselves when they feel like they are going to flip their lid. This could be regular or scented Play-Doh, a note the child writes to themselves, a stone, a crystal, a cotton ball with their favorite aromatic scent, or a note from a parent. Let the child choose what they want in this special container. Let them know this item will be safe because the lid now knows how to stay on and be protected.

NowMaps Adventure

Book
NowMaps Jr.: Adventure Stories to Help Young Kids Navigate Everyday Challenges & Grow in Caring and Kind Ways by Daniel J. Siegel (2022)

Description
NowMaps Jr. is a fun rhyming story that introduces young kids to the neuroscience of early childhood social-emotional learning through an interactive choose-your-own-adventure story. As children choose to travel through a jungle, desert, or pirate ship, they learn about three different tools that can help them better understand their present-moment experience: a pause button, a focus flashlight, and an OK monitor. Although reading *NowMaps Jr.* is an adventure in itself, this intervention expands on the book by giving the child an opportunity to create their own pause button, focus flashlight, and OK monitor. With these tools by their side, your client can learn to navigate big feelings and handle challenges with greater flexibility and confidence.

Treatment Goals
- Effectively navigate big feelings
- Practice staying in the "now"
- Learn about body sensations, thoughts, and feelings

Materials
- Paper and coloring utensils
- Full array of art supplies to decorate the tools (e.g., glitter, stickers, pom-poms)
- Air-dry clay (optional)
- Puppets or sandtray miniatures (optional)

Directions
1. Read the book with the child.
2. Have the child create a pause button, focus flashlight, and OK monitor using whatever tools they would like. They can draw them on paper or create more three-dimensional objects (using air-dry clay or another medium)—the choice is theirs!
3. Once their tools are complete, have them reenact one of the adventures included in the book (or act out a different adventure of their choosing). They can complete this role-play with you as well as the caregiver, if they are present in the session. The child can also act out the story with puppets or sandtray miniatures if they prefer.
4. As the child role-plays the story, ask them how they would use these tools to overcome the various challenges the character in the book was faced with. Prompt them to identify the thoughts, feelings, and body sensations they are having in response to this challenge. Offer different scenarios if they can't come up with anything.
5. Another option is for them to create a new adventure or chapter and make it into a book.

The Power of Neurons*

Books

- *Your Fantastic Elastic Brain: A Growth Mindset Book for Kids to Stretch and Shape Their Brains* by JoAnn Deak, illustrated by Sarah Ackerley (2010)
- *Good Night to Your Fantastic Elastic Brain: A Growth Mindset Bedtime Book for Kids* by JoAnn Deak and Terrence Deak, illustrated by Neely Daggett (2022)

Description

With its captivating illustrations and examples, *Your Fantastic Elastic Brain* presents accurate information about the anatomy and functions of the brain in a way that is understandable for parents, teachers, and kids alike. This book shows how, like the rest of our body, the brain may grow through exercise. *Good Night to Your Fantastic Elastic Brain* explains the crucial functions that the brain performs while we sleep at night, including retaining what is learned during the day, and emphasizes the value of getting adequate sleep. Both books are great resources for teaching children about mirror neurons, growth mindset, and brain development! This intervention utilizes direct teaching to provide an understanding of mirror neurons and neural communication in order to promote psychological development, stress management, empathy, and self-regulation.

Treatment Goals

- Provide the child with the language to understand how their brain recognizes the emotions of others
- Explore how neurons communicate throughout the nervous system and body
- Understand the brain-body connection and its impacts on emotions and behaviors

Materials

- Energy Stick®
- Craft chenille stems (pipe cleaners)
- Plastic pony beads

Directions

1. Read either *Your Fantastic Elastic Brain* or *Good Night to Your Fantastic Elastic Brain* with the child.
2. Introduce the activity with the following script:
   - We just read how neurons send messages to other cells in your body to tell them what to do. They also help us understand our feelings and the feelings of others. See this cool Energy Stick? It lets us see how energy works, which is how our brains communicate through

---

* Intervention by Jennifer Lefebre, PsyD, TCTSY-F, RYT-500, RCYT, NASM-CPT, ATA-AIT

electrical impulses. [*Hold the metal end in one hand, and then touch the other end—the toy lights up when the circuit is complete.*]

- Now watch this! My brain [*place one end of the stick on your forehead*] can communicate with your brain [*place the other end on the child's forehead, lighting up the toy*] to let me know how you're feeling. These are mirror neurons! We see our mirror neurons in action when someone yawns—and then we automatically yawn! Our mirror neurons help us understand each other through electrical signals!

3. Allow the child time to play with the Energy Stick and ask questions if needed.

4. Next, create neurons by bending and folding pipe cleaners into the shape of neurons, being sure to include the cell body, dendrites, and axon. Place various color beads around them. Use the following script to explain to the child what you are doing:

    - These are neurons that we're making. They release special chemicals to talk to each other called *neurochemicals*. Electrical impulses send out these chemicals from here [*point to axon*] into this little space called a *synapse*, and then the chemical messages are picked up by other neurons here [*point to dendrites*].

    - These colorful beads represent neurochemicals like dopamine and serotonin—our happy chemicals! Having a healthy neurotransmitter balance is important because they influence our learning and memory, our stress levels, our mood and behavior, and much more.

5. Encourage the child to place the beads on the ends of the neurons, exploring how the neurotransmitters are sent back and forth between cells, discussing the roles of each.

6. If the child is on medication or struggling to understand the need for a family member to take medication, you may explore that also through this model. You can use the following script:

    - Getting enough sleep, food, and exercise helps us balance our brains. But sometimes our brain has a little trouble making and using these chemicals, which can lead us to have big emotions or behaviors. If this happens, our doctor might have us take medication [*use another color bead*] to help our neurons communicate with each other and to keep our brain balanced.

7. If using this to help a child understand medication, make sure to have certain color beads representing neurotransmitters and medication. For example, dark pink might represent serotonin, bright blue dopamine, and light pink the "helper" medication. Move the beads around so that they are balanced in number. For example, there may be 10 bright blue beads and only 6 dark pink, but then you bring in an additional 4 light pink beads to help balance the brain.

Sensory and Somatic "Ception" Party*

Book

Neuro & the Ception Force Friends: A Special Team of Receptor Neurons That Help Your Body & Brain with Regulation by Dora Henderson, illustrated by Heather Worley (2022)

Description

Neuro & the Ception Force Friends is an exciting book that teaches children about the special helpers inside our bodies called *neurons*. Neurons are tiny messengers that send important messages to the brain. It's as if we have lots of friends inside us, and each friend has a special job. Some friends help us see things with our eyes, some help us taste yummy foods, some help us feel soft or bumpy things, and others make sure we're safe and balanced. All these friends work together to help us understand the world around us. It's like having a superpower inside us that helps us explore and enjoy the world every day! The book introduces several characters, representing different "ceptions" in the body: exteroception, interoception, nociception, thermoception, equilibrioception, and proprioception. These characters, the Ception Force Friends, are always with us, helping us understand our bodies and emotions better. In this fun intervention, children will have a chance to get to know the Ception friends and learn how they help us feel calm and in control when we have different feelings.

Treatment Goals

- Increase awareness of the body and the senses
- Become body detectives of the nervous system

Materials

- Set up a discovery station for every Ception Force Friend (see below)

Directions

1. Read the book with the child so they can get to know their Ception friends.

2. Then act as an adventure guide for the child, guiding them to explore the discovery stations for each Ception friend. These stations are like magical spots where they can find hidden treasures of knowledge. Explain how at each station, the child will meet a friendly Ception friend who will help them learn fun things about their body and feelings. It's like uncovering the secrets of a fantastic treasure island!

3. Here are some ideas of what you might have at each station:
   - **Extero-Ception:** Offer fun foods in a variety of flavors and textures (e.g., sour, salty, sweet, slimy, squishy, crunchy), making sure to check with the caregiver first for food allergies (*taste*). You can also have the child experiment with sandpaper and other textured items (*touch*), breathe in the scent of cotton balls infused with different essential oils (*smell*), look

---

* Intervention by Dora Henderson, LMHC, RPT-S, CTP, CST

at various cut-out pictures or images (*sight*), or listen to various nature recordings or other soothing music while they take in the sounds and journal or color about them (*sound*).

- **Intero-Ception:** Include an image of a gingerbread man and ask the child to draw what they sense internally (e.g., hunger, thirst, fatigue, urge to use the bathroom) on the figure. Encourage them to pause, breathe, and draw what is happening inside of them.

- **Noci-Ception:** Create an empathy station that encourages your client to notice and nurture themselves. If they are hurting anywhere, they can put a bandage on themselves and talk about some moments when they have been injured.

- **Thermo-Ception:** To increase temperature and body awareness, you can create a hat and scarf station, asking the child to stop and notice whether they are hot or cold. You may also want to include weighted blankets, a bowl of ice, and warm fun things the child can hold (e.g., glove warmers).

Polly Vagale and the Vagus Nerve Superhighway*

Book
Neuro & the Ception Force Friends: A Special Team of Receptor Neurons That Help Your Body & Brain with Regulation by Dora Henderson, illustrated by Heather Worley (2022)

Description
This intervention builds on the previous one by using *Neuro & the Ception Force Friends* to help children learn about different nervous system states. In the book, the main character, Polly Vagale, introduces the Vagus Nerve Superhighway and the states of the autonomic nervous system. She takes readers on a ride through Vagale Valley, where the body is depicted as a vast roadway connecting various inner systems. Throughout this journey, Polly goes to three main roads representing different autonomic nervous system states: Ventral Vagal Road, Sympathetic Road, and Dorsal Vagal Road, showing the reader what their emotions might look like on each of these roads. This intervention playfully draws on the book by giving children an opportunity to learn about and role-play the three different autonomic nervous system states.

Treatment Goals
- Increase body awareness of ventral vagal, sympathetic, and dorsal vagal states
- Promote emotion regulation and self-awareness
- Enhance empathy and understanding of others who may experience nervous system states differently

Materials
- Paper
- Coloring utensils
- Matchbox cars (optional)
- Pillows, blankets, and sand tray (optional)

Directions
1. Read the book with the child.
2. Explain the various "roads" or autonomic nervous system states to the child, helping the child connect these states to their own experiences:
    - **Ventral Vagal Road:** "Imagine this as Happy Road. It's when you feel happy and friendly, like when you're playing with your friends and having fun. Your body feels calm and safe. What makes you feel happy and engaged?"
    - **Dorsal Vagal Road:** "Think of this as Sad Road. Sometimes, you might feel sad or tired, like when you miss someone you love or when you're really tired after a busy day. Your body might feel slow and quiet. What makes you feel sad or shut down?"

---
* Intervention by Dora Henderson, LMHC, RPT-S, CTP, CST

- **Sympathetic Road:** "This is Mad Road. Sometimes, you might feel angry or frustrated, like when you can't get your way or something doesn't go as planned. Your body might feel like it has lots of energy, like a race car! What makes you feel frustrated or angry?"

3. Explain how these roads represent different feelings our bodies can have. We all travel on these roads at different times, and that's okay. Discuss how it's important to know how we feel and what to do when we're on these roads to help ourselves feel better.

4. Have the child role-play the various nervous system states to show how they feel when they are in each state:
    - Ventral vagal state (happy)
    - Dorsal vagal state (sad, shut down, or frozen)
    - Sympathetic nervous system state (frustrated or angry)

5. Then have them draw what each state looks like for them. For example, they might draw certain facial expressions, body postures, or symbols to represent these states.

6. When they are done, take a moment and invite the child to think of which Ception friend they might choose (from the previous *Sensory and Somatic "Ception" Party* activity) to help them feel better when they are in a sympathetic nervous system or dorsal vagal state. Use hypothetical scenarios to explore how different Ception friends might provide support and comfort in these situations.

Variation

1. Gather some small matchbox cars and find a place to play, like a carpet or a sand tray. Place the cars nearby.

2. Use materials like pillows, blankets, or sand to create different types of roads for the cars to drive on. You can make one road bumpy by placing pillows and cushions in a zigzag pattern, another road smooth and straight, and a third road with a tricky part, like a puddle or a small hill.

3. Explain to the child that just like cars can go on different roads, people can have different feelings. For example, feeling happy is like driving on a smooth road, feeling worried is like driving on a bumpy road, and feeling stuck or unsure is like driving on the tricky road.

4. Let the child pick a car and place it on one of the roads. Encourage them to show how the car is feeling by making it drive fast, slow down, or even stop. For instance, if the car is on the bumpy road, it might go slowly and wobble like it's a little worried.

5. Along the way, explain that the cars can take breaks, just like people need breaks when they're doing something hard or when they feel a lot of emotions.

6. Introduce a part of the play area as a gas station or rest stop. This is a place where the cars and the child can take a little brain break to relax and feel better. Have the cars stop at this special rest area to take a break, breathe deeply, and calm down.

7. Keep playing and switching the cars between the different roads, exploring how each road makes the child feel. Talk about the cars' feelings and help the child understand that it's okay to have different emotions.

Autonomic Nervous System States

VENTRAL VAGAL ROAD

Name a coping tool that helps you relax to stay on Ventral Vagal Road.

SYMPATHETIC ROAD

Name a coping strategy that helps you feel better when you are having big emotions on Sympathetic Road.

DORSAL VAGAL ROAD

What or who helps you feel better when you have shut down or feel sad?

Mirror, Mirror

Book
The Fabulous Fight or Flight Stress System: Neuroscience & Polyvagal Theories Through Animal Metaphors by Jennifer Lefebre (2021)

Description
Through nature and animal metaphors, *The Fabulous Fight or Flight Stress System* helps children understand how their brains, bodies, and nervous systems function. By providing a rich, developmentally appropriate, and engaging discussion of the stress response system through rhymes and colorful pictures, this book provides playful, trauma-sensitive, and child-friendly embodied movement and yoga activities to help children up-regulate and down-regulate, while connecting with others. This intervention utilizes the therapeutic relationship to encourage attunement, co-regulation, safety, and connection within the caregiver-and-child dyad.

Treatment Goals
- Provide child-friendly language regarding the stress response system and the brain-body connection
- Support co-regulation and connection within the family

Materials
- None needed

Directions
1. Read the book with the child and their caregiver (or the whole family). Alternatively, someone from the family unit may read the book, or they may take turns reading pages out loud.

2. Introduce the activity as follows:
    - In this activity, you'll have an opportunity to practice mirroring each other's movements. Think of what happens when you look in a mirror: Your reflection does exactly what you do, at the same pace and in the same way. By mirroring each other's movements, we are letting each other know that we are paying attention and that we are seeing, hearing, and understanding each other. This can help us feel safe and supported, especially when we've experienced times when we felt all alone and like no one was there to take care of us.

3. Prompt the child and the caregiver to utilize the animal metaphors from the book as their movements:
    - We will take turns being the mirror reflection using the animals and their movements we just read about. When you are the person deciding on the moves, try to move at a steady pace. That way, your partner will have a chance to get used to the way you move. You also want

to make sure you are not doing "trick" moves. You want to make sure your partner is able to follow along with your moves!

4. Encourage the child and caregiver to engage in various representations offered in the book, as there are metaphors for the fight-or-flight response as well as regulatory possibilities.

5. If time allows (or possibly in a different session), the child and caregiver may be prompted to incorporate real-life scenarios into the movements, such as:
    - A bunny (flight) getting ready for school or work
    - A lion (fight) doing their homework or chores
    - An opossum (freeze/shutdown) at the store

My Seven Sensational Senses Self-Care Kit

Book
Seven Sensational Senses for Little Sprockets: Part of the Fabulous Fight or Flight Stress System Series by Jennifer Lefebre (2023)

Description
Through an inclusive framework, *Seven Sensational Senses for Little Sprockets* provides a multifaceted exploration of the senses and sensory system so that all children may access this information. Written for children with sensory-related disabilities as well as those without, this book provides information about the ways our sensations may be similar or different from one another. It also includes playfully embodied sensory and adaptive strategies to help children self-regulate so they can feel safe and connected within their bodies and with others. This intervention allows the child to understand the signals that their body is sending to their brain and to realize that not everyone experiences the world in the same way. It also takes them on an interoceptive journey of self-discovery and provides them with an opportunity to build a sensory-based self-care kit that is unique to their own experience.

Treatment Goals
- Provide the child with language to understand their unique sensory stress system and interoceptive cues
- Support self-regulation and intrapersonal connection within the child

Materials
- A plastic pencil box
- Sensory-related items of the child's choosing (various textures, smells, colors, sounds, etc.)

Directions
1. Read the book with the child.
2. Introduce the activity with the following script, pausing for a bit after each prompt to allow the child time to answer. If the child experiences their senses in an adaptive manner, make sure to modify the script to fit their unique experience:
   - If you'd like to, we can go on a little mindful meditation journey. You may choose to sit or lie down for this journey. Bring a gentle awareness to your body and your surroundings. What are some things you see? Is your body experiencing any sensations? What are some things you hear? Can you smell anything? Are you tasting anything?" [*If the child has difficulty answering, you may provide an example or two to help them along.*]
   - When you are ready, draw a small circle with your nose in the air, making a gentle circle as you move your head and neck. Gently move your fingers and toes as well.

3. Introduce the next part of the activity as follows:
   - Now we are going to create a sensory self-care kit, which will help you use your senses if you get stressed out. I have so many sensory items to choose from. Which ones would you like to start with?
4. Encourage the child to find sensory items that elicit positive thoughts and feelings (e.g., a piece of silky fabric, something that crinkles or crunches, a cotton ball that smells like vanilla, lotion that smells pleasing, lip balm, playdough) and have them place these items in the pencil box.
5. It is important to try various items that represent different sensations, as what may be calming to one child may activate a different child. It is up to the child, not the therapist, to include different items. If the child is struggling, you may offer different ideas for the child to explore.

CHAPTER 5

Neurodiversity

People are described as neurodivergent when their thought patterns, behaviors, or learning styles fall outside of what is considered "normal" or neurotypical. This might include individuals with autism, attention-deficit/hyperactivity disorder (ADHD), Tourette's syndrome, and other learning differences. Working with this population is one that is dear to my heart. Many of these children teach me new facts each week, as they think of projects and games through a lens I had never considered! These children are also sure to remind me of everything that I have forgotten from the week before.

Unfortunately, neurodivergent children often receive negative messages about their differences, which only makes their challenges harder to overcome. As clinicians, it is thus critical that we celebrate the gifts of neurodivergence and deepen our understanding of how the brain works, which empowers children and families to see their differences as strengths. We must help them grow their self-esteem by providing them with opportunities to express their uniqueness, rather than viewing differences as barriers. We want to provide them a safe space where they can be themselves and provide opportunities for play that "speak" their language. This involves offering interventions with several different sensory, movement, and connection options. Be aware that for some neurodivergent children, an abundance of toys may be overwhelming—in these cases, less can be more. Remember that what is "just right" for one child may not be "just right" for another since we all process sensory information differently and have different sensory preferences.

It is important to note that many children who have experienced trauma are misdiagnosed with ADHD and autism and placed on medication. Trauma and anxiety can mirror these disorders because some of the symptoms (e.g., distractibility, hyperactivity, impulsivity) overlap. You always want to dig deeper and question the diagnosis since the treatment for neurodivergent children is different from the treatment of trauma. If your client is getting evaluated for ADHD or autism, make sure the evaluator considers the child's trauma history so they can make an appropriate diagnosis and formulate a plan for the child to be most successful.

If you work with neurodivergent children and love play therapy, make sure to also check out the brilliant books and resources from Robert Jason Grant, developer of Autplay® and author of *Play Interventions for Neurodivergent Children and Adolescents* (2024).

Suggested Materials

- Expressive art supplies (e.g., paint, markers, paper, clay)
- Sand tray with more realistic-looking miniatures (and rakes, funnels, shovels, chopsticks, or wooden tongs for kids who have sensory sensitivities and do not want to touch the sand)*
- Sensory toys
- Sensory sequence pillows
- Weighted stuffed animals or a weighted lap pillow
- Tunnels and forts
- LEGO®
- Toy trucks and cars
- Games—there are so many, but here are a few I love for these kids: mancala, Operation®, chess, Scrabble®, Twister®, obstacle course, charades

Suggested Books

Featured in This Chapter

- *My Brain Is a Race Car: A Children's Guide to a Neuro-Divergent Brain* by Nell Harris (2023)
- *All Cats Are on the Autism Spectrum* by Kathy Hoopmann (2020a)
- *All Dogs Have ADHD* by Kathy Hoopmann (2020b)
- *Some Brains: A Book Celebrating Neurodiversity* by Nelly Thomas, illustrated by Cat MacInnes (2020)
- *Every Bunny Can Learn: A Tail of Inclusion* by Amy Nelson, illustrated by Yogesh Mahajan (2023)
- *Just Ask! Be Different, Be Brave, Be You* by Sonia Sotomayor, illustrated by Rafael López (2019)
- *Miss Piper's Playroom: Helping Aiden with His ADHD* by Lynn Louise Wonders, illustrated by Uliana Barabash (2022a)
- *When Things Get Too Loud: A Story About Sensory Overload* by Anne Alcott (2021)

Also Recommended

- *Happy Dreamer* by Peter H. Reynolds (2017)
- *I'm Here* by Peter H. Reynolds (2011)
- *My Brain Is Magic: A Sensory-Seeking Celebration* by Prasha Sooful, illustrated by Geeta Ladi (2023)
- *ADH-Me!* by John S. Hutton, illustrated by Lisa Griffin (2016)
- *Different—A Great Thing to Be!* by Heather Avis, illustrated by Sarah Mensinga (2021)
- *The Secret Life of Rose: Inside an Autistic Head* by Rose Smitten (2021)
- *Congratulations, You're Autistic!* by Katie Bassiri and Alex Bassiri, illustrated by Dylan Zinn (2022)
- *It's Hard to Be a Verb!* by Julia Cook, illustrated by Carrie Hartman (2008)
- *Too Much! An Overwhelming Day* by Jolene Gutiérrez, illustrated by Angel Chang (2023)

---

* For alternatives to sand when working with kids with sensory sensitivities, you can use jasmine rice, Kay-Kob®, lentils, pasta noodles, or confetti instead. You can find other fantastic alternatives by watching Robert Jason Grant's YouTube video: https://www.youtube.com/watch?v=OJSn2395yL8&t=2s.

Red Light, Green Light Scribble Drawing*

Book
My Brain Is a Race Car: A Children's Guide to a Neuro-Divergent Brain by Nell Harris (2023)

Description
This a great book that many children and adults can relate to. I know I can relate to the metaphor of my brain being a race car that sometimes runs out of gas! This is especially the case for many neurodivergent children, who often feel like their brakes do not work, making everyday tasks more challenging. Although the book itself provides some tools to help children regulate and slow their minds and bodies, I like to pair it with the following intervention, which is based on D. W. Winnicott's Interactive Squiggle Game. The version included here has the added component of Red Light, Green Light, which makes it helpful for clients who would benefit from focus, concentration, and connection. The intervention works best when done in a group and is a great way for the caregiver or whole family to participate in session.

Treatment Goals
- Improve impulse control, listening skills, focus, and self-regulation
- Promote flexibility and collaboration
- Enhance creativity and problem-solving
- Provide psychoeducation on the neurodivergent brain

Materials
- Large paper
- Markers or other coloring utensils

Directions
1. Read the book with the child.
2. Talk about what it feels like for your brain to be a race car, and then introduce the activity by saying, "We are going to see how fast *your* car can go! Can it slow down when it needs to? Do its brakes work to stop at the red light?"
3. Introduce the first part of the activity by placing a large piece of paper and markers on the table or floor. Ensure there is enough space for each family member to reach the paper comfortably.
4. Have each person in the family pick a marker, and instruct one person to draw a scribble on the large piece of paper. Then the next person continues where the last person left off by adding to their scribble, followed by the next person, so on and so forth. The scribble becomes a continuous line of connections, with the lines going in whatever direction they choose.

---
* This original intervention features welcome additions from Paris Goodyear-Brown (2022).

5. When the family is done, say, "This is too easy, so we are going to make it harder" and turn the paper over. Ask the family if they are familiar with the game Red Light, Green Light. Explain that red light means stop, green light means go, yellow means slow down, and purple means go super fast.

6. Then pick someone in the family to start as the leader who will be calling out the commands, and explain that the family's goal is to connect their scribbles together (similar to before), but each person cannot go until the leader says "green light." They should also change the speed at which they draw in response to the commands (i.e., using slower strokes in response to yellow and faster strokes in response to purple). Play several rounds, switching the leader in each round so each family member has a turn, until the scribble is complete.

7. Once the scribble creation is complete, invite the family to use markers or whatever other art supplies they want to create a picture from the scribbles. They can color in any images they see and expand on them. This is a fun time for the family to work together, quiet their minds, reset, and just color together.

8. At the end of the activity, make observations regarding the child's ability to focus, listen, and not get a speeding ticket. You might ask questions like "Was it hard to wait for the green light and be patient?" and "What speed did you like the most? Super fast (purple), regular (green), or slow (yellow)?"

9. Have everyone sign the creation and allow them to take it home. Encourage the family to continue playing this at home, as well as the basic version of Red Light, Green Light.

My "About Me" Book

Books
- *All Cats Are on the Autism Spectrum* by Kathy Hoopmann (2020a)
- *All Dogs Have ADHD* by Kathy Hoopmann (2020b)

Description
I adore *All Cats Are on the Autism Spectrum* and *All Dogs Have ADHD*—you cannot help but fall in love with Kathy Hoopmann's books. These two books explain autism and ADHD to children through a variety of adorable animal photographs. It allows neurodivergent children to relate to these animals and reframe their challenges as strengths. I have clients who want to read these books over and over again, or at least look at the pictures. Any child who loves animals will appreciate this book, as it is even beneficial for children who are not neurodivergent in helping them better understand their peers or siblings. In this intervention, your client will have an opportunity to create their own "about me" story that is based on these books and that reframes their challenges from a positive, strength-based lens.

Treatment Goals
- Provide psychoeducation on autism and ADHD
- Empower the child to see their challenges as strengths
- Build self-esteem and pride

Materials
- Coloring utensils and a premade blank page book (or paper that can be stapled or tied together with yarn to make a book)

Directions
1. Read whichever book is most appropriate for your client.

2. Invite the child to create their own book about themselves. Instruct them to write down the qualities they most relate to in Hoopmann's story and then, in their book, have them give examples of how they possess that quality. For example, in *All Dogs Have ADHD*, one page says, "An ADHD child can be fearless." If the child relates to that quality, they would write "fearless" on a blank page in their book and draw a picture to represent how they are fearless. Make sure they also give their book a title and sign their name as the author and illustrator.

3. When the client is done creating their book, they can read it back to you and then take their special book home to share with others.

Adaptation for Telehealth
- Create a Google doc or use another app that allows the child to create their book digitally. You can check out https://app.bookcreator.com for ideas or search online for other book creator apps for kids.

Brain Power*

Book
Some Brains: A Book Celebrating Neurodiversity by Nelly Thomas, illustrated by Cat MacInnes (2020)

Description
This book provides a thorough presentation of neurodiversity and includes illustrations of several different children with various sensitivities, needs, and ways of being in the world. There are also messages on each page that describe what neurodiversity is and recognize it as a positive part of society ("My neuro is not typical—what a cool part of me!"). This intervention draws on the book by giving the neurodivergent child an opportunity to explore the way their brain works differently than others and to identify how these differences can actually be strengths. It also provides them with a fun visual reminder they can take home with them to celebrate these differences. You can complete this intervention with an individual child or as a family activity.

Treatment Goals
- Provide psychoeducation on the concept of neurodiversity
- Explore how the neurodivergent brain works differently
- Help the child view neurodivergence in a positive way and improve their sense of self

Materials
- Paper
- Coloring utensils

Directions
1. Read the book with the child. You can take turns reading, read to the child, read the whole book, or select certain pages to read.
2. Process the book with the child by asking questions such as "What do you think this book was about?" "What do you think was the message of this book?" "What in this book reminded you of yourself?"
3. After processing these questions, provide the child with a piece of paper and coloring utensils, and invite them to draw an outline of a person to represent themselves. For the head, ask them to draw a large brain inside. They can color the person however they like, even with specific clothing.
4. In the large brain head, ask the child to draw pictures, write words, or use colors to represent the ways they believe their brain is different. If the child is struggling to think of ideas, help them brainstorm.

---
* Intervention by Robert Jason Grant, EdD, LPC, NCC, RPT-S

5. Once the child has completed their drawing, talk to them about each of the differences they identified. As part of this discussion, reinforce the notion that differences are important and okay—in fact, they are often a source of strength! For example, children with visual sensory differences may struggle with certain lighting being distracting and painful, yet they are also able to notice small details in a room or perceive movement from long distance. Another example is a child who only has one main interest area that they want to study, think, and talk about, yet they are very knowledgeable in this area and may have the opportunity to turn their interest into a very fulfilling career.

6. Make sure to provide time for the child to ask questions and process the experience. You can even refer back to parts of the book to help reinforce the message.

7. At the end of the session, the child can take their paper creation home to remind themselves of their awesome neurodivergent self!

My Neuro Is Not Typical

Book
Some Brains: A Book Celebrating Neurodiversity by Nelly Thomas, illustrated by Cat MacInnes (2020)

Description
This intervention is a wonderful complement to the previous activity that further reinforces the idea that neurodiversity is a normal, essential part of human diversity. You can do this as a stand-alone intervention or ask the client to write their answers to each question inside of the brain they created in the previous *Brain Power* activity. Either way, this intervention will remind your client that "all brains are special, all brains are smart" and help them understand that brains are all unique—just like fingerprints!

Treatment Goals
- Empower kids to see their strengths
- Provide psychoeducation on neurodiversity
- Celebrate differences and highlight the gifts of the amazing brain

Materials
- *My Neuro Is Not Typical* worksheet (included at the end of this intervention)
- Coloring utensils
- Paper
- Playdough, model magic, or clay

Directions
1. Read the book with the child. You can take turns reading, read to the child, read the whole book, or select certain pages to read.

2. Have the child complete the following *My Neuro Is Not Typical* worksheet, or ask the child to respond to the following prompts on plain paper:
    - My brain thinks like this . . .
    - My brain does stuff that others can't, like . . .
    - How do you see things differently?
    - How is your "neuro" a superpower?
    - What are some things that you really like?
    - What are some things that you don't like?
    - Do you prefer being in a big crowd or being alone?
    - How does noise make you feel?
    - Is your brain more creative or do you like numbers and facts? Or maybe both?
    - What do you do at school to make you feel better?
    - How do you give yourself a brain break so your brain isn't "hurty"?

3. Once the child is done, invite them to make a replica of their brain! They can use playdough, model magic, clay, markers and paper, or whatever they choose to celebrate their beautiful brain.

My Neuro Is Not Typical

Write or draw your answers to the prompts below.

My brain thinks like this . . .

My brain does stuff that others can't, like . . .

Is your brain more creative or do you like numbers and facts? Or maybe both?

Do you prefer being in a big crowd or being alone?

What do you do at school to make you feel better?

How do you see things differently?

How is your "neuro" a superpower?

How does noise make you feel?

How do you give yourself a brain break so your brain isn't "hurty"?

What are some things that you really like?

What are some things that you don't like?

Animal Allies*

Book
Every Bunny Can Learn: A Tail of Inclusion by Amy Nelson, illustrated by Yogesh Mahajan (2023)

Description

Every Bunny Can Learn is the sweet rhyming story of a young neurodivergent bunny named Mimi who is navigating her first day at school. With her teacher's help, Mimi learns that it's okay to be different and that every bunny can thrive at school and be a successful learner with the right accommodations. The book provides valuable insights and practical strategies to foster inclusion and embrace unique strengths and learning preferences for young children.

This intervention builds off the book by inviting the child to create a puppet of the character they most identify with in the story, who represents their animal ally. This ally is a symbol of support and inclusion for the child, which reinforces the message and theme of the book. This intervention is flexible and can be adjusted based on the child's age, developmental level, and available resources. Miniatures or stuffed animals may replace the art activity if it better supports the child's preferences. The focus is on providing a safe and engaging environment for exploration, self-expression, and reflection. This intervention can be done during any phase of treatment and can be used with the child individually or in a small group, with or without a teacher or other caregivers.

Treatment Goals

- Teach concepts of neurodiversity and inclusion
- Help the child identify their unique learning preferences and needs
- Strengthen the child's ability to express their unique learning preferences and needs

Materials

- Paper lunch bags
- Coloring utensils
- Glue
- Child-safe scissors
- Craft supplies (e.g., googly eyes, yarn, fabric scraps, feathers, stickers, pom-poms)
- Cardstock or construction paper

Directions

1. Read the book with the child.
2. While reading the book, pause and highlight key moments to discuss the various animal characters' qualities, strengths, and learning preferences. Explore how the characters demonstrate inclusivity and acceptance. Explain that neurodiversity means everyone's brains are different, and that's okay! Just like everyone looks different on the outside, everyone's brain works differently on the inside too.

---

* Intervention by Amy Nelson, LCSW, LSCSW, RPT-S

3. Afterward, ask the child to choose the animal character they feel most connected to or identify with from the book. Provide the child with a paper bag and a variety of art supplies and instruct them to use these supplies to transform the paper bag into a puppet representing their chosen animal ally. Encourage creativity and self-expression in their puppet design.

4. Once the puppet is assembled, encourage the child to talk about why they chose that animal, how they relate to it, and how they feel about inclusion and self-acceptance. Processing questions may include:

    - Which animal character did you choose? Why did you choose that animal?
    - What qualities or strengths of that animal do you see in yourself?
    - How does your animal ally represent what makes you unique and special?
    - What supports do you think your animal ally might need to learn best? How does that relate to your learning needs and preferences?
    - What would you want your teacher to know about how you learn?
    - What did you learn about including others and accepting differences from the book?
    - How can you help others feel included and accepted, just like the animals did in the story?

    The answers to these questions may be summarized and written on cardstock paper to be added to the puppet for the child to take home and share, if they choose, with their caregivers.

5. Reiterate that everyone is unique and has a special way of experiencing the world. Encourage the child to embrace and communicate their differences and learning preferences. Conclude the session by affirming the child's unique qualities and highlighting how their understanding of inclusion and self-awareness can positively impact their interactions.

What's Your Question?

Book
Just Ask! Be Different, Be Brave, Be You by Sonia Sotomayor, illustrated by Rafael López (2019)

Description
Just Ask! is a book that empowers children to have a voice. So many kids feel different or are curious about others who are different, but they are often afraid to ask questions and may stay in a place of curiosity and confusion. This book explores children of different ages and with different abilities, including children with diabetes, Down syndrome, ADHD, and autism, and looks at the special powers these kids have as well. This intervention draws on the book by inviting your neurodivergent client to participate in a pretend news segment where they come up with questions other people can "just ask" to get to know them. I have also enjoyed doing this intervention with transgender clients who are afraid that kids will ask questions about their gender or bully them. It provides a wonderful opportunity for children to role-play how they can respond to questions with confidence and self-respect. Although you can do this intervention alone with the child, it's also a great way for the caregiver to participate in session.

Treatment Goals
- Celebrate diversity and encourage curiosity
- Provide psychoeducation about differences
- Build resilience and empowerment

Materials
- Toilet paper roll and foil (or a toy microphone)
- Camera, phone, or computer with a video camera
- Backdrop materials (e.g., colorful silk scarves, blankets, curtains, large rolls of paper)

Directions
1. Read the book with the child.
2. Help the child create an imaginary news stage in your office. You can create a background together using colorful silk scarves, blankets, curtains, or large rolls of paper.
3. Invite the child to make a list of questions they want to be interviewed about. These might be questions they have been asked at school or that they have felt uncomfortable answering in front of their peers. You can help the child brainstorm potential questions if they have difficulty coming up with ideas.

4. Have the child make a microphone using a toilet paper roll and foil ball. They can also use a plastic toy microphone if you have one available (or they can even talk into their hand and pretend it is a microphone!).

5. Interview the child using the questions they created.

6. If you are recording the interview, make sure to obtain a signed release and permission from the child's parent or guardian. Although your client can role-play the interview without being recorded, some kids find it helpful to watch it back. Make sure to also follow HIPAA guidelines and do not record anything on your personal computer or device.

Adaptation for Telehealth

- Create a fun background on the computer using the various options available on your selected telehealth platform.

Funneling and Focusing BIG Energy*

Book
Miss Piper's Playroom: Helping Aiden with His ADHD by Lynn Louise Wonders, illustrated by Uliana Barabash (2022a)

Description
This book tells the story of a boy with ADHD named Aiden, whose therapist supports him in channeling all his hyperactive energy through games and play-based activities. So often, children diagnosed with the hyperactive subtype of ADHD have an experience of having big energy that can feel and appear to resemble an ungrounded live electric wire. This intervention supports children with ADHD by helping them recognize their big energy as a superpower that can be channeled, or "funneled" and "focused," so they can learn to better manage and regulate themselves.

Treatment Goals
- Promote self-regulation skills
- Empower the child to see their challenges as strengths
- Enhance the child's ability to focus their attention

Materials
- Timer and materials for four activity stations (see below)

Directions
1. Read the book with the child.
2. Create a series of four activity stations in the room:
   - A ring toss game with a blue painter's tape line on the floor. The child will stand with their toes on the line to enhance body awareness and keep a focused distance from the pegs.
   - An assortment of pom-poms and clear plastic cups. The child will sort the pom-poms by color, with one cup for each pom-pom color.
   - A memory matching card game that is set up with cards face down ready to find matches.
   - A large exercise ball that the child can bounce on to discharge energy.
3. Explain to child that you will set a timer for three minutes for each station. During those three minutes, the child will participate in each activity with you until the timer goes off and then shift to the next station. When the child gets to the bouncy ball, they will sit on the ball and bounce in place while sharing with you what they liked about the previous activities.
4. Each activity helps the child to focus their mind, eyes, and body on the given activity, strengthening and sharpening their ADHD superpowers.

---
* Intervention by Lynn Louise Wonders, LPC, CPCS, RPT-S

When Things Get Too Loud*

Book
When Things Get Too Loud: A Story About Sensory Overload by Anne Alcott (2021)

Description

When Things Get Too Loud follows the story of Bo, a boy with sensory processing differences that impact how he feels moving through the world. Using his "Feel-O-Meter," Bo is able to identify how comfortable or uncomfortable he is experiencing different sensory inputs. When Bo gets overwhelmed by too much sensory input and the unexpected introduction of a new friend, he finds a place to hide that drowns out the overwhelming sensory environment around him. With the help of a little snail, Bo finds just the tool that works for his individual differences to calm his nervous system and re-engage with the world around him in a calm, confident, and comfortable way! This intervention builds off the book by helping children tune into their own body cues, identify the body sensations associated with various levels of arousal, and start to identify triggers for sensory overload.

Treatment Goals

- Build interoceptive awareness
- Connect body sensations with certain feeling states
- Promote sensory regulation

Materials

- Paper and coloring utensils
- *Feel-O-Meter* worksheet (included at the end of this intervention), or have the child create one

Directions

1. Read the book with the client.
2. Introduce the Feel-o-Meter and the concept of interoception (i.e., internal body signals) using developmentally appropriate language tailored to the client. Note that many neurodivergent children are hyporesponsive to interoceptive cues, meaning that they may not be able to identify body-based cues of arousal until the level of arousal is very intense. In this case, it is important to support the development of interoceptive awareness prior to using this specific intervention.
3. Assist the child in identifying the colors they associate with different levels of arousal in the body and have them color these in on the Feel-o-Meter accordingly.
4. Have the child identify the body-based cues they experience with various levels of arousal. Label these on the Feel-o-Meter using words or pictures (as developmentally appropriate).
5. Ask the child to identify situations where they experience these different levels of arousal or stress.

---

* Intervention by Rebecca O'Neill, LCSW, CAS

Feel-O-Meter

Feeling Feelings from the Inside Out*

Book
When Things Get Too Loud: A Story About Sensory Overload by Anne Alcott (2021)

Description
When Things Get Too Loud follows the story of Bo, a boy with sensory processing differences that impact how he feels moving through the world. Using his "Feel-O-Meter," Bo is able to identify how comfortable or uncomfortable he is experiencing different sensory inputs. When Bo gets overwhelmed by too much sensory input and the unexpected introduction of a new friend, he finds a place to hide that drowns out the overwhelming sensory environment around him. With the help of a little snail, Bo finds just the tool that works for his individual differences to calm his nervous system and re-engage with the world around him in a calm, confident, and comfortable way! This intervention builds off the book by helping children connect certain body cues with feeling states and identify situations that trigger sensory overload (as well as situations that help them feel calm).

Treatment Goals
- Build interoceptive awareness
- Connect body sensations with certain feeling states
- Promote sensory regulation

Materials
- Coloring utensils
- Large roll of paper to trace a body
- Standard-sized paper
- Scissors

Directions
1. Read the book with the client.

2. Discuss how the different situations that Bo experiences make him more and more uncomfortable in his body to the point that he has to get away from everything to calm his body down. Ask the child how they know from the illustrations that Bo is getting uncomfortable. You can also point out the physical cues of Bo's dysregulation if the child is unable to identify these body-based cues themselves.

3. Introduce the concept of interoception in developmentally appropriate terms and assist the child in identifying the signals their body gives them when they are feeling a variety of feelings.

---
* Intervention by Rebecca O'Neill, LCSW, CAS

4. Ask the child's permission to trace an outline of their body on the large piece of paper. Touch is not necessary in this activity, but obtaining consent is important to ensure the child's sense of safety and bodily autonomy.

5. Using the separate, smaller pieces of paper, work with the child to create pictures, words, or colors that represent how their body feels in different feeling states. Cut these out. It may be helpful to make a number of copies of the images the child creates before cutting them out.

6. Using the images the child created, have the child place these images on their body outline to identify where in their body they feel these emotions.

7. Introduce different scenarios that might cause sensory overload and have the child place the feeling states images on their body outline to illustrate their experiences of those situations. Make sure to also include scenarios that are pleasant and calm to build the client's awareness of their body cues when in those states.

My Calming Snail Fidget*

Book

When Things Get Too Loud: A Story About Sensory Overload by Anne Alcott (2021)

Description

When Things Get Too Loud follows the story of Bo, a boy with sensory processing differences that impact how he feels moving through the world. Using his "Feel-O-Meter," Bo is able to identify how comfortable or uncomfortable he is experiencing different sensory inputs. When Bo gets overwhelmed by too much sensory input and the unexpected introduction of a new friend, he finds a place to hide that drowns out the overwhelming sensory environment around him. With the help of a little snail, Bo finds just the tool that works for his individual differences to calm his nervous system and re-engage with the world around him in a calm, confident, and comfortable way! This intervention builds off the book by helping children develop tools to calm their bodies down when the sensory input around them feels like too much.

Treatment Goals

- Build interoceptive awareness
- Provide tools to calm sensory overload
- Promote sensory regulation

Materials

- Oven-bake polymer clay, such as Sculpey®, in a variety of colors
- Necklace chain or string (optional)

Directions

1. Read *When Things Get Too Loud* with the client.
2. Discuss Bo's response to the snail in the story and the way that he is able to use the snail to calm his body down.
3. Introduce the idea of fidgets (small items we can manipulate with our hands for extra sensory input for regulation purposes) and the ways in which fidgets can be used to help us feel good in our bodies. Normalize the need for input and movement for regulation.
4. Discuss the aspects of the snail that Bo found interesting and calming, and assist the child in identifying the types of sensory input they find calming.
5. Introduce the activity and explain to the child that they will be creating their very own snail shell fidget out of clay. Explain that the colors and texture of the clay will be a way that they can get the input that feels good to them through touch, sight, and even smell.

---

* Intervention by Rebecca O'Neill, LCSW, CAS

6. Have child pick out a variety of colors that they find calming to include in the creation of their shell.
7. Make pea-sized balls of each color that the child chooses (6 to 8 balls total). Roll the pea-sized balls together to create a larger ball.
8. Placing the clay ball on the table, begin to roll the ball into a snake-like string. Use the palms of both hands to roll the string of clay into the child's preferred length and width.
9. Once the clay is the length and width the child likes, take one end of the clay and begin rolling it into a spiral. The finished shape will look like the spiral of a snail's shell. You might choose to poke a straw-sized hole into the clay so the finished product can be made into a pendant.
10. Bake the clay according to the package instructions. Once it is cool, work with the client to explore the sensory aspects of the shell fidget and how they might use it. If you added a hole before baking, the client can string their fidget pendant on a necklace for easy access.

CHAPTER 6

Trauma and Attachment

There are many different types of trauma that children and families experience, from a single traumatic experience to multiple traumas that occur over an enduring period of time. Often, this trauma can involve attachment ruptures when children are separated from their caretakers due to mental health issues, addiction, deployment, incarceration, loss, divorce, or the caregiver's inability to manage the pressures of parenthood. We know that children's brains are profoundly affected by these experiences, leading their stress response system to get stuck in a state of hypervigilance or immobilization. As a result, traumatized children are often on alert—scanning their world for cues of danger and safety.

The treatment in these situations is to repair attachment wounds, which we do by facilitating co-regulation and establishing a safe, nurturing relationship with the child. In the context of a trusting relationship, children can achieve that felt sense of safety and connection, which regulates their nervous system and returns them to a ventral vagal state. As Stephen Porges (2017) has described, safety *is* the treatment and the treatment is safety. Books provide that safety and work as a co-regulator, especially when read by a safe, supportive adult.

When working with children who have witnessed or endured physical or sexual abuse, they also need to know that touch can be nurturing and safe. They may associate any type of touch as a cue of danger, so your job is to help them understand what safe touch feels and looks like. For example, I have been involved in international service work in migrant camps in India. When we worked with children in the camps, we traced letters and numbers on their backs. This served a dual purpose: It not only helped them learn English but also emphasized the significance of positive and safe physical contact with other people. Engaging in this activity, the children exhibited focused attention, emotion regulation, and genuine delight.

Similarly, there are special considerations when working with children who are in foster care, who have been adopted, who are living with other family members, or who have experienced any other breaks in attachment. In these situations, it is vital to have the caretakers participate in the bibliotherapy interventions. Having the caregiver read the book with the child is part of the therapeutic process of holding that safe space for them. I am a strong advocate that parents participate in the process, especially when dealing with attachment trauma. When there is a loss or other traumatic event in the family system, the whole family is traumatized, and books assist in healing the entire system.

The books I have included in this chapter are beautifully written and pair well with play therapy interventions for trauma, attachment ruptures, and other forms of grief and loss. They have brought so much healing to my clients. Additionally, if you are a play therapist who works with attachment issues, I highly recommend that you seek training in Theraplay® (Booth & Jernberg, 2010) as this was a game changer for my clients. I also recommend reading *Beyond Behaviors* (Delahooke, 2019), *The Boy Who Was Raised as a Dog* (Perry, 2006), *Dibs in Search of Self* (Axiline, 1964), *Raising Kids with Big, Baffling Behaviors* (Gobbel, 2023), and *What Happened to You?* (Perry & Winfrey, 2021), which all significantly impacted my work as a therapist.

Suggested Materials

- Medical toys and supplies (e.g., first-aid kit, bandages)
- Play food and play kitchen
- Baby dolls
- Baby bottles and sippy cups
- Small snacks and juice boxes (giving children juice or snacks with the caregiver's permission can help create nurturing and safety)
- Cotton balls
- Bubbles
- Sand tray and miniatures
- Expressive art supplies (e.g., paint, markers, paper, clay)
- Therapeutic board games (my favorite is the Nurturing Game: https://www.childtherapytoys.com/products/nurturing-game)

Suggested Books

Featured in This Chapter

- *A Safe Circle for Little U* by Paris Goodyear-Brown, illustrated by Eric Gott (2016)
- *Understanding Neglect: A Book for Young Children* by Beth Richey and Paula Wood (2021)
- *When a Grown-Up You Love Hurts You: A Book for Children Who Have Experienced Physical Abuse* by Beth Richey and Paula Wood (2019)
- *Penelope the Peacock* by Paris Goodyear-Brown, illustrated by Eric Gott (2018)
- *Daddy's Waves* by Chandra Ghosh Ippen, illustrated by Erich Ippen Jr. (2021)
- *Mama's Waves* by Chandra Ghosh Ippen, illustrated by Erich Ippen Jr. (2020)
- *We're All Not the Same, But We're Still Family: An Adoption and Birth Family Story* by Theresa Fraser and Eric E. W. Fraser (2019)
- *Maybe Days: A Book for Children in Foster Care* by Jennifer Wilgocki and Marcia Kahn Wright, illustrated by Alissa Imre Geis (2022)
- *Letting Us into Your Heart* by Dorothy Derapelian, illustrated by Sharon Toh (2017)
- *My Grief Is Like the Ocean: A Story for Children Who Lost a Parent to Suicide* by Jessica Biles and Jillian Kelly-Wavering, illustrated by Jessica Biles (2022)
- *When Someone Dies: A Children's Mindful How-to Guide on Grief and Loss* by Andrea Dorn (2022)
- *Family Forest* by Briana Quinlan, illustrated by Patricia F. Braga (2022)
- *The Heart and the Bottle* by Oliver Jeffers (2010)
- *The Invisible String* by Patrice Karst, illustrated by Joanne Lew-Vriethoff (2000/2018)
- *In Grandpaw's Pawprints: A Story of Loss, Life & Love* by Lauren Mosback, illustrated by Nino Aptsiauri (2022)
- *Jungle Journey: Grieving & Remembering Eleanor the Elephant* by Barbara Betker McIntyre, illustrated by Michael O. Henderson (2000)
- *Rabbityness* by Jo Empson (2012)
- *The Very Lonely Firefly* by Eric Carle (1995)
- *The Magic Rainbow Hug: A Fun Interactive Storyteller-Child Activity* by Janet A. Courtney (2013a)
- *The Magic Rainbow Hug Activity Book* by Janet A. Courtney (2013b)

Also Recommended

- *No Matter What* by Debi Gliori (1999/2014)
- *You Are Never Alone: An Invisible String Lullaby* by Patrice Karst, illustrated by Joanne Lew-Vriethoff (2020)
- *I Love You Like No Otter* by Rose Rossner, illustrated by Sydney Hanson (2020)
- *Gabby the Gecko* by Paris Goodyear-Brown, illustrated by Brian Hull (2003)
- *A Terrible Thing Happened* by Margaret M. Holmes, illustrated by Cary Pillo (2000)
- *Brave Bart: A Story for Traumatized and Grieving Children* by Caroline H. Sheppard (1998)
- *The Fabulous Fight or Flight Stress System: Neuroscience & Polyvagal Theories Through Animal Metaphors* by Jennifer Lefebre (2021)
- *Amazing You! Getting Smart About Your Private Parts* by Gail Saltz, illustrated by Lynne Cravath (2005)
- *An Exceptional Children's Guide to Touch: Teaching Social and Physical Boundaries to Kids* by Hunter Manasco, illustrated by Katharine Manasco (2012)
- *My Body Is Private* by Linda Walvoord Girard, illustrated by Rodney Pate (1984)
- *The Goodbye Book* by Todd Parr (2015)
- *The Kissing Hand* by Audrey Penn, illustrated by Ruth E. Harper and Nancy M. Leak (1993/2006)
- *Gentle Willow: A Story for Children About Dying* by Joyce C. Mills, illustrated by Cary Pillo (1993)
- *Tear Soup: A Recipe for Healing After Loss* by Pat Schwiebert & Chuck DeKlyen, illustrated by Taylor Bills (1999/2005)
- *Miss Piper's Playroom: Helping Lily with Her Loss* by Lynn Louise Wonders, illustrated by Uliana Barabash (2021b)
- *Once I Was Very Very Scared* by Chandra Ghosh Ippen, illustrated by Erich Ippen Jr. (2016)
- *You Weren't with Me* by Chandra Ghosh Ippen, illustrated by Erich Ippen Jr. (2019b)
- *Holdin Pott* by Chandra Ghosh Ippen, illustrated by Erich Ippen Jr. (2019a)
- *I Love You Rituals* by Becky A. Bailey (2000)

Recommended for Adoption, Foster Care, and Kinship Care

- *Argo and Me: A Story About Being Scared and Finding Protection, Love, and Home* by Chandra Ghosh Ippen, illustrated by Erich Ippen Jr. (2022)
- *A Mother for Choco* by Keiko Kasza (1982/1999)
- *Motherbridge of Love* by Anonymous, illustrated by Josée Masse (2007)
- *A Handful of Buttons* by Carmen Parets Luque (2018)
- *I Don't Have Your Eyes* by Carrie A. Kitze, illustrated by Rob Williams (2003)
- *We Belong Together* by Todd Parr (2007)
- *Between Us and Abuela: A Family Story from the Border* by Mitali Perkins, illustrated by Sara Palacios (2019)
- *A Grandfamily for Sullivan* by Beth Winkler Tyson, illustrated by Adam Walker-Parker (2019)
- *Murphy's Three Homes: A Story for Children in Foster Care* by Jan Levinson Gilman, illustrated by Kathy O'Malley (2008)

A Safe Circle for You*

Book
A Safe Circle for Little U by Paris Goodyear-Brown, illustrated by Eric Gott (2016)

Description
The delightful book *A Safe Circle for Little U* is about the process of reconnecting and learning to trust again after loss. After losing Big O as a reliable caregiver and companion, Little U finds the courage to connect and trust Q. Likewise, Q finds a way to stretch to forge a relationship with Little U. A story of hope and reconnection, the metaphor provides a foundation from which reconnection can be explored via symbols and images. This intervention draws on the book by helping the child identify safe people and connections that bring them comfort. When used as a part of EMDR, this bibliotherapy intervention can also be used for resourcing.

Treatment Goals
- Identify social support and reduce isolation
- Explore safety in the context of relationships
- Help the child find connection again after trauma, loss, or abandonment

Materials
- Paper and coloring utensils or a sand tray and miniatures

Directions
1. Read the book with the client.
2. Invite the client to create an image or select a sandtray miniature to represent connection and strong relationships with the people in their life who offer support.
3. Once the child is done, you can use the broad directive "Tell me about what you have created" to begin processing. Ask the child to expand on how these people make them feel safe and supported or give an example (e.g., "My grandmother never missed a soccer game" or "Whenever I feel scared, my aunt lets me know I can call her").
4. Ask the child to visualize being in the arms of one of these people and ask them what it feels like. They may associate a certain smell, voice, or feel with a particular person. Encourage them to bring in all the senses and breathe in this visualization.

---

* Intervention by Sueann Kenney-Noziska, MSW, RPT-S

Understanding Neglect*

Book
Understanding Neglect: A Book for Young Children by Beth Richey and Paula Wood (2021)

Description
This book helps young children understand the complexities of neglect and subsequent involvement in the child welfare system. It gently explores the various categories of needs that every child has in order to grow up safe and happy: housing, food, education, supervision, medical care, safety, and love. This intervention helps kids further understand which of their basic needs are being met or not met as a result of their current circumstances. It should be completed during the psychoeducation phase of treatment, with the involvement of a safe caregiver if that is an option. This can help the child gain a concrete understanding of their situation and provide answers as to why they were removed from their home or why Child Protective Services became involved due to neglect.

Treatment Goals
- Explain the concept of neglect in a non-stigmatizing, non-shaming manner
- Provide a basic understanding of neglect and how it relates to the child and their specific family situation
- Teach the child about different basic needs

Materials
- Blank paper or a copy of the house outline (included at the end of this intervention)
- Coloring utensils

Directions
1. Read the book with the child.
2. Draw a basic house shape on a piece of paper or use a photocopy of the provided house outline. Write the child's name on it (example: Beth's House).
3. Based on the categories of needs that are mentioned in the book (food, education, supervision, body care, safety, love, housing), have the child draw a picture inside the house that represents how each of these needs are being met where they live now. For added engagement, you can ask the child to focus on their favorite in each category (e.g., favorite food, favorite beverage, favorite teacher, favorite nurse, most trusted person who keeps them safe, favorite babysitter, favorite room in the house).

---
* Intervention by Beth Richey, LCSW, RPT-S

4. Read aloud the "For Therapists" questions at the back of the book to encourage further exploration and discussion:
    - Tell me some ways you are lovable. What are good things about you?
    - What are some examples of things kids need?
    - What were some things in your home you did not have enough of?
    - What are your feelings about what kids need?
    - What are your feelings about living in a new home?
    - Whose fault do you think it is that your caregiver was not able to give you everything you need?
    - Can you still love the grown-up who did not give you all the things you need?
    - Who is the grown-up who gives you all the things you need now?

Adaptation for Telehealth

- Using the screen share function on your telehealth platform, show a PDF of the house outline or draw one yourself. Direct the child to write or draw a picture of their answers inside the house.

_____'s *House*

Draw a picture of how each of these needs are met at your current home: food, education, supervision, body care, safety, love, and housing.

When a Grown-Up You Love Hurts You*

Book
When a Grown-Up You Love Hurts You by Beth Richey and Paula Wood (2019)

Description
When a Grown-Up You Love Hurts You helps young children process and gain a greater understanding of physical abuse by a trusted adult. The book uses friendly animal imagery to explain that anger is a normal emotion, but that some grown-ups have problems with anger that cause them to be physically aggressive toward others, including their children. It goes on to further explore children's reactions to physical abuse and explains how abuse is never the child's fault. In this intervention, children will combat the negative self-image and internalized emotions that can arise following caregiver abuse. It is most appropriate during the psychoeducation phase of treatment (with the involvement of a safe caregiver as well).

Treatment Goals
- Help the client understand that physical abuse is never the child's fault
- Explain physical abuse as a grown-up problem
- Reinforce the child's inherent lovability and positive qualities

Materials
- Paper or photocopy of the body outline (included at the end of this intervention)
- Coloring utensils

Directions
1. Read the book with the client.
2. Draw a basic body shape on a piece of paper or use a photocopy of the provided body outline. Write the child's name at the top.
3. Together, come up with a list of the child's strengths and positive qualities. Ask the child to fill in the body outline with all these positive qualities using words or pictures.
4. Read aloud the "For Therapists" questions at the back of the book to encourage further exploration and discussion:
    - Tell me some ways you are lovable. What are good things about you?
    - What are ways some parents keep their children safe?
    - Is it okay for people to be angry? Do all angry people hurt other people? What are safe ways to show angry feelings?

---
* Intervention by Beth Richey, LCSW, RPT-S

- What unsafe behaviors did you see in your home?
- Do you think it's your fault that your grown-up showed unsafe behavior and hurt your body?
- What kinds of feelings have you had about your grown-up after they hurt your body?
- Can you still love the grown-up that hurt your body?
- How is it helpful to talk to a safe grown-up about your feelings and memories?

Adaptation for Telehealth

- Using screen share on your telehealth platform, show a PDF of the body outline or draw your own. Ask the child to write or draw a picture of the lovable things about themselves inside of the outline.

_____'s **Strengths**

Inside the body, write or draw pictures of your strengths and positive qualities.

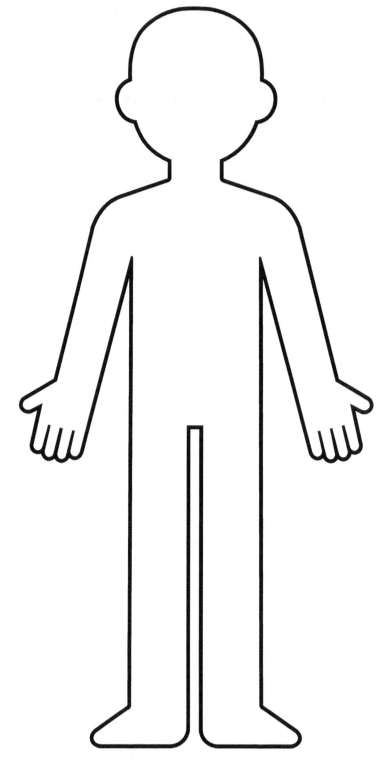

Plucking the Peacock*

Book
Penelope the Peacock by Paris Goodyear-Brown, illustrated by Eric Gott (2018)

Description
During a TraumaPlay™ training for house-parents of children who were rescued from human trafficking situations, one house-parent asked, "In our group home, we serve a mother and child who were rescued from a brothel in India. The mom became pregnant after one of many rapes. She kept the baby and after she gave birth, she would hide him under the bed when she was forced to have sex with customers. They were rescued when the little boy was only one. He is nine years old now and keeps asking his mother, 'Who is my daddy?' His mother then cries and leaves the room. What shall I tell her to tell him?"

    Penelope the Peacock provides the answer to questions like these. The book shares the story of a beautiful peacock who is sold to a Feather Farm and has her feathers plucked by customers, one by one. She loses hope that life will ever change, that she could ever feel real and whole again. Just then an egg appears and becomes her baby, giving her renewed hope and purpose. This story can be used with child sexual abuse survivors and with children who have survived other forms of maltreatment and neglect. Children deserve answers to their questions, and they deserve a storykeeper who will unflinchingly hold the space for them to name the hurt and have it witnessed and honored. In this intervention, which is most appropriate for the working phase of treatment, each plucked feather represents one of the child's trauma memories. The plucked feathers may help you identify trauma targets and aid you in designing a treatment plan that integrates TraumaPlay and EMDR. The simple act of naming events can also function as a titrated dose of trauma narrative work, serving as both an initial approach and containment of trauma content.

Treatment Goals
- Identify the child's traumatic events
- Titrate doses of trauma narrative work
- Identify the child's resiliencies
- Provide targeted psychoeducation about boundaries, consent, and the trauma that comes from boundary violations

Materials
- Peacock feathers
- A variety of other colorful feathers
- Clay

---

* Intervention by Paris Goodyear-Brown, LCSW, RPT-S

Directions

1. Read the story to the child.

2. Explain that our bodies belong to us and that just like people took Penelope's feathers without asking, sometimes people will take things from us—emotionally, physically, psychologically, or relationally—without asking.

3. Invite the child to create a peacock body by molding clay and attaching multiple peacock feathers to it.

4. When the child is done, invite them to name individual boundary violations they have experienced as they pluck individual feathers from their clay peacock. Each plucked feather represents a traumatic experience and can become a trauma target for reprocessing and integration work. You can use the following script:

    - "Penelope's feathers were her pride and joy. They made her feel beautiful and worthy. But people came and stole them from her. Are there things in your own life that you feel were taken from you? These could be hurtful thoughts, feelings, or beliefs that a grown-up shared with you. These might be scary events that made you feel small, ashamed, scared, embarrassed, or alone. Pull out a feather for each of the hurts you want to name with me. In the future, we might draw pictures, create sandtrays, or tell stories that help these hurts to get smaller."

5. After the child has pulled out as many feathers as they like, you can offer the other varieties of bird feathers and explain the following: "When hurts happen, it helps to share them with a trusted adult. In the story, Penelope's child became a source of strength and comfort for her. What are your sources of strength and comfort?"

6. Have the child name one coping strategy or new nugget of wisdom they've learned as they add new feathers into the empty holes. These are concrete reminders that they are healing. In the end, they will have created a beautiful new creature, not quite the same as before but equally beautiful and stronger than they knew might emerge.

Adaptation for Telehealth

- Use your telehealth platform's whiteboard feature to draw a peacock with feathers. Have the child individually erase feathers from the drawing as hurts are named. The child can draw new feathers in vibrant colors as resiliencies are identified.

Riding Daddy's Waves

Book
Daddy's Waves by Chandra Ghosh Ippen, illustrated by Erich Ippen Jr. (2021)

Description
Daddy's Waves is an excellent book that was written specifically for children whose parents have struggled with addiction or mental illness, whether they live together or not. So many children are affected by parents who struggle with these issues. The book is about a little girl, Ellie, whose father does not show up for their visit, leaving her sad, confused, and filled with questions. The safe adults in Ellie's life help her through this difficult time by using the metaphor of the waves—helping Ellie understand that her father has highs and lows and reminding her to hold on to the good memories. This intervention uses the same metaphor of a wave to help the child talk about and understand their father's* ups and downs, recognize and hold on to loving memories, and know that they are not alone.

Treatment Goals
- Provide the child with the language to understand the challenges that parents face
- Allow the child to talk about tough times and good times—keeping the good memories alive
- Help the child understand why their parent may not be around

Materials
- Balancing board

Directions
1. Read the book with the child.
2. Introduce the board and have the child practice balancing on it as if they are riding the waves.
3. You can prompt the child on how big the wave is and instruct them to turn left, turn right, duck, sail through calm waters, or jump off the board before the wave gets too big. This active and playful game incorporates the full body.
4. After the child has acclimated to the balancing board, give different examples of what is going on with their father and have them describe what type of wave accompanies this situation. For example:
   - Can you tell me about a good memory with Daddy? Is this a big scary wave, a fun wave, or a calm wave?
   - When was a time when the wave was so big that it was scary?
   - Can you think of a question you have for the wave?
   - Do you think the wave has a message for you?

---

* If the child's trauma involves a maternal caregiving figure, you can use the alternate version of the book, *Mama's Waves*, which was also written by Chandra Ghosh Ippen and illustrated by Erich Ippen Jr. (2020).

We Are Still Family*

Book
We're All Not the Same, But We're Still Family: An Adoption and Birth Family Story by Theresa Fraser and Eric E. W. Fraser (2019)

Description
We're All Not the Same, But We're Still Family was written by a play therapist and adoptive parent together with her adult child. It is a book that describes one child's journey of reconnecting with his birth family while being supported by his adoptive family in doing so. This intervention will also support the child in reconnecting with their biological family as long as certain prerequisite conditions are met. You must first meet with the adoptive parents and develop therapeutic rapport while investigating factors necessary for this reunification process, such as:

- Where is the biological family geographically located?
- What were the circumstances of the adoption?
- Is it likely that the biological family will provide the adopted child with a positive message about their birth?
- Is the biological family likely to maintain healthy contact?
- Is the biological family able to accept the adoptive family's role in the child's life?
- Are the adoptive parents able to accept the biological family if they have different values, cultures, faiths, and so on?
- Are the adoptive parents willing to make the time and effort needed for this process? It will involve working with you in parents-only sessions, communicating with and potentially coordinating visits with the biological family, and supporting the child through experiences that could be difficult for both the child and the adults.

It is only once you achieve acceptable answers to these questions that you should pursue this intervention.

Treatment Goals
- Support the child in identifying questions they would like to ask their biological family
- Identify positive commonalities the child shares with their family of origin

Materials
- Paper
- Collage materials (scissors, glue, markers, magazines, etc.)
- Sand tray and miniatures

---
* Intervention by Theresa Fraser, CYC-P, CPT-S, MA, RP, RCT

Directions

1. Help the adoptive parents role-play how to initiate contact with the child's birth family. What will they say? How will the adoptive parents explain why they are initiating contact now? How will they explain how they want to proceed? How will they explain the reasons why they think it might be good for the child to have contact with the birth parents now? Ask the adoptive parents if there might be any indicators that might convey to them that they, the biological parents, or the child might not be ready for the next steps.

2. With your support, connect the adoptive parents with the identified birth family to ensure that the birth family is in an emotional place to engage with the child. It is paramount that the biological family can provide the child with positive messages about their birth. You must determine if they can explain why the attachment rupture occurred, ensuring that the child is given the message that they are in no way responsible for the rupture and that adult circumstances precipitated the separation from the biological family.

3. After this meeting, consult with the adoptive parents and discuss if this information should be shared with the child via a letter from the biological family to be processed in therapy, via a face-to-face meeting, or not at all. If you decide not to proceed, then do not continue with the intervention and do not read the book to the child (though you may have already shared the book with the parents for their own preparation).

4. You should also identify whether a safety plan needs to be implemented so the child's privacy can be maintained if reunification is not suitable at this time. For example, depending on where the biological family lives, are they likely to make contact without the permission or support of the adoptive parents? Do the adoptive parents know of other people connected to the child who may be in contact on behalf of the biological parents? If the child is old enough to use social media, is their usage supported in case biological family members reach out electronically? If any of these things are possible, do the adoptive parents have a plan to address these concerns?

5. If you proceed with the intervention, future meetings between the adult members of the adoptive family and the biological family may need to be arranged—without the child present—to gain further information and also create a positive connection.

6. As you move forward, make sure that the biological family is interested in collaborative contact and is not interested in undermining the child's adoptive placement. If they are not able to provide reassurance of this, then perhaps the adoptive family only provides limited updates about the child's functioning to the biological family until the child is an adult and emotionally prepared to deal with the anger the biological family may have about the systems that facilitated the child's apprehension or surrender.

7. Once a visitation or access plan is determined, you and the adoptive parents can read the book to the child before sharing the information that has been found. You can then share the letter from the biological parents, or plan a phone call or video call. The child needs to be reassured that they don't need to make contact, or continue with contact, at any stage of the process.

8. If the child does not want to have contact with their birth parents, the adoptive parents can hold on to the letter provided by the biological family and let the child know that it will be there for them if at any time in the future they decide they would like to make contact (or to consider

making contact). The child should also be asked to provide consent regarding what information about them can be shared with biological family.

9. If the child does choose to move forward, let them know they will receive support from you and their adoptive family as appropriate. Then invite the child to make drawings or collages about themselves or their biological family as they identify any questions they have about their birth family. Conversely, the child can use the sand tray to process their feelings and ask questions while you write them down. Either way, this process provides the child with the opportunity to create a list of questions in advance, as they are likely to forget these during first contact.

10. If you or the adoptive family decide to seek out the answers to these questions on behalf of the child, the biological family can provide answers in a video or a written letter to be shared with the child as determined by the adoptive parents.

Maybe Days*

Book

Maybe Days: A Book for Children in Foster Care by Jennifer Wilgocki and Marcia Kahn Wright, illustrated by Alissa Imre Geis (2022)

Description

This book provides exceptional, developmentally appropriate psychoeducation and support to children placed in foster care. For these children, the answer to questions such as "Will I live with my parents again?" and "Will I stay with my foster parents forever?" is often "maybe." In the book, the author addresses these questions and normalizes the often-conflicting feeling states that children experience in response to the "maybes." In this intervention, you will help your client learn how to cope and reach out for help whenever they have a "maybe day"—those days when they are feeling lost, frustrated, or hopeless with this transitional period of intense distress and unpredictability. Maybe their visits with their biological family keep getting rescheduled without any explanation and they're expected to go about the rest of their day like nothing happened without having any concrete date to look forward to. Part of this process involves creating a safety plan they can use in the midst of a crisis.

Treatment Goals

- Develop a safety plan for "maybe days"
- Reduce distress in response to uncertainties associated with foster placement
- Improve the child's ability to communicate during a crisis through the use of visual aids

Materials

- Watercolor paper with two holes punched at the top (so it can be hung up)
- Yarn
- Scissors
- Lined paper
- Coloring utensils and watercolors (or magazines and scissors)
- Glue or tape

Directions

1. Read the book with the child.
2. Assist the child in creating a safety plan that includes the following:
   - A list of their triggers (specific behaviors, situations, or circumstances) that put them at risk for a crisis
   - Warning signs (bodily sensations, thoughts, behaviors) that a crisis is developing
   - Internal coping strategies they can use to take their mind off the problem

---

* Intervention by Kelsey Dugan, MPS, ATR-BC, LCPAT

- External support network (three trusted adults they can call on a "maybe day" and the contact information for each)*
- Crisis hotlines for both the child and foster parent and the nearest emergency room
- A reminder to use the script "I'm having a maybe day" to ask for help

3. Create at least three copies of the safety plan: one for the child to keep in a safe place of their choosing (such as on their nightstand or in their backpack), one for the foster parent, and one to keep in your office.

4. Offer the coloring utensils (e.g., crayons, markers, colored pencils) and ask the child to draw a shape in the middle of the watercolor paper to represent themselves. This can be a circle, blob, scribble, square—whatever they choose!

5. Inside the shape, ask the child to draw what they are feeling inside—along with the phrase "I'm having a maybe day."

6. Then invite the child to use watercolors to depict the "maybe" environment outside of their shape. Some children may become frustrated with the properties of the watercolors since they are a fluid art material. If the child shows severe distress in response to the lack of control, intervene immediately and help ground them before replacing the watercolors with a more controlled material or with magazine clippings they can use to make a collage. Children with extensive sexual trauma may require limit setting when it comes to material choice, as the use of fluid materials can be flooding to them without proper containment provided by the clinician. Children with trauma benefit from clarity and predictability so they feel safe and less overwhelmed.

7. On a piece of lined paper, help the child write out the names and roles of each supportive adult in their life. It is strongly encouraged that they use a pencil, as those assigned to the child's case may change over time. Then write the following mantra: "Any day can feel like a maybe day, and today was one of those days. But kids do the best they can in the middle of all the maybes. Today was a maybe day and I did my best. I won't be perfect, but I can trust that I am safe and loved on both my good days and my maybe ones. I'm proud of myself for making it through another maybe day."

8. Attach the lined paper to the back of the child's watercolor creation using glue or tape.

9. Help the child string a piece of yarn through the hole-punched circles at the top of the watercolor paper so they can hang it on their bedroom door. Explain to the child that they now have a bedroom door sign they can use to signal to their foster parent when they're having a "maybe day" and are in need of support and patience.

10. If possible, laminate the door sign and safety plan to serve as a protective measure against any destruction that may occur during a crisis. If the client does destroy the door sign during a crisis episode, avoid shaming them, as this can and does happen. It's best to respond by reestablishing safety and promptly scheduling a therapy session to safely process the crisis before helping the child to create a new door sign and/or safety plan.

---

* Children may want to list their biological caregivers in their support network, which may not be realistic depending on the situation. If the biological caregiver is not available, avoid falling into a power struggle with the child and empathize with the child's situation before offering alternatives. For example, you can encourage the child to use a transitional object that reminds them of their biological caregiver instead.

Catch the Feather*

Book

Letting Us into Your Heart by Dorothy Derapelian, illustrated by Sharon Toh (2017)

Description

Letting Us into Your Heart is the young child version of Core Attachment Therapy© (CAT; Derapelian, 2015, 2019), which is a therapeutic process to facilitate secure attachment among children who have been adopted or experienced any other type of attachment rupture or developmental trauma. It gives the child firsthand experiences of utilizing the love and emotional responsiveness of their new parents. CAT involves a two-component prescriptive play therapy process. The first is the Nurtured Heart Approach® in which the parent learns how to focus on what is going right rather than on the chaos the child brings. This puts the parent in the driver's seat of the energy in the house. The second component involves a series of mommy/daddy games that replicate the attachment development process, which allows the parent to form a loving bond with the child in the language of children—play! This intervention describes one of the games illustrated in *Letting Us into Your Heart*. It involves the caregiver and child blowing a feather back and forth.

Treatment Goals

- Allow the child to feel a separate sense of self
- Facilitate attunement between the parent and child

Materials

- Feather

Directions

1. Ask the parent and child to sit on the couch or floor facing one another.
2. Explain to the child and caregiver that they will be playing a game called "Catch the Feather." The game starts with the parent blowing the feather from the palm of their hand to the child to catch. The child then blows the feather back to the parent.
3. The game continues in this fashion, with the parent deciding when the game is over. In CAT games, the parent is in charge, as secure attachment can only occur when the child relinquishes control to the parent. It conveys trust.
4. If there is time, the parent can read the book *Letting Us into Your Heart* with the child so the child can recognize the attachment game they have just played.

---

* Intervention by Dorothy Derapelian, MEd, LCMHC

"My Grief Is Like the Ocean" Mantra*

Book
My Grief Is Like the Ocean: A Story for Children Who Lost a Parent to Suicide by Jessica Biles and Jillian Kelly-Wavering, illustrated by Jessica Biles (2022)

Description
My Grief Is Like the Ocean tells the story of a boy whose father has died by suicide. This gently illustrated book uses the metaphor of the waves to promote dialogue about the narrator's complex grief experience. When read together with a caring adult, it helps normalize and encourage the expression of the many emotions that children face after a loss due to suicide. This heartfelt book also promotes the development of healthy coping skills and provides resources to grieving caregivers. The intervention that accompanies this book is intended only for children who have experienced complex grief due to a loved one's suicide. It should be completed at the beginning of treatment and revisited each week in subsequent sessions. During the process of treatment, you can keep the drawings the child has created, ultimately forming a book that they can then take home at the end of treatment.

Treatment Goals
- Normalize the varied emotions a child may feel after loss due to suicide
- Provide caregivers with a coping skill to use at home
- Give the child a safe distance in explaining their complex grief through a metaphor

Materials
- Paper
- Coloring utensils
- Stapler

Directions
1. Read the book with the client.
2. On the top of a blank piece of paper, write the phase "My grief is like _____. Today _____," and then help the child brainstorm which nature-based metaphor will become their mantra. For example, they might say:
   - My grief is like the ocean. Today the waves feel huge.
   - My grief is like a mountain. Today it feels hard to climb.
   - My grief is like a cactus. Today it feels sharp.
3. Ask the child to draw an image that reflects the mantra they chose to write and describes how their grief feels that day.

---
* Intervention by Jessica Biles, LCSW-R, RPT

4. When the child is done, write the date on the bottom of the page. Repeat this activity at the start of each subsequent therapy session as a feelings check-in. You can also encourage caregivers to use this check-in at home.

5. At the end of treatment, gather each page in order, from the first date to the last date, and compile them together into a book for the child to take home. Encourage the child to make a cover for their book and a dedication page that you can add to the front. Staple the completed book together.

Adaptation for Telehealth

- You can either send art materials to the child to use at home or check in with the caregiver to see if they have these materials already.
- An alternative to a tangible book is to use the illustration feature on the whiteboard function of your telehealth platform. You can take a screenshot of the artwork each session and then print them, compile them into a book, and mail it to the client at the end of treatment.

Grief Parts*

Book
When Someone Dies: A Children's Mindful How-to Guide on Grief and Loss by Andrea Dorn (2022)

Description
When Someone Dies describes grief as "all the feelings we have when someone dies" and provides steps for working through these tricky feelings. The following intervention, which is inspired by the internal family systems (IFS) model, encourages children to consider how these grief feelings are "parts" of themselves that emerge and each have unique needs. You can do this intervention with the child during any phase of treatment, but it may be most helpful during the initial psychoeducational stages to create greater awareness of grief feelings and help the child identify what they need in order to heal. It is also a wonderful opportunity to invite the caregiver into the session.

Treatment Goals
- Identify and acknowledge difficult emotions
- Identify and acknowledge the child's various parts
- Explore protective parts and strengthen the child's connection to their inner self
- Empower the child to develop healthy coping strategies and self-compassion

Materials
- Paper or *Grief Parts* handout (included at the end of this intervention)
- Coloring utensils

Directions
1. Read the book with the child.
2. Discuss how grief feelings can be distinct compared to how we feel when we are peaceful and at ease. In this way, grief feelings can almost feel like other parts of us, or even like other people or characters.
3. Use a piece of paper to draw the child's grief parts, or use the provided *Grief Parts* handout. In the center of the page, depict the child's peaceful "self" (using either their name or a self-drawing). Add the grief parts that emerge most often as parts surrounding the child's self. You can use the expanded feelings chart in the back of *When Someone Dies* to help identify recurring grief feelings.
4. For each identified part:
    - Name or draw an image of the part.
    - Discuss any messages that part wants the child or others to know.

---
* Intervention by Andrea Dorn, MSW

- Discuss what that part needs to feel better when it is activated.
- Create a feel-better plan for any grief part the child identifies as needing extra support. Use the "feel-better steps" in *When Someone Dies* as a guide if needed. Some parts may have the same feel-better plan.

5. Suggestions for optional discussion questions:
    - What do you notice about your grief parts? How are they the same? How are they different?
    - How does it feel in your body when each grief part emerges?
    - Are there any thoughts, feelings, or situations that trigger specific grief parts?
    - Which parts have an easier time reaching out for help from others?
    - Which parts can support other parts of you that may need support?

Variation

- Have the child pick stuffed animals or characters from a TV show or movie to represent their peaceful self and each grief part.

Adaptation for Telehealth

- Use the telehealth platform's whiteboard feature as a drawing space.

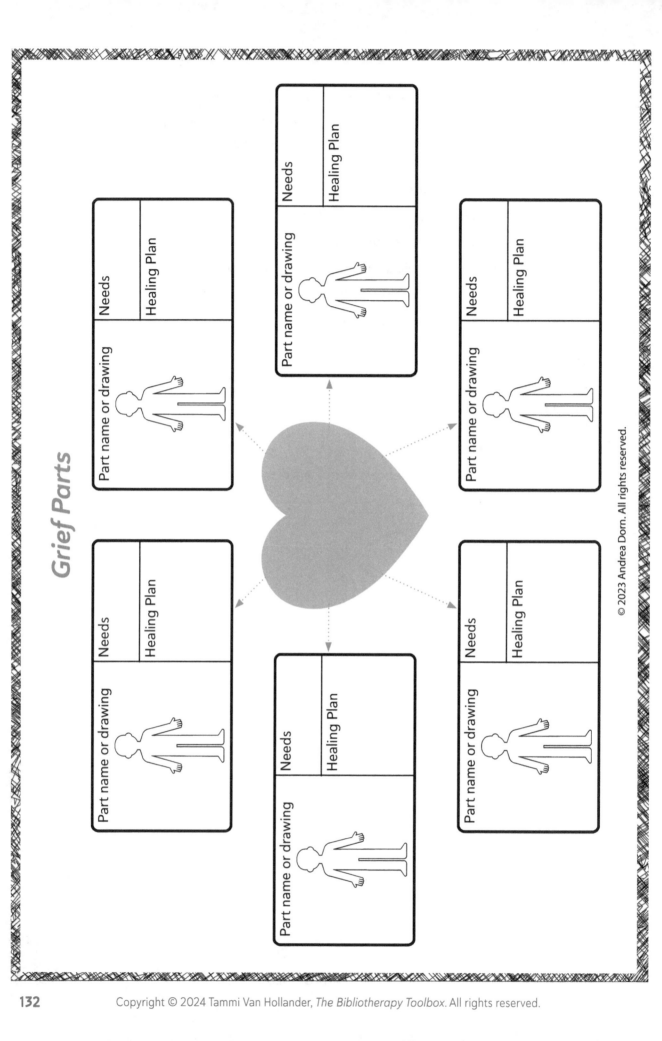

Family Forest*

Book
Family Forest by Briana Quinlan, illustrated by Patricia F. Braga (2022)

Description
Family Forest helps children create awareness and understanding of what it means to have a family. It moves beyond the traditional "family tree" model of the family system and allows children to see the diversity of what a family can comprise—including the idea that family is whom you choose. Through the beautifully illustrated woodland characters, the book provides concrete language around the gifts that family gives us that are not tangible yet imperative to who we are as individuals. Similarly, this intervention allows the client to create their own narrative around family while processing the different individuals with whom they have connection and ties (blood-related or not), and the gifts these individuals have given them that cannot be seen or touched. It can be done at any phase of treatment.

Treatment Goals
- Allow the child to tell their story of family and reinforce a sense of belonging
- Strengthen communication around attachment and trust
- Promote compassion, understanding, and support of differences among family systems

Materials
- *Create Your Own Tree and Forest* template (included at the end of this intervention)
- Variety of expressive art supplies—whatever the client's preference is!

Directions
1. Read the book with the child.
2. Invite the child to create their own family forest with any medium they would like (e.g., paper and pencil, markers, canvas, paint, pastels, iPad and iPencil, clay, diorama). It can be fun to use fingerpaint to create leaves using their fingerprints! The sky is the limit with supplies here.
3. Utilize the *Create Your Own Tree and Forest* visual to help the child brainstorm what items to put in the roots, trunk, and branches of their tree. The roots include places and people they have grown from, the trunk is made up of what they value, and the branches contain what they want to build for themselves, their future, and their family based on the gifts they have received from others. You can also find a tree coloring page online to print and build off if that would allow the client to feel more comfortable in the creative stage.

---
* Intervention by Briana Quinlan, LCSW-C

4. Process the activity together. Some processing questions could include:
    - Who did you include in your own unique tree and why?
    - What places did you include in your own unique tree and why?
    - Whose tree might you be a part of?
    - Trees have a really long lifeline. Do you think your tree and forest have changed, will change, or will remain the same?
    - There are all different types of trees all over the world. What type of tree would yours be and why?
    - Who gets to decide what is in your tree and in your forest and why?

Adaptation for Telehealth

- Use your telehealth platform's whiteboard feature or share screens with the client to brainstorm ideas for the roots, trunk, branches, and leaves. Then invite the client to create their family forest on the screen or to use whatever art medium they have at their disposal.

Create Your Own Tree and Forest

Branches
The branches make up the "crown" of the tree. They are responsible for converting sunlight into energy for the tree. Some branches are thick and other branches are more like twigs.

Trunk
The trunk of a tree provides support. It connects the crown of the tree with its roots. The trunk transports the nutrients from the roots to the top of the tree.

Roots
The roots anchor the tree to the ground—this helps it to remain in place for a long, long time and weather storms as well as other conditions. The roots provide nutrients from the ground to the tree itself. They also keep the tree from eroding or being destroyed. There can be tons of roots to a tree. Some are short and some are up to 20 feet long!

The Heart and the Bottle: Heavy and Light*

Book
The Heart and the Bottle by Oliver Jeffers (2010)

Description
The Heart and the Bottle deals with the topics of death, loss, and grief. Utilizing a metaphor, the author takes us on a developmental journey from childhood through adulthood. To begin, the child in the story places their heart in a bottle in an attempt to cope with grief and loss. The child keeps the bottle safe by carrying it around their neck, but over time, it becomes heavier and heavier, and they miss out on life around them. As time passes, the child becomes an adult and they eventually meet a small child who helps them feel the joy of life again. The adult is able to free their heart from the bottle while still holding on to memories of their loved one in their body and thoughts. Similarly, this role-play intervention helps the child recognize that when hard feelings stay for a long time, it can make them forget how to experience joy, wonder, and curiosity. It allows them to recognize that we sometimes need other people to help us with hard feelings and to live fully again while holding on to memories.

Treatment Goals
- Identify feelings that occur in response to loss
- Illustrate how big feelings can turn into difficult (heavy) behaviors over time
- Learn strategies to allow big feelings to return to the child's heart and memories

Materials
- Paper
- Coloring utensils
- Scissors
- Bottle
- Lanyard
- Calendar or clock
- Materials that can serve as "heart rescue" props (e.g., long tweezers, tongs, straws)

Directions
1. Read the book with the child.
2. Help the child cut out a variety of paper hearts and place these inside the bottle. For a greater challenge, use a bottle with taller neck, and for less of a challenge, use a bottle with a wide opening, like a mason jar.

---
* Intervention by Mary Anne Peabody, EdD, LCSW, RPT-S

3. Tie a lanyard around the neck of the bottle and place it around your neck.
4. Act out the events from the book to illustrate how time is passing. Use a calendar or clock to illustrate this passage of time with the child.
5. Have the child solve your problem (i.e., take the hearts out of the bottle) using a selection of heart rescue tools.
6. Discuss how we sometimes need other people to give us support and suggestions for coping with hard feelings. You might ask additional processing questions like "What does this story tell us about difficult/heavy feelings over time?"
7. You can extend this activity by creating a poster of other healthy strategies the child can use to cope with sad feelings (e.g., read a book, draw a picture, talk to a trusted grown-up).

Adaptation for Telehealth

- Let the child be the teacher and problem-solver by having them suggest how to get the hearts out of the bottle with the available materials. Or using the Zoom whiteboard, identify difficult feelings—and coping strategies to manage those feelings—and draw hearts around the ideas.

Heart to Heart

Book
The Invisible String by Patrice Karst, illustrated by Joanne Lew-Vriethoff (2000/2018)

Description
The Invisible String is a story about how we are all connected by a series of invisible strings, so we know we are never alone. This book is an excellent resource when working with children who have experienced grief, divorce, separation, life transitions, and so much more. It reminds the child that even if someone is not physically by their side, that person is still with them in their heart. This intervention draws on the book by having the child create a visual representation of all the connections in their life. For more invisible string activities, I highly recommend that you check out *The Invisible String Workbook* (Karst & Wyss, 2019).

Treatment Goals
- Process grief and loss
- Create feelings of safety and connection
- Identify and strengthen the child's support network, both within and outside their family

Materials
- Large paper
- Markers
- Sand tray and miniatures (optional)
- String, stones, or pick-up sticks (optional)

Directions
1. Read the book with the child.
2. In the middle of a large piece of paper, ask the child to draw a heart with their name inside it.
3. Then ask the child to write all the people they are connected to (e.g., relatives, favorite teachers, neighbors, good friends, people who have died, pets) around them, circling each name with a heart.
4. Invite the child to draw lines that connect each person to them, showing that they are always connected and they are never alone.
5. Alternatively, you can have the child choose a miniature that represents themselves and have them place it in the center of the sand tray.
6. Then invite the child to choose miniatures that represent loved ones and have them place these in the sand tray as well.

7. The child can then use string, pick-up sticks, or stones to connect each person to them, color-coding the connections that are most important to them.

8. Encourage the child to take their drawing home (or take a picture of their sandtray creation) and to revisit it when they need a reminder of the special people in their life.

In Grandpaw's Pawprints*

Book
In Grandpaw's Pawprints: A Story of Loss, Life & Love by Lauren Mosback, illustrated by Nino Aptsiauri (2022)

Description
In this adorable children's story, Bethany the Bear's beloved Grandpaw dies, leaving her feeling very sad and lost. With the help of her friends, Bethany learns that she can celebrate the life of her Grandpaw by sharing his special qualities with others. By following in Grandpaw's pawprints, she can carry on and expand the mark he left on the world. On her journey toward healing, Bethany discovers that Grandpaw's love is still with her—it never left! This intervention draws on the story by having the child create a large pawprint where they can record all the special marks their loved one left on the world.

Treatment Goals
- Provide a safe opportunity for the child to talk about the person who has died
- Encourage the child to remember the positive impact this person had on them and the world
- Offer different ideas to celebrate the life of the person who has died

Materials
- Paper and coloring utensils
- Scissors

Directions
1. Read the book with the child.
2. Ask the child to create the outline of a large pawprint. You can also search online for images of pawprint outlines if that would be more appropriate for your client.
3. Inside the pawprint, invite the child to write down or draw special memories about the person who has died, and what they miss about them. They can also write down or draw the unique qualities and traditions this individual shared with others or share how the individual impacted the world in positive ways.
4. When they're done, ask the child to share what they wrote, either visually or by using their words. Encourage the child to bring this pawprint activity home to place in a special spot in their room or home.
5. There is also a resource section at the end of book that you can use for additional suggested activities that offer hope and encouragement, as well as tools and tips for adult caregivers on discussing grief and loss.

---
* Intervention by Lauren Mosback, LPC

Jungle Journey: Grieving and Remembering Eleanor the Elephant*

Book
Jungle Journey: Grieving and Remembering Eleanor the Elephant by Barbara Betker McIntyre, illustrated by Michael O. Henderson (2000)

Description
This book shares the grief journey that the animals in the jungle take when they are faced with the death of Eleanor the Elephant. It validates the many ways we mourn and the many ways we can learn to cope with our grief. The jungle animals each react in their own way to the death of Eleanor as they gather and bury Eleanor with twigs and leaves. The animals then continue their jungle journey where they share their fears and help each other through the stages of grief. This intervention provides a similar opportunity for your client to embody the role of an animal as they grieve their loved one's death. It can be done with just the child or with the whole family.

Treatment Goals
- Normalize the grieving process
- Allow the child and family members to share the ways they are grieving
- Identify ways family members can support each other through the grieving process

Materials
- Sand tray and animal miniatures (e.g., elephants, parrots, zebras, rhinos, lions, monkeys, boars, snakes—or another representation of the animals such as pictures or puppets)
- Twigs and leaves (optional)

Directions
1. Read the book with the child (and the family if they are participating).
2. Have the child (and the family, if they are participating) choose an animal miniature featured in the book to show how they grieve like that animal. For example, the elephants in the book asked "why" and stayed together as they mourned, while the rhino felt all alone and was unable to reach out, so she mourned by herself.
3. Place an elephant miniature in the middle of the sand tray to represent the loved one who died. If the client would like, they can choose to cover the miniature with twigs and leaves like the African elephants do.

---
* Intervention by Lyla Tyler, LMFT, RPT-S

4. The child can then use the animal miniatures to describe something they remember about the person who died and what they will miss about them. If family members are participating in session, have them do the same with their chosen miniatures.

5. Have the child and family members think of things they can do to help themselves or others as they grieve their loss. For example, in the story, the elephants help the animals cross the river on the jungle journey, while the lions teach the other animals to roar when they feel afraid. A child may choose to draw pictures for grieving family members, or a caregiver may sing a special lullaby to help a child sleep.

6. Talk about how everyone grieves in their own way and how there is no right or wrong way to grieve. For example, some people feel very sad and cry, while others become agitated and need to get outside and play. Similarly, some people want to spend time with others, while others want time alone.

7. At the end of the activity, take a picture of the sandtray if the child or family would like to.

The Gifts They Left Us

Book
Rabbityness by Jo Empson (2012)

Description

Rabbityness is a very special book—especially if you appreciate the expressive arts, creativity, play, and metaphor—that follows Rabbit's friends on a journey after Rabbit disappears. They find that Rabbit has left behind some very special gifts, like musical instruments and art supplies, for them to help them discover their own "unrabbity" talents. This beautiful story starts in black and white, but as the friends find things that Rabbit has left behind, they color the forest with paint, music, play, and song. This book inspired me to use my *Greatness Cards*™ to really sit and reflect on the beautiful qualities that my mother left behind for me to continue to hold and cherish (as seen in the photographs at the end of this intervention). Using sandtray therapy for grief work is always so powerful and very therapeutic. In this intervention, your client will have an opportunity to create a sandtray to celebrate the person who died or is no longer with them (e.g., because they moved away or there was a rupture in the relationship, like divorce or family cutoff).

Treatment Goals

- Normalize the grieving process
- Honor the positive qualities of loved ones who have died
- Allow the child to name how their loved one made a difference in their world

Materials

- Sand tray and miniatures
- Greatness cards or greatness sticks*

Directions

1. Read the book with the child.
2. Invite the child to create a sandtray to remember their loved one, using the following prompt: "What were the things the person who died left behind for you to remember?"
3. Encourage them to use the greatness cards or greatness sticks as they make their creation. The following are questions you can use throughout this process:
   - What is your favorite quality about your loved one?

---

* Premade *Greatness Cards* and *Greatness Sticks* can be purchased at https://www.mainlineplaytherapy.com/shop. You can also create your own using the Greatness Sticks intervention (p. 44).

- What qualities do you have in common?
- What quality do you think that person would want you to have more of? Or what do you think they would say is their favorite quality about you?

4. After the sandtray creation and process questions, invite the client to give their sandtray a title and take a picture of it.

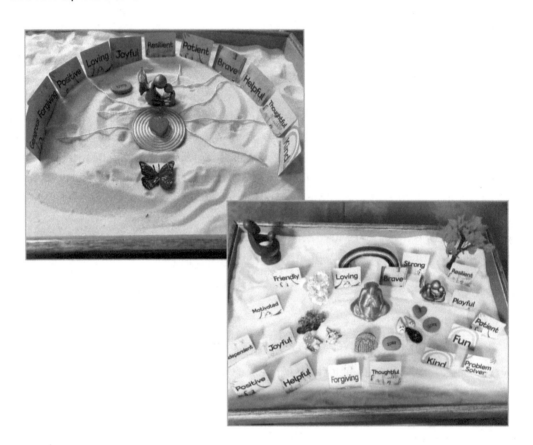

Searching to Belong*

Book
The Very Lonely Firefly by Eric Carle (1995)

Description
The title character in *The Very Lonely Firefly* searches various places for other fireflies. The firefly works hard to find its group, something we all feel as humans. This story resonates with the universal experience of seeking connection and belonging. Just as the firefly in the tale diligently searches for its group, children, too, are on a quest to find their place in the world where they feel safe, understood, and connected. This book becomes a valuable tool for facilitating discussions about the complex emotions associated with loneliness and separation anxiety, especially in situations involving family separations, divorce, adoption, friendship challenges, or other life events. It offers an opportunity to explore the resilience it takes to continue seeking connections even when it feels challenging. Depending on the child's needs, you can either directly relate the book's narrative to the specific challenges in the child's life or maintain a more metaphorical approach. This intervention can be effectively incorporated into early or mid-stage treatment, involving both the caregiver and child in meaningful discussions about their experiences.

Treatment Goals
- Create a connection between caregiver and child
- Identify groups in the child's life where they feel they belong
- Explore the emotions of loneliness, belonging, and separation anxiety

Materials
- **Glow-in-the-dark activity:** Glow-in-the-dark toys or tape and several flashlights
- **Dress-up activity:** A variety of dress-up clothing and several flashlights
- **Art activity:** Paper, markers, and colorful, glittery bandages

Directions
1. Read the book with the client and their caregiver.
2. Choose one of the following activities, based on the client's interests and the materials available:
    - **Glow-in-the-dark activity:** Before the session, place glow-in-the-dark items or pieces of glow-in-the-dark tape around the playroom. After reading the book, explain to the child and caregiver, "The firefly kept flying toward the light to find others. I have several glow-in-the-dark items around the playroom. Is it okay if we dim the lights in the room** and use

---
* Intervention by Rose LaPiere, LPC, RPT-S, ACS
** Always ask the child's permission when turning off or dimming lights. Consider the safety of the environment, such as tripping hazards, and the child's traumatic experiences.

these flashlights as fireflies to find the glow-in-the-dark items? Let's notice how we feel as we search for them and how it feels when we find them." Help the child and caregiver notice the feeling of searching and being found, belonging, and connecting. You can also encourage the caregiver and child to search for fireflies at a park or outside their home.*

- **Dress-up activity:** Invite the caregiver and child to dress up by choosing from the clothing items available. Then give each person a flashlight and explain, "The firefly kept flying toward the light to find others. Is it okay if we dim the lights in the room and use these flashlights as fireflies to find each other? Let's notice how we feel as we search and how it feels when we find each other." Ask them to begin moving or dancing around the room, turning their flashlight on and off, moving toward and away from each other. Explore the feelings of being apart and coming close together. This is a playful way to work on separation anxiety, and the caregiver and child can also play it at home together.

- **Art activity:** Invite the child and caregiver to create images of fireflies using paper, markers, and colorful, glittery bandages (see the example provided). After everyone completes their fireflies, encourage the child and caregiver to share a story about their fireflies.

3. After completing the chosen activity, facilitate discussion with these process questions:

    - The firefly was flying around for so long, looking for other fireflies. Did you think the firefly found what they were looking for?
    - Have you ever felt lonely before? Talk about it or draw a picture of what that felt like when you were lonely.
    - When and where do you feel like you belong? Talk about it or draw a picture of what it feels like when you belong.
    - What can kids do when they feel lonely? (You might help them get started with some suggestions: Talk about it. Find someone to play with, like a caregiver, friend, sibling, or pet. Draw how you feel.)

Adaptations for Telehealth

- **Dress-up activity:** Give the caregiver advance notice to have flashlights and dress-up clothes available during the session.
- **Art activity:** Use a whiteboard tool to create fireflies with the client.

---

* Be sure to check your area to find out when fireflies emerge (in the US, this is typically early summer). Also explain to the caregiver that it's possible they will not find any fireflies; in this case, they can explore how that feels and choose an alternative nature activity, such as making a firefly from sticks, leaves, and other loose nature items.

The Magic Rainbow Hug*

Books

- *The Magic Rainbow Hug: A Fun Interactive Storyteller-Child Activity* by Janet A. Courtney (2013a)
- *The Magic Rainbow Hug Activity Book* by Janet A. Courtney (2013b)**

Description

The Magic Rainbow Hug is a FirstPlay Somatic Storytelling intervention that combines metaphoric storytelling with playful activities that can be simultaneously drawn on a child's back. Some children may come to know these stories as "back stories." The story opens with a mother telling her daughter how she learned about the magic of a Rainbow Hug© from her own mother. Intrigued, the little girl asks, "What's a rainbow hug? How can I get hugged by a rainbow? What will it feel like?" Following a weather theme, a story within a story unfolds, and the little girl (along with her brother and a playful puppy) discover the amazing heartfelt peace of a healing rainbow.

This parent-child intervention uses the power of nurturing touch to reduce fears and anxieties in children while helping them grow feelings of comfort, calm, and relaxation. Research has shown that touch can help reduce stress in children while also increasing levels of empathy and parent-child bonding. When we give caring touch, the feel-good "love" hormone oxytocin is released, while the stress hormone, cortisol, is decreased. There are several touch-based activities included in *The Magic Rainbow Hug* with instructions, located in brackets on the bottom of each page, on how to perform each technique. As the child is listening to the story and receiving nurturing touch on their back, they are engaging their imagination while at the same time connecting to an awareness of sensation by feeling the story. Through the story, children learn relaxation methods to self-regulate while also enhancing their receptiveness to positive caring touch.

Treatment Goals

- Lower anxiety
- Strengthen self-regulation skills
- Build the parent-child attachment relationship
- Increase awareness of respectful touch for self and others

Materials

- Large pillow or stuffed animal
- Coloring utensils and a copy of the template from the end of this intervention (optional)

---

* Intervention by Janet A. Courtney, PhD, RPT-S
** Spanish editions of these books are also available: *Abrazo Mágico del Arcoíris* and *Libro de Actividades del Abrazo Mágico del Arcoíris*.

Directions

1. Follow the instructions for the kinesthetic activities found at the bottom of each page in *The Magic Rainbow Hug*. There is also a short version of the story with activities located in the back of the book.

2. Guide the parent and child through the touch-based activities in the book while demonstrating the techniques on a large pillow or stuffed animal.

3. Always ask permission from a child prior to engaging in any of the activities. You can do this by simply asking, "Hey, would you like for me to tell you a 'back story'?" This sends a powerful message to the child that they are respected. Know that the interactive part is always optional.

4. Some of the instructions in *The Magic Rainbow Hug* suggest that the storyteller participates in the relaxation methods along with the child. For example, the instructions may indicate for the storyteller to also take a breath in and out, or to sing a sound such as *ahhhhh*. By modeling relaxation, you can increase a child's eagerness to practice while also increasing a level of mutual attunement.

5. To further ground the self-regulation concepts in the book and put them into action, you can also provide the child with coloring utensils and the coloring template on the next page, which contains a coloring activity from *The Magic Rainbow Hug Activity Book*.

Adaptation for Telehealth

- Guide parents through the nurturing touch-based techniques by demonstrating the activities on a large stuffed animal or pillow while the parent simultaneously follows along with their child.

Magic Rainbow Hug Coloring Template

In the bubble beside each picture, write the word that says how you feel in each kind of weather.

Copyright © 2024 Tammi Van Hollander, *The Bibliotherapy Toolbox*. All rights reserved.

CHAPTER 7

Separation, Divorce, and Sibling Rivalry

Children can face numerous challenging separations, ranging from a parent's deployment or a caregiver's work-related travel to a parent's incarceration, the departure of loved ones, or the experience of separation and divorce. All separations may be difficult on children, but they are even more difficult when children are unable to say goodbye. When it comes to separation and divorce, some children are relieved because it means their parents are no longer fighting, while many others struggle still. Children may blame themselves, feel isolated, get lost in the shuffle, or feel like they are caught in the middle. They may also worry that their parents will "fall out of love" with them just as they fell out of love with each other. This is not to mention that living in two homes is exhausting—both emotionally and physically. The most important thing that children need to know in this situation is that it was not their fault and that they are loved unconditionally. When this is done in a way that provides clarity, love and safety, children can thrive rather than just survive.

Some things to consider when working with children of divorce are age and developmental level. Remember, a child may chronologically be 10 years old but developmentally 4 years old, so consider the appropriate level of the book. In addition, you want to help parents and children learn how to set healthy boundaries and avoid triangulation. Look out for parents who attempt to alienate a child from the other parent. Children are already facing numerous changes in their lives, making it essential to acknowledge their emotions and to equip them with coping strategies to navigate these new stressors effectively.

If you are a clinician or professional working with families who are navigating a difficult separation, I highly recommend reading *When Parents Are at War* (Wonders, 2019), which is filled with valuable information and advice about how to competently and ethically work with clients in high-conflict divorces, as well as *Cory Helps Kids Cope with Divorce: Playful Therapeutic Activities for Young Children* (Lowenstein, 2013). A great book for families in this situation is *Mom's House, Dad's House* (Ricci, 1997).

In addition to separation and divorce, another family issue that I frequently encounter in my office is sibling rivalry, particularly among siblings who are close in age. Although sibling rivalry can be part of growing up, in some cases the fighting is worse than in others. Parents will come into my office stressed out, exhausted, and at the end of their rope. My own kids used to wear me out with their fighting! The bickering would not stop, and I worried that they would never learn to tolerate each other. Thankfully, I am happy to report that my children, now in their twenties, are pretty close. They have a love and respect for each other that I could have never foreseen when they were in elementary or middle school. So what was happening when they were younger?

When it comes to sibling fighting, it is important to remember that we do not choose our family members. We are forced into a relationship with these people—whom we sometimes don't like—yet we are expected to be nice to them! Imagine if your significant other brought home an annoying neighbor to move in with you.

You were not asked permission before they walked in the door, ate all your food, grabbed your favorite spot on the sofa, and interrupted the live season finale of your favorite show. How would you react? Chances are, not very well.

The same is true with children. If creating chaos is a way for a child to be seen or heard, they will continue. Remember that all behaviors have meaning. Yes, many siblings fight, but it is important to pause and assess the meaning underneath this behavior. Many kids are trying to communicate that they don't feel like they are being treated fairly. So often, kids will come into my office saying, "My parents just don't understand" or "They like my brother or sister more than me." Birth order is often a contributing factor in these situations. For an older child, who used to be the sole object of their parents' loving attention, it can be destabilizing when a new baby comes along and the attention shifts. Then there is the middle child who just does not know where to fit in, and the youngest child who has more freedom and fewer rules. These are just some of the many family dynamics to be thinking about.

Since I am a big believer that children are seeking connection, not attention, I strongly recommend that caregivers in this situation set aside special time with each child. I know this can be challenging, but it can be a game changer when they set aside just 20 to 30 minutes for uninterrupted playtime where their child gets to make the rules. When a caregiver's buttons are constantly pushed, sometimes staying patient and cool is tough, but co-regulating with the child and staying in relationship with them is paramount. As Dan Siegel and Tina Payne Bryson (2011) describe in *The Whole-Brain Child*, the caregiver must "connect to redirect." If caregivers are looking for additional parenting resources to navigate challenges such as these, I also recommend that they read *Siblings Without Rivalry* (Faber & Mazlish, 2012) and *Good Inside* (Kennedy, 2022).

Suggested Materials

- Two large dollhouses
- Nurturing toys (e.g., baby dolls, baby bottles, play food)
- Court gavel and miniature courtroom set
- Sand tray and miniatures featuring blended families, two homes, soldiers, villains, and superheroes
- Expressive art supplies (e.g., paint, markers, paper, clay)
- Anger thermometer
- Emotional release toys (e.g., pool noodles for sword fighting)
- Games like Jenga®, mancala, or LEGO® (these are excellent tools for promoting co-regulation and reciprocity, as they encourage the child to take turns, work collaboratively, and slow down)
- Bubble wrap or bubble fidget toy for popping

Suggested Books

Featured in This Chapter

- *A Paper Hug* by Stephanie Skolmoski, illustrated by Anneliese Bennion (2006)
- *Miss Piper's Playroom: Helping Danny with His Parents' Divorce* by Lynn Louise Wonders, illustrated by Uliana Barabash (2021a)
- *Two Homes Filled with Love: A Story About Divorce and Separation* by Steve Herman (2020)
- *The Invisible String* by Patrice Karst, illustrated by Joanne Lew-Vriethoff (2000/2018)
- *Where's My Pajommy, Mommy Mommy? A Tongue Twisterommy* by Neal King, illustrated by Eva John (2022)
- *Sometimes I'm Bombaloo* by Rachel Vail, illustrated by Yumi Heo (2005)
- *Brobarians* by Lindsay Ward (2017)
- *Here and There* by Tamara Ellis Smith, illustrated by Evelyn Daviddi (2019)
- *Mom and Dad Glue* by Kes Gray, illustrated by Lee Wildish (2009)
- *Step One, Step Two, Step Three and Four: A Picture Book Story About Blending Children from Two Families to One* by Maria Ashworth, illustrated by Andreea Chele (2016)
- *Maple & Willow Together* by Lori Nichols (2014)

Also Recommended

- *Two Homes* by Claire Masurel, illustrated by Kady MacDonald Denton (2001)
- *Two-Hug Day* by Rebecca Honig-Briggs, illustrated by MaryBeth Nelson
- *The List of Things That Will Not Change* by Rebecca Stead (2020)
- *The Family Book* by Todd Parr (2003)
- *You Make Your Parents Super Happy! A Book About Parents Separating* by Richy K. Chandler (2017)
- *Lily Hates Goodbyes* by Jerilyn Marler, illustrated by Nathan Stoltenberg (2012)
- *Far Apart, Close in Heart: Being a Family When a Loved One Is Incarcerated* by Becky Birtha, illustrated by Maja Kastelic (2017)
- *The Night Dad Went to Jail: What to Expect When Someone You Love Goes to Jail* by Melissa Higgins, illustrated by Wednesday Kirwan (2013)
- *When My Parents Forgot How to Be Friends* by Jennifer Moore-Mallinos, illustrated by Marta Fabrega (2005)
- The *I Have* series by Colleen LeMaire, illustrated by Marina Saumell:
  - *I Have Two Homes* (2014)
  - *I Have a Stepmom* (2015)
  - *I Have a Stepdad* (2016)
  - *I Have Two Dads* (2019a)
  - *I Have Two Moms* (2019b)

A Paper Hug

Book
A Paper Hug by Stephanie Skolmoski, illustrated by Anneliese Bennion (2006)

Description
A Paper Hug is a sweet little book about a child whose dad is going into the military and who creates a paper hug as the best goodbye gift. Many children in military families encounter situations where a caregiver is deployed and they need to say goodbye for an extended period of time. Sometimes they may even not know how long that caregiver will be away. In my practice, I have used the following paper hug activity for children going through deployment as well as many other types of separation and loss. For example, during the COVID-19 pandemic lockdowns, my clients would make paper hugs and mail them to grandparents or other loved ones because they were separated from so many loved ones during this time.

Treatment Goals
- Connect with loved ones from a distance
- Create a feeling of safety during difficult separations
- Build resilience and allow the child to talk about the loved one they are missing

Materials
- Large roll of paper to trace a body (or construction paper)
- Scissors
- Markers
- Tape
- String
- Paint

Directions

Option 1
1. Read the book with the child.
2. Ask the child to lie down on the large roll of paper with their arms extending out on the paper. Make sure the paper is large enough for the child to open their arms out.
3. With the child's permission, trace the child's head and arms. (If the child is uncomfortable with having their body traced, you can use the second option for this activity instead.)
4. Then invite the child to cut out, paint, and decorate their self-portrait.

5. Once the client's self-portrait is dry, roll it into a large envelope to mail to their loved one.

6. When the loved one receives the paper hug in the mail, they can wrap it around their body and take a picture to show the child that they received their hug. (It may be helpful to include a note explaining the intention of the paper hug within the envelope.)

Option 2

1. Read the book with the child.

2. Trace each of the child's hands on a piece of construction paper, then invite the child to cut out, paint, and decorate their handprints.

3. Ask the child to open their arms as wide as they can and, using a piece of string, measure the distance between their hands.

4. Cut the string to that size, then tape each end of the string to each cut-out hand, once they are dry.

5. Place the client's paper hug into a large envelope to mail to their loved one.

6. When the loved one receives the paper hug in the mail, they can wrap it around their body and take a picture to show the child that they received their hug. (It may be helpful to include a note explaining the intention of the paper hug within the envelope.)

I Can Love and Be Loved by Both of My Parents*

Book

Miss Piper's Playroom: Helping Danny with His Parents' Divorce by Lynn Louise Wonders, illustrated by Uliana Barabash (2021a)

Description

This story in the *Miss Piper's Playroom* series features a young boy who begins attending therapy because of the difficulties he is experiencing in the midst of his parents' conflictual divorce. With Miss Piper's support, the boy is able to understand the changes happening in his family and begin feeling better again. Similar to the book, this intervention helps children cope with all the big changes and big emotions that happen when parents get divorced. It is especially useful for children who may be suffering from loyalty conflict, which is internalized anxiety about having to "choose" one parent over the other when parents are having high levels of conflict.

Treatment Goals

- Provide relief from internalized anxiety
- Relieve the pressure of having to choose one parent over the other
- Help the child realize they can love and be loved by *both* parents even if the parents don't love each other anymore

Materials

- 3 clear glass or plastic jars with lids
- 3 plastic cups
- White sand or fine white salt
- Chalk pastels
- Funnel

Directions

1. Read the book with the child.
2. Together with the child, select three different colors of chalk: one to represent the child and one color for each parent.
3. Pour sand or salt into the three jars, filling halfway.
4. Break off a piece of each chosen colored chalk and drop one color into each jar.
5. Gently shake the jars until the sand or salt turns the desired color.
6. Pour the colored sand or salt into three different plastic cups.

---

* Intervention by Lynn Louise Wonders, LPC, CPCS, RPT-S

7. Explain to the child that the colored sand represents the love each person has in their heart. While the parents may no longer share love between each other, the love they have for their child—and the love the child has for *both* parents—is still there and still available.

8. Designate which jar represents the child and which jar represents each parent. Set the corresponding colored sand cup by each jar.

9. Using a funnel, invite the child to pour some of the colored sand that represents each person into that person's jar.

10. Then have the child pour some of the child's colored sand into both parent jars. Affirm aloud that there is enough love in the child's heart for both parents.

11. Next, have the child pour a layer of one parent's sand into the child's jar and then another layer of the other parent's sand on top of that.

12. Repeat this process—pouring a layer of each person's own sand into their own jar, then a layer of sand from the child to both parents, then a layer from both parents into the child's jar—until there is no more sand.

13. The finished sand jars represent the love the child has for both parents and the love both parents have for the child. Explain again that even though the child's parents may no longer share love for each other, they both have love for the child and the child can love both parents.

Two Homes*

Book
Two Homes Filled with Love: A Story About Divorce and Separation by Steve Herman (2020)

Description
Two Homes Filled with Love is a story about a little boy and his dragon, Diggory Doo, who support a friend, Mikey, whose parents are going through a difficult divorce. This book helps children comprehend and cope with parental divorce and separation. Similar to the story, this intervention normalizes the many common feelings that children have related to divorce. It also includes an interactive element, in which the client physically hops on one foot back and forth between the pictures of their two homes, which is an engaging way to facilitate discussion of the stressors involved in living in two homes. The use of sticky notes also encourages the client to focus on the story and reinforces key concepts.

Treatment Goals
- Normalize feelings related to divorce
- Verbally express feelings about living in two homes
- Cope with the stress of living in two homes

Materials
- Sticky notes
- Paper
- Coloring utensils
- Scissors
- Small, inexpensive prize (optional)

Directions

1. Prior to the session, read through the book and prepare questions related to its content. Write each question on a separate sticky note and place it on the appropriate page in the book. Examples include:
    - Does Mikey live in one home or two?
    - Did Mikey do something wrong or bad to make his parents get a divorce?
    - What's something good about living in two homes?
    - What can Mikey do when he's with his mom and he misses his dad (or vice versa)?
    - Can Mikey talk to Diggory Doo about his thoughts and feelings?
    - Does a family love you just as much whether it's in one home or two?

---

* Intervention by Liana Lowenstein, MSW, RSW, CPT-S

2. Cut out several paper circles. These will be the potholes that make the journey of going back and forth between two homes bumpier or more difficult.
3. At the next session, read the book with the client. As you're reading, give the child an opportunity to answer the sticky note questions on each page. As an optional engagement strategy, you can offer a small prize once the client has answered all the questions.
4. When you're finished reading, ask the client to draw a picture of each caregiver's home on separate sheets of paper, and then place the drawings at each end of the room (or at least 10 feet apart).
5. Explain to the client that there are things that make living in two homes more difficult. Read the scenarios below, and using the paper potholes you created earlier, write down any that apply to the client. Invite the client to add to the list.
    - I miss the parent that I'm not with.
    - I forgot to pack something that I need.
    - My parent is late picking me up.
    - My parents argue at drop-off or pick-up time.
    - I miss my neighborhood friends when I'm at my other parent's home.
    - It's hard to adjust to the different rules/routines at each home.
    - It's hard to pack and unpack my stuff.
    - I hate how long it takes to get to my other parent's home.
    - Sometimes my parent misses or cancel visits.
    - I like being at my other parent's home much better.
6. Place the potholes on the floor, between the drawings of the two homes.
7. Next, have the client stand beside the picture of one parent's home, and ask them to hop on one foot to the drawing of the other parent's home. Repeat until the client has hopped back and forth several times. As the child is hopping and getting out of breath, reflect that it can be hard going back and forth between two homes. When the client hops into a pothole, emphasize that this makes the journey bumpier or more difficult.
8. Allow the client to share their thoughts and feelings about living in two homes by asking questions such as:
    - Is it easy or hard for you to go back and forth between homes? What makes it easy? What makes it hard?
    - Who decided on the visitation schedule? How do you feel about this schedule?
    - Are there times when you don't want to go to your other parent's home? How come?
    - Are there different rules and routines at your two homes?
    - What's something positive about living in two homes?
    - What advice would you give to another child who is having a hard time going back and forth between two homes?

9. Offer the client a variety of coping strategies that will make it easier going back and forth between two homes. The following are some examples (modify to suit the client's age and circumstances):

    - Put a calendar in your room. Write "Mom" on days you are with your mom and "Dad" on days you are with your dad. This will help you keep track.
    - Create a private space at each home for your clothes, toys, books, and other belongings. Ask your parents to help by saying, "This is my home with you. Can we find a private space just for my stuff?"
    - Keep certain things at each home so you don't have to pack as much, like a toothbrush, pajamas, and some clothes.
    - Have a favorite toy, book, or game at each home so you always have something fun to do.
    - Keep something comforting at each home, like a stuffed animal or special blanket, so you feel safe and comforted no matter where you are.
    - Follow the same routine at each home so it's easier to adjust. For example, get up and go to bed at the same time at each home.
    - When you are at your mom's house, keep a picture of your dad with you. When you are at your dad's house, keep a picture of your mom with you. This will help you feel close to both your parents when you are apart from them.
    - Think positive thoughts like "I have two parents who love me" or "It's fun getting two of some things, like two birthday cakes."

A Piece of My Heart*

Book
The Invisible String by Patrice Karst, illustrated by Joanne Lew-Vriethoff (2000/2018)

Description
The Invisible String reminds us that we are all connected by a series of invisible strings, so we know we are never alone. This book is an excellent resource when working with children who have experienced grief, divorce, separation, life transitions, and so much more. It reminds the child that even if someone is not physically by their side, that person is still with them in their heart. This intervention is based on *The Invisible String Workbook* (Karst & Wyss, 2019), which includes an activity called "Piece of My Heart Puzzle." In this activity, your client will create a family art piece to remind them of the unique gifts that each of us brings to the world.

Over the years, I have used this activity in several family sessions to honor family members who are separated (whether by divorce, job circumstances, military deployment, incarceration, or death). For divorced families, this activity can be done with each family unit creating their own heart pieces, or you can make a copy of the same art piece to be displayed at the different homes. For families experiencing grief in response to death, you can complete this activity before the loss (e.g., when someone is sick leading up to their death), as well as after to support your clients and help them process the loss. For military or job circumstances, the family can do the activity together and then carry a copy with them wherever they go.

Treatment Goals
- Increase family bonding and rapport even when separated
- Provide a tangible transitional object for the whole family
- Remind family members that they are never alone

Materials
- 2 large pieces of poster board (or multiple pieces of paper or smaller poster board)
- Art supplies (e.g., markers, crayons, oil pastels, paint)
- Glue
- Scissors
- Pencil

---

* Intervention by Dana Wyss, PhD. Adapted from *The Invisible String Workbook*, © 2019 by Patrice Karst, published by Little, Brown Books for Young Readers.

Directions

1. Read the book with the child.

2. On one large piece of poster board, draw a large heart using a pencil, then cut the heart shape out. Sometimes families will choose a flower instead, or another image that is really meaningful to them.

3. Cut the heart into enough puzzle pieces to represent the number of people in the family, including any family members from whom the child is separated (e.g., due to divorce, deployment, incarceration, death). If there is a dangerous or contentious situation and the family is not ready to add the missing member, just cut out enough pieces to represent the rest of the family. To help you put the puzzle back together, especially if there are more than four pieces, you can number the pieces on the back for reference later. (If you are using smaller poster board or paper, take enough pieces for all the family members and arrange them into a grid with their edges together. Draw the shape across the entire grid so that each piece of paper is now a puzzle piece.)

4. If the whole family is participating in the session, have each person decorate their piece of the heart by drawing or describing the unique qualities they bring to the family. For example, love, hugs, playfulness, good food, laughter, music—anything you can think of! For the missing family member, the family will all work together to complete that heart piece. If you are doing this activity in an individual session with a child, they can draw or describe all the qualities that the other family members bring. Each person can decorate their heart piece however they would like. The only rules are (1) do not cut into or attach anything over the edges of the puzzle pieces (or, if using smaller paper, do not cover the lines of the heart) and (2) do not throw any pieces away. These rules are to ensure the heart can be reassembled.

5. Once all the pieces are decorated, put the heart puzzle back together and then use the other piece of posterboard to glue it down.

6. At the end of the activity, you can use these possible processing questions:
   - Tell me about your piece of the heart.
   - What do you notice or what stands out?
   - Is there anything missing or that you would like to add?
   - What does each family member give to you?

Adaptation for Telehealth

- Draw a heart (or use a premade heart shape) using your telehealth platform's whiteboard feature. Make lines on the screen to divide the heart into pieces for the number of people in the family. Using the annotate feature, have each family member fill in their part of the heart.

"Silly Bone" Chart*

Book
Where's My Pajommy, Mommy Mommy? A Tongue Twisterommy by Neal King, illustrated by Eva John (2022)

Description
Where's My Pajommy, Mommy Mommy? is a purposefully very silly rhyming book that creates tongue twisters by forcing words to rhyme with "ommy." This book, whose story can offer lessons in resilience and self-regulation, carries itself on the *reader's* energy (and whether and how that energy is conveyed to the listener). Observing how parents and children interface with this book, with or without prompting, is the basis of the intervention. By asking the caregiver to read the book to the child in session, you'll get a better understanding of the family's dynamics. For some caregivers, there is a long bridge to their "silly bone." They find it challenging to be as silly as their child needs them to be in order for the book to do its magic, which is to take life from the silliness that is put into it.

Treatment Goals
- Glean useful insights into family dynamics, including parents' attitude toward silliness in the home
- Address the concept of silliness within the family
- Teach children to stretch the boundaries of silliness without breaking general household rules of respect for others

Materials
- Paper and writing or drawing utensils

Directions
1. Ask the caregiver to read the book with the child in session. As they do, observe how the parent and child respond to the book and to each other.

2. Comment on the silliness of the book and invite the child to create a "silly bone" chart. This chart is the child's representation of their family members (pets too!). Ask the child to rate how silly each family member is on a scale of 1 to 10 (with 10 being the silliest).

    For example:

Silly Bone Chart				
Mommy	**Daddy**	**Charlie**	**Grandma**	**Fido (dog)**
5	7	9	3	10

3. Share your observation of the parent and child's interaction while reading the book, plus the child's creation of the silly bone chart. For example, if the caregiver (let's assume it is the child's

---
* Intervention by Neal King, LCSW

father in this case) was able to join the child in silliness, you can ask the child, "Is Daddy silly? Is Daddy silly at home? Who do you wish was as silly as Daddy?" and so on—with your experience informing more questions. What you observe may help to inform other parts of family dynamics.

4. On the other hand, if the caregiver struggled to be silly, you can follow the same line of questions and also ask the child, "If you could choose how silly you want Daddy to be, what would it be?"

5. This intervention can also prompt discussions related to "When is silliness not okay?"

My Bombaloo

Book
Sometimes I'm Bombaloo by Rachel Vail, illustrated by Yumi Heo (2005)

Description
Katie is a well-behaved child who, most of the time, exemplifies good behavior, like many other kids. However, there are moments when she loses her cool, like after her little brother knocks down her meticulously crafted castle despite her clear instructions not to touch it. In these moments, Katie transforms into a character she refers to as "Bombaloo," where her anger takes over and she acts out with her feet and fists rather than words. With a moment to calm down and the love and understanding from her mother, she resets to the Katie we know and love. This intervention draws from the book by helping the child to name and identify their own Bombaloo, who might come out during sibling or parental conflict. The goal is to increase the child's emotional intelligence and help them become more aware of what triggers their anger.

Treatment Goals
- Provide strategies to cope with difficult emotions like anger, frustration, and jealousy
- Encourage siblings to understand and empathize with each other's perspectives
- Recognize and identify feelings of anger
- Assist the child in developing strategies for calming themselves when they become angry

Materials
- Modeling clay
- Paper
- Coloring utensils

Directions
1. Read the book with the child.
2. Ask the child if they ever turn into Bombaloo (or if their sibling does). You can also ask if their parent turns into Bombaloo—maybe this happens when the child fights with their siblings.
3. Ask the child to give their Bombaloo a name, then have them create a visual representation of their anger by using modeling clay or drawing it.

4. Have the child play out a scenario when their Bombaloo emerged in response to challenging family dynamics. Ask processing questions to determine what makes their Bombaloo bigger and what they need to calm it down—for example:
    - What does Bombaloo need?
    - Does it want to be near people or left alone? If it wants to be near people, then who?
    - What does it feel like when you are Bombaloo?
    - How does it feel in your body? Are there any signs that Bombaloo is erupting?
    - What do you want to say to your Bombaloo?
5. Ask the child to give their Bombaloo love and anything it needs to feel safe and protected.

Adaptation for Telehealth

- The child can make their Bombaloo on the whiteboard feature of your telehealth platform and draw out the scenarios that make their anger emerge.

The Epic Battle

Book
Brobarians by Lindsay Ward (2017)

Description
This book tells the imaginative and playful tale of Iggy the Brobarian, who seized control of all the land. The question remains: Can his brother, Otto the Big Brobarian, reclaim it? Alternatively, perhaps, and with a touch of assistance, these two brothers can find peace and reconciliation instead of going into a battle. Similar to the book, this intervention provides two siblings the opportunity to create an epic battle, only this time, they are on the same team.

Treatment Goals
- Enhance communication and problem-solving among siblings
- Develop conflict resolution skills
- Explore and address family dynamics

Materials
- Miniature toys that can represent battles or conflict (e.g., army soldiers, superheroes)
- Large paper
- Markers or other coloring utensils
- Sand tray (optional)

Directions
1. Read the book with both siblings.
2. Ask them to identify their favorite parts of the book. What characters do they relate to the most?
3. Then invite them to create an epic battle where they must strategize together to creatively defeat the opposing side. The battle may be over land (as in the book) or another conflict the siblings choose. Do not fall into the rabbit hole of trying to tell kids they must be the "good guys" in this fight. Children often identify as the villains, so allow them to decide—keep it client centered. The siblings may need coaching to problem-solve if they find it difficult to agree on a side, a theme, or other details of the battle.
4. Offer them the miniature toys and let them know they can collect what they need from the playroom to create this battle.
5. After the battle is set up, it is time to make a plan. Offer them a large piece of paper with markers and ask them to map out strategies they will use to win this battle. They may give themselves different superpowers and give each other roles. All ideas are welcome.

6. When working with young children, battle themes are common. The children may spend the entire session setting up for the battle and never actually playing. This can be frustrating for the therapist, but it is important to understand that the setup and organization of the battle is just as important as the battle itself. Follow their lead. They are doing their work.

7. When the siblings are ready, have them play out the battle. Remind them that they need to be safe: Toys cannot be broken on purpose, they have to keep their hands and feet to themselves, they cannot grab each other's toys, and they must ask permission if they want to use the other person's selected toys.

8. This battle may not have an ending and it may be a "to be continued" situation, as some battles can last longer than others, which is a metaphor for our own internal conflicts and relationships, especially between siblings.

Here and There[*]

Book
Here and There by Tamara Ellis Smith, illustrated by Evelyn Daviddi (2019)

Description
This book is a creative and developmentally appropriate way to educate families about divorce while offering support to children who are processing their new and big feelings around change. It is best introduced to clients during the early stages of parental divorce. In the story, the main character, Ivan, is able to start healing and find hope during his parents' separation through the use of music and nature. Whether he's "here" or "there," he discovers that music can be heard all around him, no matter where he is, if he takes the time to notice. In this intervention, children will create a transitional object to remind them that beauty is everywhere they look, even if it can feel difficult to find at times. It offers the child a new way to understand divorce, whether through nature's music, beauty, or anything else they make a connection with. It affords them a path to freedom and joy during times of change. Personal growth is a key element in this story.

Treatment Goals
- Mitigate sadness and other big feelings around life changes
- Enhance the child's sense of empowerment
- Offer a tangible transitional object to use in between sessions

Materials
- Scissors
- Sandwich bag
- Cardstock or construction paper
- Coloring utensils
- Tape or glue stick (optional)

Directions
1. Read the book with the child.
2. Invite the child to select the type of paper and coloring utensils they'd like to use. Then have them draw a shape on the piece of paper that is big enough to fill most of the page.
3. Within this shape, ask them to draw or squiggle any images that represent what brings them joy when living with each parent.
4. Once they're done, have the child cut along the outline of the shape they drew, then cut the shape into several smaller pieces (5–10, depending on the child's age and dexterity). You or the caregiver can also assist with this part by directing the child where to cut.
5. Mix the pieces up so they no longer create the same shape.

---

[*] Intervention by Laci Radford, CPC student

6. Ask the client to put these "puzzle" pieces back together. If they'd like, they can use tape or glue to hold the puzzle together, but forgoing this step allows them to revisit this intervention as needed. The pieces can be stored in a sandwich bag for later use.

7. Observe how well the pieces still fit together to make the original shape. This reflects the idea that even when things feel like they're being broken into pieces, like when there is a separation or divorce in a family, you can find a way to make things feel whole again. It also serves as a reminder of the things that bring the child joy—a reminder we all need at times.

Variation

- Ask the client to take some time to notice the music they hear in nature. They can incorporate their other senses by noticing the temperature outside, or maybe the wind. What colors do they see? What textures do they feel around them?

- They can compare this experience at each home and begin to identify similarities that provide comfort. If possible, they can also collect pieces of nature that represent each home (e.g., leaves, pebbles, sticks, flowers, pine cones) and put them all into the same box. They can treat this as a treasure chest to revisit when they need a reminder of how nature's beauty is all around us, no matter where we are.

Feel-Better Glue

Book
Mom and Dad Glue by Kes Gray, illustrated by Lee Wildish (2009)

Description
Mom and Dad Glue is a beloved book in my collection that is particularly suited for children whose parents are going through separation or divorce. This heartwarming, simple, and easy-to-read rhyming story revolves around a young boy's search to find a special kind of "parent glue" to mend his parents' marriage. It reassuringly conveys the message that the child is cherished unconditionally, emphasizing that the separation is not their fault. This intervention helps the child understand that although they cannot find parent glue, they can do other fun things with glue to make them feel better and alleviate their anxiety.

Treatment Goals
- Help the child process feelings about their parents' separation or divorce
- Alleviate anxiety by reassuring the child that they are loved unconditionally
- Validate any desires the child might have to find a remedy for their parents to get back together

Materials
- Glue
- Heavy stock paper or watercolor canvas
- Place mat, drop cloth, or trash can
- Salt
- Watercolor paints and paintbrush
- Cup of water

Directions
1. Read the book with the child.
2. Let the child know that although there is no such thing as parent glue, they can use glue to make their heart feel better in other ways.
3. You may wish to put a place mat or drop cloth down, or have a trash can ready, for easy cleanup.
4. Have the child use glue to draw a picture on the stock paper of something that makes them feel better. They can also draw a picture of their parents' homes, or a picture of a heart. Although these are suggested prompts, you can also just suggest that they draw whatever they want to keep it playful and creative. The focus is more about opening up their imagination and allowing them to get creative with glue, as bringing fun and creativity into the session can mindfully quiet their anxiety.
5. Before the glue is completely dry, sprinkle salt onto the glue. Shake off any excess salt onto the mat or cloth or into the trash can.
6. Then invite the child to use watercolors to gently paint over the glue however they want. The color will be absorbed from the paintbrush and spread up the salt like magic!
7. Invite child to share their creation with you and their parents.

Peeling Feelings

Book
Mom and Dad Glue by Kes Gray, illustrated by Lee Wildish (2009)

Description
This is a second activity that I like to do with *Mom and Dad Glue* for clients who may be neuro-divergent or who struggle with anxiety or sensory issues. (Some children with sensory issues will still respond negatively to this activity, so it is not for everyone.) It is also a great intervention for kids with trichotillomania, as it offers a replacement activity to hair pulling or skin picking. For this intervention, the child will peel dried glue off their hand as they visualize peeling away their tricky thoughts and feelings related to the divorce or separation. I have so many fond memories as a kid of painting my hand with glue and peeling it off. I was also an antsy sensory-seeking kid who needed to keep my hands busy, as I was a "picker." Kids love this activity and will say, "It is *so* satisfying and feels so good!" The sensation of peeling the glue off can also help them make connections to things that feel good on the outside and inside, like a safe hug.

Treatment Goals
- Reduce feelings of anxiety
- Promote the understanding that feelings do not last forever
- Connect the satisfaction that the child gets from peeling off the glue with other times they felt that way

Materials
- Glue
- Paintbrush
- Permanent marker

Directions
1. Read the book with the child.
2. Ask the caregiver if they give permission for you to put glue on the child's hand.
3. Then you (or the caregiver) will use a paintbrush to paint glue on the child's hand. The child can also put the glue on their own hand if they'd prefer—the decision is theirs. Make sure the paint is only one coat, as it will take longer to dry if the glue is painted on too thick. As the glue gets painted on, you will typically find that the child is engaged and open to talking about their thoughts and feelings, because they are feeling safe and in relationship with you or their caregiver through safe touch.
4. Ask the child how the glue feels on their hand. Do they like it or not like it?

5. Say, "Now is the hard part. We can't do the next step until the glue on your hand dries." You can ask the child to problem-solve what to do to speed up the drying process. Use a fan? Flap their hands like a bird? The child can be playful and move around. They do not have to be still.

6. Once their hand is dry, you (or the caregiver or the client) will use a permanent marker to write on the child's hand different feelings related to the divorce or separation. You might even draw a broken heart.

7. Then allow the child to peel off the glue. Not only is this fun and satisfying, but the magic is that the ink does not stick to their hand. Let the child know that their emotions about the situation are real, and it can sometimes feel like these emotions will stick with them forever, much like permanent ink. However, when they can show their feelings and talk about them, it can help "peel away" their hurts. Help the child visualize peeling away any hard feelings and feeling better.

Cooperative Jenga

Book
Step One, Step Two, Step Three and Four: A Picture Book Story About Blending Children from Two Families to One by Maria Ashworth, illustrated by Andreea Chele (2016)

Description
This is a fun, Dr. Seuss-like book that expresses a little girl's big feelings about gaining stepsiblings and her fear of losing that special time with her mom. Blended families can be challenging for children and the whole family system. Children have to adjust to a new family structure, possibly a new home, a new parent, new siblings, and new rules. Some children may be excited about this new family, but they fear if they let themselves get too attached, there could be another divorce or separation. They may also feel sad for their other parent, who may be alone without a partner. This block-building intervention is wonderful for families in this situation because it increases cooperation, attunement, and co-regulation—enhancing the felt sense of safety within the family and allowing you to observe family dynamics that might enhance individual work with the child. It is also a great activity to do with *all* families or in sibling sessions, not just blended families.

Treatment Goals
- Help the child adjust to the new family system
- Improve communication and verbalization of feelings within the family
- Enhance relationships and cooperation

Materials
- Giant Jenga®

Directions
1. Read the book to the child (or have a family member read it to them).
2. Dump the Jenga blocks onto the floor and let the family set up the blocks to prepare for the game. Take a mental note of who is taking the lead, who is left out, and other ways the family members are communicating with one another.
3. Let the family know that this is a game of cooperative Jenga, and they can do whatever they need to do to make the Jenga tower as tall as possible. That means helping another person is okay. It is also okay to hold the top of the tower to keep it from falling down. The rules are that they need to take turns and no criticism is allowed—only words of encouragement, like "Good job," "Wow, you were really brave taking the bottom block," "You've got this!" or "I believe in you."
4. If the tower falls, simply have the family rebuild it. Let the family know that the best thing about Jenga is that they can always rebuild the tower. Sometimes, the second tower is even stronger

because they know what the building needs and they learn what the members of the family need for support.

5. When the family is done, use the following prompts to process the activity:
   - What did you like best about the activity?
   - When in the building process did it get hard or scary?
   - Were there times when you wanted to give up or quit?
   - What made you push through although it was hard?
   - Go around and say one positive statement about each person in the family and one positive statement about yourself regarding the activity.

Maple and Willow Fairy Houses

Book
Maple & Willow Together by Lori Nichols (2014)

Description
This book beautifully portrays the power of imagination and creative play, highlighting the unique bond between siblings and their knack for problem-solving and compromise. Just looking at the illustrations in the book makes me feel happy and at ease. In the story, Maple and Willow are inseparable sisters, sharing their joy in outdoor adventures year-round, whether in the sun, in the rain, amidst fallen leaves, or even in the snow. However, even the closest sibling relationships can have their moments of conflict, as big sisters tend to assert their authority, and little sisters can become exhausting. Since making fairy houses is one of the activities in the book that Willow and Maple enjoy, this intervention also invites siblings to make fairy houses while adding in elements of mindfulness, problem-solving, and autonomy.

Treatment Goals
- Strengthen sibling bonds by identifying strengths and weaknesses in the relationship
- Develop the child's sense of autonomy
- Strengthen communication and problem-solving skills
- Promote imaginative play and safe spaces

Materials
- Nature elements (e.g., leaves, sticks, pine cones, stones)
- Wooden miniature fairy doors (you can make your own or buy them online)
- Markers or colored pencils

Directions
1. Read the book to both siblings. Note that this could take two sessions.
2. Ask them some processing questions:
    - What were the things that Willow and Maple loved to do together (e.g., make fairy houses, catch grasshoppers, play hide-and-seek)? What do you both love to do together? What do you have in common?
    - What bothers Maple and Willow about each other? What bugs you about your sibling?
    - What are the things that make you different from your sibling?
3. As part of this discussion, make sure to acknowledge that it is okay to have different interests. It is okay to be different and like different things.

4. Next, ask each child to pick out a wooden fairy door and invite them to decorate their door using markers or colored pencils. If you have permission from the parents to go outside, let them know that they are going to create these fairy houses in nature. (If not, you can also create them inside).

5. After they complete their doors, give each child a basket and ask them to collect items in nature for their fairy house. Make sure to explain, "This is something you are going to create together."

6. Once items have been collected, they can find a nature space to start creating and building their fairy spaces with their fairy houses. They need to problem-solve for their creation and cooperate with one another.

7. The only rule is that each sibling has to ask permission to touch the other sibling's fairy house and items they picked out, so they can create boundaries and show respect for each other's items.

8. After they have completed their fairy houses, ask the siblings to create an imaginary mutual story and write it down for them. You can say, "Create a once-upon-a-time pretend story of your fairy house creation." Ask the children to take turns, with each sharing one sentence at a time while you write down the story. Both children can create their own ending and title to the story.

CHAPTER 8

Anxiety, Fear, Perfectionism, and OCD

We are in a widespread mental health crisis, so it is perhaps not surprising that anxiety disorders are on the rise in today's world. I often feel like there are more people who suffer from anxiety disorders than do not, as there are many things in this world for people to become anxious about, especially in childhood. Little ones today can experience anxiety about a variety of issues in the modern world. Academic stress and perfectionism are common culprits, as children may constantly worry about school performance, homework, and tests, leading to self-imposed pressure and negative thought patterns. Social anxiety can also be a heavy weight, with children fearing bullying, exclusion, or difficulty making friends.

As discussed in the last chapter, family stressors can shake a child's sense of security and stability, too, as can exposure to distressing news, like school shootings, war, or natural disasters. Health concerns have been amplified by the COVID-19 pandemic, with children fearing illness or the loss of family members. The pressure to excel in sports, arts, and other extracurricular activities can lead to performance anxiety, driven by high expectations from both the child and their parents. Anxious children can also present with symptoms of obsessive-compulsive disorder (OCD), including checking behaviors, a need for order and symmetry, hoarding tendencies, counting and repetitive behaviors, magical thinking, excessive handwashing, and more. Some kids with OCD do not present with symptoms while they're in the playroom because they are at ease in this environment, but the behaviors occur when they leave the office.

These types of anxiety disorders often function within the family system, meaning that anxious parents equal anxious kids. It often starts with a child who is experiencing anxiety, whether due to school, social pressures, or other concerns. In the parent's attempt to help and protect their child, they may become overly involved, inadvertently reinforcing the child's fears and anxieties. This overinvolvement can lead the child to become more reliant on their parents for reassurance and avoidance of anxiety-inducing situations, causing the child's anxiety to escalate as they struggle to navigate daily life independently. In response, parents become increasingly anxious themselves, and the cycle continues, with anxiety oscillating between the child and the parent. As Howard Glasser, creator of the Nurtured Heart Approach®, says, "Children read energy like braille." When children have anxious parents, they can feel that energy and their anxiety increases.

Play therapy is well-suited for the treatment of anxiety in childhood, as it provides a safe space to quiet and calm the child's nervous system, providing them with the tools to battle their fears in the safety of the playroom. Anxiety is stored in the body, so a highly anxious child may feel stuck and shut down when you directly ask them about their anxiety. They may be having somatic reactions and not even know what they are feeling anxious about. Play therapy operates on the foundation of a bottom-up approach, which prioritizes establishing a sense of safety and regulation within the therapist-child and caregiver-child relationship. This enables children to express themselves through play, which is their natural language, and gradually lowers their guard to play out their anxieties. In this clinical setting, children can not only express their anxieties but also develop the skills and confidence needed to confront, boss back, and conquer their fears.

Because anxiety is not typically rational, it is common for children with anxiety disorders to feel like there is something wrong with them, making them feel different from their peers. Therefore, it is important to have a variety of psychoeducational and therapeutic books that normalize and remove the stigma of anxiety to help children learn that anxiety is common and manageable among people of all ages.

Suggested Materials

- Sandtray miniatures (e.g., fences and traps to compartmentalize the anxiety)
- Dollhouse
- Expressive art supplies (paint, markers, clay, etc.)
- Sensory toys and fidgets to promote regulation
- Relaxing music
- Peacock feathers (for balancing)

Suggested Books

Featured in This Chapter

- *Hey Warrior: A Book for Kids About Anxiety* by Karen Young, illustrated by Norvile Dovidonyte (2017)
- *Transforming Anxiety: Grow Resilience and Confidence* by Lauren Mosback, illustrated by Chiara Savarese (2021)
- *Fear Not! How to Face Your Fear and Anxiety Head-On* by Christina Furnival, illustrated by Katie Dwyer (2022)
- *Ash's Handwashing Adventure* by Omisa Shah (2023)
- *Beautiful Oops!* by Barney Saltzberg (2010)
- *Creatrilogy* series by Peter H. Reynolds (also available as a box set):
  - *The Dot* (2003)
  - *Ish* (2004)
  - *Sky Color* (2012)
- *The Girl Who Never Made Mistakes* by Mark Pett and Gary Rubinstein, illustrated by Mark Pett (2011)
- *Some Days I Make Mistakes: How to Stay Calm and Cool When Your Day Is Not So Great* by Kellie Doyle Bailey, illustrated by Hannah Bailey (2022)
- *Mr. Worry: A Story About OCD* by Holly L. Niner, illustrated by Greg Swearingen (2004)

Also Recommended

- *Scaredy Squirrel* series by Mélanie Watt:
    - *Scaredy Squirrel* (2006)
    - *Scaredy Squirrel Makes a Friend* (2007)
    - *Scaredy Squirrel at the Beach* (2008)
    - *Scaredy Squirrel at Night* (2009)
    - *Scaredy Squirrel Has a Birthday Party* (2011)
    - *Scaredy Squirrel Prepares for Christmas* (2012)
    - *Scaredy Squirrel Prepares for Halloween* (2013)
    - *Scaredy Squirrel Goes Camping* (2021)
    - *Scaredy Squirrel Visits the Doctor* (2022)
- *My Monster and Me: A Reassuring Story About Sharing Worries* by Nadiya Hussain, illustrated by Ella Bailey (2021)
- *Miss Piper's Playroom: Helping Sal with Social Anxiety* by Lynn Louise Wonders, illustrated by Uliana Barabash (2022b)
- *Amir's Brave Adventure: Exploring Confidence, Mindfulness and Attachment* by Carmen Jimenez-Pride, illustrated by Tanja Varcelija (2019)
- *Don't Feed the WorryBug: A Children's Book About Worry* by Andi Green (2011)
- *You've Got Dragons* by Kathryn Cave, illustrated by Nick Maland (2003)
- *The Kissing Hand* by Audrey Penn, illustrated by Ruth E. Harper and Nancy M. Leak (2007)
- *The Invisible String* by Patrice Karst, illustrated by Joanne Lew-Vriethoff (2000/2018)
- *Wherever You'll Be* by Ariella Prince Guttman, illustrated by Geneviève Godbout (2021)

My Wonderful Warrior*

Book
Hey Warrior: A Book for Kids About Anxiety by Karen Young, illustrated by Norvile Dovidonyte (2017)

Description
Hey Warrior provides exceptional, developmentally appropriate psychoeducation and support to children about anxiety. The book provides a simple definition of anxiety, describes the purpose of the amygdala, identifies psychobiological and somatic responses to anxiety, encourages self-control through diaphragmatic breathing, and offers compassionate, normalizing messages to the child. This intervention expands on the book by inviting the child to create their own amygdala warrior who can assist them in applying the anxiety-reducing messages discussed in the book. It can be completed during any phase of treatment.

Treatment Goals
- Mitigate anxiety symptoms
- Offer a tangible, transitional object the child can use between sessions to reinforce the emotion regulation techniques discussed in the book

Materials
- Scissors
- Hot glue
- Writing utensil
- Toilet paper roll
- Paint and paintbrush
- Cardstock paper
- Lined paper
- Art supplies to decorate the toilet roll (e.g., googly eyes, pom-poms, pipe cleaners)

Directions
1. Read the book with the child.
2. Invite the child to paint a toilet paper roll using whatever colors they would like. Depending on the paint type, several layers might be preferable and some time to dry might be necessary prior to proceeding to the following steps.
3. Once the paint is dry, trace the base of the roll on a piece of cardstock paper, cut out the circle, and hot glue the circle to one end of the roll so that end becomes closed off.
4. Invite the child to decorate the toilet paper roll with the other art supplies (googly eyes, pipe cleaners, pom-poms, etc.) to construct an amygdala creature.
5. On lined paper, write the following message from the book and place it inside the roll: "Hey Warrior [*or whatever cool name the child has given their amygdala*]. We're okay. You can relax now.

---

* Intervention by Rachel Altvater, PsyD, RPT-S

Thanks for looking out for me, but we're all good here." Based on the child's developmental ability or preference, you can also type and print the message instead.

6. If you'd like, you can also add a note reminding the child to breathe strong, deep breaths whenever they are feeling anxious.

Adaptation for Telehealth

- If possible, send or have the child obtain the art materials prior to the session so they can construct a physical version of the craft. If they are unable to obtain supplies or a virtual intervention is preferable, you and the child can work together to create their warrior in Google Slides:
  - When first creating a Google Slides presentation, make sure to adjust the permissions settings so you can share it with your client. Click the "share" button in the top-right corner, and make sure the link information is set to "anyone with link" and that the viewer access is set to "editor." This will allow the child to create in this space with you from a different device. Copy the link and provide it to the child via your telehealth platform's secure chat box.
  - Delete all the text boxes from the slide so your client has a blank slide to start from.
  - Have your client go to "insert," then "shapes" to choose various shapes to create their warrior creature. They can use the paint can icon to color in the shape however they want. Optionally, they can add facial features and accessories by going to "insert," "image," then "search the web."
  - When they're done, go to "insert," then "text box" and add the message provided in the book (see step 5 of the in-person directions).
  - The child can save and print the slide at home if desired.

Bravery Ladder*

Book

Transforming Anxiety: Grow Resilience and Confidence by Lauren Mosback, illustrated by Chiara Savarese (2021)

Description

This story is about Ben, a young boy who struggles with a powerful feeling that he doesn't understand and that he can't quite escape: anxiety. Luckily, Ben's friends help him better understand his anxiety and introduce him to "super skills," which are social-emotional strategies intended to help him work through his anxiety instead of fighting against it. One of these tools is a bravery ladder, which allows Ben to start small and progressively work his way up the fear hierarchy as he confronts his fears. In this intervention, the client will have an opportunity to create their own bravery ladder to help them overcome feelings of worry and anxiety.

Treatment Goals

- Educate children about anxiety and how it feels
- Identify social-emotional strategies to work through anxiety
- Overcome worries and fears

Materials

- Toothpicks or popsicle sticks
- Construction paper or *Bravery Ladder* template (included at the end of this intervention)
- Glue
- Coloring utensils

Directions

1. Read the book with the child.
2. Invite the client to design their own bravery ladder by gluing toothpicks or popsicle sticks onto a piece of construction paper to form a ladder. You can also use the provided *Bravery Ladder* template if this would provide more structure.
3. Ask the client to identify one goal they'd like to achieve but have been unable to because of anxiety. For example, if a child has a fear of talking to people they don't know, their goal might be to "feel confident enough to make new friends." Have them draw or write this goal at the top of the paper.

---

* Intervention by Lauren Mosback, LPC

4. Then help them break down their goal into five smaller steps, beginning at the bottom of the ladder and going up from easiest to hardest. For example, if their goal is talking to people they don't know, you might break down the goal into these steps:

    - *Step 1:* Practice smiling and saying hello in front of the mirror.
    - *Step 2:* Smile and make eye contact with new people.
    - *Step 3:* Say hello to someone new.
    - *Step 4:* Use affirmations to remind yourself that you're a kind and caring person and a good friend: "I am kind and caring," "I am a good friend."
    - *Step 5:* Start a conversation with a new person at school.

5. Let the child know that naming their worries and breaking down their goals into smaller steps makes it more comfortable and easier to overcome anxiety. They can do it!

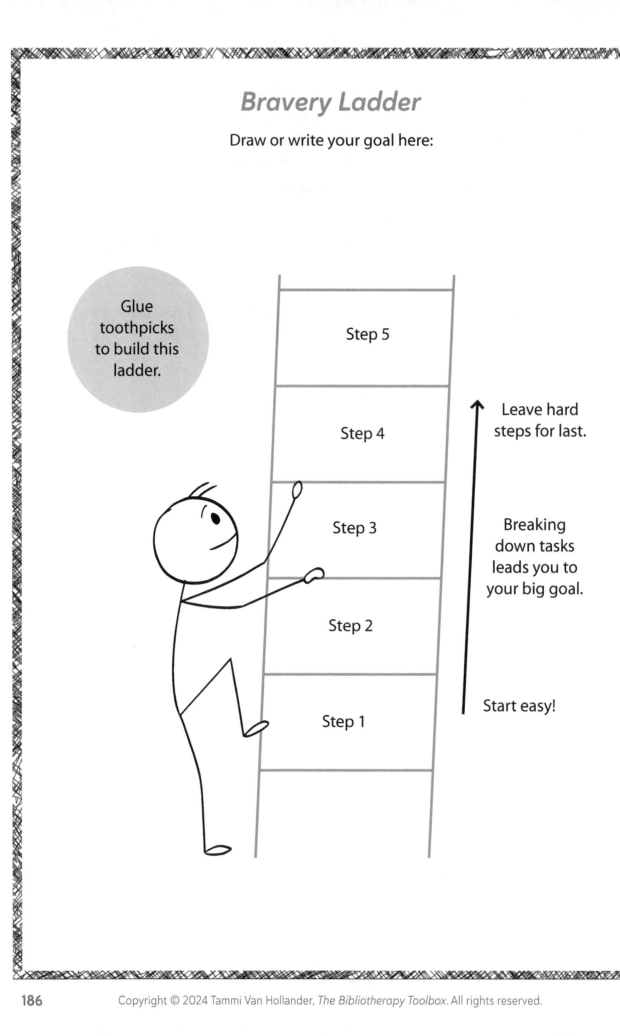

Face My Fears with Coping Skills*

Book
Fear Not! How to Face Your Fear and Anxiety Head-On by Christina Furnival, illustrated by Katie Dwyer (2022)

Description
Fear Not! normalizes children's experiences with fear and anxiety while teaching them a practical three-step lesson to work through these difficult emotions. They learn that they can strip fear of its power by (1) noticing the fear and naming it out loud, (2) reminding themselves that this feeling will pass, and (3) using coping skills to help them regain their cool. Similarly, this intervention provides psychoeducation regarding the nature of fear and anxiety and gives examples of coping skills that kids can put in their toolkit. It is recommended for children who are experiencing avoidance behaviors as a result of their fears. For additional psychoeducation, activities, and coping skills to help kids work through fear and anxiety (as well as other emotions), see *The Big Feelings Flip Chart*, also by Christina Furnival (2023).

Treatment Goals
- Gain an understanding of what fear and anxiety are
- Recognize symptoms of anxiety
- Understand why avoidance behaviors are ineffective
- Identify healthy coping skills to confidently face fear and anxiety head-on

Materials
- *Coping Skills* template pages (included at the end of this intervention)
- Coloring utensils
- Scissors
- Glue

Directions
1. Read the book with the child. Use the conversation starters and discussion questions at the end of the book to discuss what fear and anxiety are.
2. Ask the child to describe some of their fears and worries. Some additional questions you might ask include:
   - How do you feel when you have these worries and fears? Does your heart race or head hurt like the main character in the book?
   - What happened when the main character avoided his worries? Does pretending you don't have those fears or worries help or make things worse?

---
* Intervention by Christina Furnival, MS, LPCC

3. Help your client understand that they can overcome their fears by confronting them instead of avoiding them: "Did you know facing your fears makes them smaller? That's right! When you can face your fears little by little, they lose their power."

4. Explain what coping skills are and how they can help the child face their fears: "Coping skills are any actions that help you calm your body and brain. They help you regain your cool so you can handle uncomfortable situations. This can include doing a puzzle, moving your body in a fun or silly way, taking deep breaths, and more! What coping skills help you?"

5. Invite the child to use the following *Coping Skills* templates to color in and cut out their favorite coping skills. Or they can draw their own!

6. When they're done, glue the coping skills on the toolbox page so your client has a reminder of all the skills they can use to cope with their fears.

Coping Skills!

Color in and cut out your favorite coping skills—or draw your own!
Tape or paste them in your Coping Skills Toolbox!

Drinking cold water

Going outside

Playing with toys

Reading

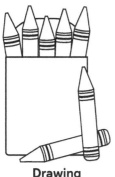

Drawing

Deep breathing

Spending time with loved ones

Listening to music

_____'s Coping Skills Toolbox

These coping skills help me when I feel scared, worried, or anxious!

I am capable of feeling and working through my big feelings!

Washing Our Worries with Soap's Superpowers*

Book
Ash's Handwashing Adventure by Omisa Shah (2023)

Description
While many books are written about handwashing, *Ash's Handwashing Adventure* explains the science behind soap's powers—explaining how instead of killing germs, like alcohol or other antibacterial agents, soap simply renders germs powerless as the germs slip off our skin and down the drain. In this intervention, the science behind soap's superpowers will be used as a powerful metaphor for helping kids wash off their worries. Additional options are also included to extend the metaphor in session and at home during bath time.

Treatment Goals
- Develop coping strategies to reduce anxiety and worry
- Enhance well-being and improve relaxation
- Identify areas of conflict in the child's life

Materials
- Bar of soap**
- Sink or basin of water
- Dry-erase marker, eraser, and board (or laminated sheets)
- Soap dough (optional)
- *Worry Wash Instructions* (included at the end of this intervention)

Directions
1. Read the book with the child.
2. Ask the child to identify their worries and write them on the dry-erase board.
3. Review the power of soap from the story and check for the child's understanding of the concepts.
4. Once the child is ready, ask them if they can imagine what their life would be like if they could just wash their worries away.
5. Brainstorm some strategies to address each worry, then invite the child to make the worries disappear by washing their hands with soap and/or erasing the words from the board.

---

* Intervention by Cherie Catron, LPCC-S, RPT-S
** If using a bar of soap, be mindful of its scent and the child's sensitivities. A scented bar may be relaxing to a child and enhance the power of the activity, or it could be irritating to their senses. Therefore, consult with the parent and child before doing the activity. You may want to have several soap bars available, including an unscented one, so the child can choose the one they find the most comforting.

6. You can use soap dough to further extend the metaphor. Soap dough is the same texture as play dough, but once it dries out, it becomes a hard bar of soap. In session, ask the child to mold the soap dough into a shape to represent one of their worries.

7. Explain to the child that the soap will take two to three days to fully harden into its soap form. Similarly, worries can take time to form, too, which means that before they "harden," we can sometimes shape our worries into something positive instead.

8. Ask the child to imagine what they would like their worry to become instead, and invite them to mold the soap dough into this new form. Remind them that they can take their time molding it, since it will take several days for the dough to harden in the open air.

9. The child can take their soap sculpture home and continue to mold it if they would like. Once it dries, they can use it during "worry wash" bath time. Provide caregivers with the following *Worry Wash Instructions* so they know how to facilitate this special bath time.

Worry Wash Instructions

If your child is of an age where they still need parental involvement during bath time, this can be a powerful activity to reinforce the therapy session. The instructions below are for a young child, with suggested modifications for older children or teenagers provided at the end.

1. Prepare a special soap that can be used specifically for the worry wash, such as bubble bath solution, bath bombs (especially colorful ones), a new bar of soap, or the soap dough that your child created in session. Make sure these are special items that are only used for the worry wash.

2. Tell the child that you're preparing a special bath where they can wash their body and, at the same time, wash all of their worries down the drain.

3. Review what your child learned at the previous therapy session, and encourage them to be playful and fun as they describe their worries. Then help them wash these worries down the drain, having them pay attention to the smells and senses during this special bath.

4. As the bath comes to a close, share with the child the ways that you as a parent have made your worries wash away (e.g., deep breathing, going for a walk, reading a book).

5. Try to end the bath with a calm, peaceful energy. Consider repeating a calm mantra to provide closure to the activity as the water empties down the drain, such as:
   - All of my stress has slid down the drain.
   - I'm slippery like soap. No stress or germs can stick to me.
   - I am happy, peaceful, and free.
   - Goodbye worries! (waving as the water slips down the drain)

6. Repeat this mantra as you apply lotion to your child to further reinforce feelings of comfort and safety.

Variation

- For older children who do not need assistance bathing, you can do this same activity with hand or foot washing as part of a modified manicure or pedicure.

- Another alternative is to use glitter, paint, or even dirt as a metaphor for worries that your child can wash away with real soap.

Having the Courage to Find Beauty in Imperfection*

Book
Beautiful Oops! by Barney Saltzberg (2010)

Description

Beautiful Oops! is a beautiful interactive book that allows kids to consider how mistakes and imperfections represent opportunities for growth. Each page gives readers the opportunity to explore their creativity by imagining new possibilities to turn everyday failures into artistic and personal successes. By exploring how to shift their perspectives on unwitting and unwanted errors, children can learn to flip their cognitive scripts to see things in new, positive, and even exciting ways. This intervention expands on the book by providing your client with an opportunity to make mistakes in a fun way, then create beautiful solutions to the errors they make.

Treatment Goals

- Shift negative self-talk about mistakes and errors
- Learn to see errors in a new way
- Decrease perfectionism and increase creativity

Materials

- Paper of different sizes, colors, and textures
- Scissors
- Glue
- Tape
- Expressive art materials (e.g., paint, coloring utensils, clay, glitter, string, paper towel or toilet paper tubes, recycled plastic bowls or lids)

Directions

1. Ask the client to describe how they feel when they make mistakes and what negative things they tell themselves when this happens.
2. Explain how making mistakes allows them to learn something new—both about the process and about themselves.
3. Read *Beautiful Oops!* with them. Ask them to identify their favorite pages.
4. Prompt the client to engage in destructive play by using any of the materials provided to "mess something up." Ask them to imitate one of their favorite pages—for example, by ripping paper,

---

* Intervention by Sarah Stauffer, PhD

spilling paint or glue, or doodling randomly on a page without thinking of anything in particular to draw.

5. Track their process by noticing how difficult it may be for them to make mistakes, as well as any signs that they are enjoying the process (e.g., smiling while making a mess of things).

6. Once the client comes to a stopping point (or about halfway through the session if they do not naturally stop), ask them to step back from what they were doing and to describe what they see. Notice and point out how they perceive their work and differentiate negative self-talk versus positive self-talk.

7. Ask the client to identify the "mistakes" and explore how these can be transformed together. Then ask the client to continue to make something new and different out of the "messed up" creation. They can use any of the expressive art materials provided.

8. Track their creativity, how engaged they are in the process, their consideration of new ideas and solutions, and their determination to make something different.

9. When there are about 10 to 15 minutes remaining, process the intervention by asking questions like:
    - What was easy (or difficult) about this activity?
    - What did you enjoy?
    - What did you learn about making mistakes? What did you learn about yourself?
    - What will you be able to do the next time you think you've made a mistake?
    - How will you talk to yourself differently about making mistakes?

10. Offer to keep the creation safe until the next session so the client can "put it down" for the time in between sessions (and allow it to dry, if needed).

11. Comment on the client's courage to be imperfect and their ability to keep working through the "messiness" of the activity all the way through to the end.

12. At the next session, comment on any shifts or changes to the creation that may have occurred over the last week (e.g., drying may transform the piece). Ask the client what shifts or changes they experienced during the week as well.

13. Look at the negative thoughts the client had before the activity and help them replace those thoughts with a new script that focuses on their progress during the process, not just the end result.

14. Compare their self-talk scripts from week to week, finding further beauty in their "oops behaviors," repeating the creation process as many times as needed throughout therapy.

Enhancing Oopsies

Books
- *Beautiful Oops!* by Barney Saltzberg (2010)
- The *Creatrilogy* series: *The Dot*, *Ish*, and *Sky Color* by Peter H. Reynolds (2003, 2004, 2012)
- *The Girl Who Never Made Mistakes* by Mark Pett and Gary Rubinstein, illustrated by Mark Pett (2011)
- *Some Days I Make Mistakes: How to Stay Calm and Cool When Your Day Is Not So Great* by Kellie Doyle Bailey, illustrated by Hannah Bailey (2022)

Description
Any of the books listed here can help children to understand that it is okay to make mistakes. In fact, we can learn, grow, and make beautiful things from them! In this open-ended intervention, your client will have an opportunity to practice making mistakes in whatever format they choose. The more creative, the better!

Treatment Goals
- Recognize that it is okay to make mistakes
- Increase flexibility
- Decrease perfectionism and increase creativity

Materials
- A variety of art supplies (e.g., coloring utensils, paper, slime, glitter) and other materials you have available (e.g., miniatures, game)—the sky is the limit!

Directions
1. This intervention is an "oops" in and of itself. There is not one clear directive, and it can be done in several different ways. The more mistakes, the better! Here is an "oopsie list" of ideas to help you and your client get started:

   - Close your eyes and draw a picture—without peeking!
   - Color outside of the lines in a coloring book.
   - Create quizzes for each other and answer the questions wrong on purpose! ("What color is grass? Bright pink!")
   - Design a game with rules spelled wrong and no beginning or end. Then break the rules!
   - Finger paint and make a mess.
   - Make slime without directions.
   - Rip paper.

2. Once the client creates their "oopsie project," ask them what they liked about it. Was it fun to not have so many rules and to make a mess? When they were doing this project, did any worries or stressors come up, or were they able to be in the moment and give their brain a break from things that are bothersome or stressful?

Wrong Number

Book
Mr. Worry: A Story About OCD by Holly L. Niner, illustrated by Greg Swearingen (2004)

Description
Mr. Worry is a great book to help children understand their OCD and finally feel like they are not alone. Some children with OCD may carry shame and hide it from others, but this book normalizes it. It is a snapshot of how difficult it can be when your brain cannot shut off, and it gives hope that OCD can be treated. Kevin, the main character in the story, has so many worries that he cannot sleep at night. Instead, he feels compelled to ask his mother reassurance questions, and his mind makes him check things over and over again although he knows he has the answers. Kevin begins seeing a therapist, who explains to Kevin that he's receiving too many messages from Mr. Worry. To help Kevin work through his OCD, the therapist explains that when somebody calls your house and it's the wrong number, you hang up, and that's what Kevin needs to do with Mr. Worry—hang up on him. This intervention builds off the book by inviting the child to create their own telephone that they can use to hang up on their worry thoughts. This phone intervention can be used creatively in so many ways, so keep these directions for other play-based activities enhancing communication and connection.

Treatment Goals
- Assist the child in recognizing OCD thoughts
- Empower the child to recognize and identify false alarms
- Emphasize that thoughts are not facts

Materials
- Coloring utensils
- Two paper cups
- String or yarn
- Sharpened pencil or another sharp object to poke a hole through each cup

Directions
1. Read the book with the child.
2. Identify and write down the worry messages the child experiences, and rate them on a scale from 1 to 5 (with 1 being the least worrisome and 5 being the most worrisome).
3. Invite the child to give a name to their OCD brain, similar to Mr. Worry in the book.
4. Then work with the child to make a phone they can use for the activity. To begin, use the tip of a pencil to poke a small hole at the bottom of each cup.

5. Next, thread the string through the hole of one cup and tie a knot in the string on the inside of the cup to keep it in place. Pull the string through the bottom of your second cup, securing it with a knot on the inside as well. You can then have the child decorate the phone however they wish.

6. Once the phone is made, ring a bell or pretend to make a ringing noise: "Ding, ding, ding!"

7. Have the child put the cup to their mouth and answer "Hello."

8. Whisper one of the worry messages through the cup while the child holds their cup to their ear. An example from *Mr. Worry* would be "Your mom is really an alien." While using your cup phones, make sure to keep the string tight as you whisper in it.

9. The child then can yell in the cup, "Wrong number, Mr. Worry [*or whatever name they give their OCD*]!"

10. You can then have the child do an exposure through the phone. For example, if the child struggles with the need for symmetry, you can "call" them and ask them to put a blue sock on their right foot, or if they have contamination fears, you can ask them to sit on the floor and crawl from one spot to the next.

11. Discuss with the child how difficult it was to do the exposure instead of listening to their worry messages. Explain how listening to the worry messages might give them relief in the moment, but it makes them feel worse in the long term. They will need to practice exposures all the time so it gets less hard and they can feel stronger.

12. At the end of the session, the child can leave the phone with you or bring it home to practice with their parents.

CHAPTER 9

Mindfulness and Embodiment

Mindfulness is fundamentally about embracing the present moment by simply observing what is happening right here and now. It involves a keen awareness of how your body communicates through your five senses—what you see, smell, hear, taste, and feel at any given instant. The practice of mindfulness encourages us to live in the "now," allowing the weight of regrets we have been holding on to and worries we have about the future to gently drift away.

Similarly, embodiment is a concept intimately tied to the connection between the body and mind that often involves engaging the senses. When children develop self-awareness and recognize the cues their body provides, they gain the ability to understand and address their needs more effectively. The synergy between body and mind is especially evident in play, as it's an inherently embodied activity. In play, we engage both our mental and physical competencies, and this interconnectedness fosters a deep sense of engagement with the world around us, contributing to a holistic understanding of our experiences.

Teaching mindfulness to children is a powerful means of helping them remain grounded in the present, encouraging them to slow down and find inner peace. It's a well-known fact that trying to reason with a child in the midst of a tantrum can be ineffective and draining. When a child experiences anger and a sense of being overwhelmed, their brain enters "fight, flight, or freeze" mode. To transition into logical and cognitive thinking, a child must first achieve a state of regulation. Bibliotherapy and play therapy, especially when incorporating movement, such as embodied play, assist children in finding this balance by immersing them in the here and now. You cannot play in the past or the future—it is a current experience. Activities such as dancing, singing, and yoga provide both physical movement and sensory stimulation, rendering them valuable resources for self-regulation. Most importantly, they are fun and promote a sense of curiosity and discovery.

One of my favorite activities is to take clients outdoors into nature, where our senses are heightened and we feel profoundly connected to the earth. By combining mindfulness with nature experiences, children can gain a profound sense of connection to themselves and the world around them, leading to enhanced emotional and physical well-being, as well as valuable life skills. However, when bringing children outdoors, it is advisable to have caregivers sign a release. Your liability insurance probably won't cover activities outside of your office, and once a child leaves the playroom, numerous liabilities come into play: breaches of confidentiality, encounters with dogs, bee stings, poison ivy, falls, injuries, and so forth. I frequently encourage caregivers to join us in the outdoor activities, as this minimizes the risks and enhances their involvement in the therapeutic process.

Ultimately, creating shared, authentic experiences that involve play, sensations, and movement allows us to foster connection, attunement, and co-regulation while nurturing a child's self-expression, resilience, and self-esteem. While there is a wealth of books that can create space for mindfulness and embodied play in our therapeutic settings, this chapter offers a selection of my personal favorites.

Suggested Materials

- Tibetan singing bowls or chimes
- Electric candle (or real candles, if safety allows)
- Stones, crystals, and gems
- Flowers and nature items (real or artificial)
- Sand and small rakes, paintbrushes, and balls for making designs
- Double and/or small finger labyrinth
- Peacock feathers (for balancing)
- Silk scarves
- Relaxing music
- Pillows and blankets
- *Yoga Pretzels* card deck (Guber & Kalish, 2005)
- Mandala coloring pages
- Yoga Joes and Yoga Janes (plastic army soldiers that are in different yoga poses)
- Expressive art supplies (e.g., paint, markers, clay)

Suggested Books

Featured in This Chapter

- *Let's Grow on an Adventure: Finding Calm in the Joy of Nature* by Lauren Mosback, illustrated by Svitlana Holovchenko (2024)
- *In My Body, I Feel: A Story About the Felt Sense of Emotions* by Jackie Flynn (2020)
- *Thank You Breath: Finding Peace and Power from the Inside Out* by Jennifer Cohen Harper, illustrated by Karen Gilmour (2022)
- *Listening to My Body* by Gabi Garcia, illustrated by Ying Hui Tan (2017a)
- *I Am Peace: A Book of Mindfulness* by Susan Verde, illustrated by Peter H. Reynolds (2017)
- *Calm and Peaceful Mindful Me: A Mindfulness How-To Guide for Toddlers and Kids* by Andrea Dorn (2021)
- *The Power in Me* by Meaghan Axel, illustrated by Michelle Simpson (2020)
- *Catching Thoughts* by Bonnie Clark, illustrated by Summer Macon (2020)
- *Everybody Needs a Rock* by Byrd Baylor, illustrated by Peter Parnall (1974)

Also Recommended

- *Alphabreaths: The ABCs of Mindful Breathing* by Christopher Willard and Daniel Rechtschaffen, illustrated by Holly Clifton-Brown (2019)
- *Peaceful Piggy Meditation* by Kerry Lee MacLean (2004)
- *Moody Cow Meditates* by Kerry Lee MacLean (2009)
- *Find Your Calm: A Mindful Approach to Relieve Anxiety and Grow Your Bravery* by Gabi Garcia, illustrated by Marta Pineda (2020)
- *A World of Pausabilities: An Exercise in Mindfulness* by Frank J. Sileo, illustrated by Jennifer Zivoin (2017)
- *Each Breath a Smile: Based on Teachings by Thich Nhat Hanh* by Sister Susan, illustrated by Nguyen Thi Hop and Nguyen Dong (2002)
- *A Handful of Quiet: Happiness in Four Pebbles* by Thich Nhat Hanh (2012)
- *Mindfulness Is Your Superpower: A Book About Finding Focus and Cultivating Calm* by Lauren Stockly, illustrated by Zach Grzeszkowiak (2022)

- *A Body-Based Journey Through Nature & Animal Metaphors: Trauma-Sensitive Yoga and Embodied Play to Support the Fabulous Fight or Flight Stress System* by Jennifer Lefebre (2022)
- *I Am Yoga* by Susan Verde, illustrated by Peter H. Reynolds (2015)
- *I Am Human: A Book of Empathy* by Susan Verde, illustrated by Peter H. Reynolds (2018)
- *Casey's Greatness Wings: Teaching Mindfulness, Connection & Courage to Children* by Tammi Van Hollander (2018a)

"I Spy" Mindfulness Exercise*

Book

Let's Grow on an Adventure: Finding Calm in the Joy of Nature by Lauren Mosback, illustrated by Svitlana Holovchenko (2024)

Description

Let's Grow on an Adventure tells the story of a young boy named Jay, whose mind is filled with worrisome thoughts and doubts. One special day, he is inspired to head outdoors with his dog, Jasper, where he discovers that interacting with the natural world helps him find courage, calm, and confidence—growing his self-esteem. By following alongside Jay and Jasper's story, children will experience the joy of playing in nature and learn how mindfully exploring the outdoors leads to greater mental, physical, and emotional growth—and loads of fun! The following nature-based intervention from the book is a wonderful way to introduce mindfulness to kids.

Treatment Goals

- Ease worries and grow confidence
- Foster a harmonious connection with the natural world
- Introduce mindfulness in a fun and kid-friendly way

Materials

- Coloring utensils and paper or the *"I Spy" Mindfulness* template (included at the end of this intervention)

Directions

1. Read the book with the child.

2. Invite the client to draw the numbers 5-4-3-2-1 horizontally across a page. You can also use the provided *"I Spy" Mindfulness* template if this would provide more structure.

3. With the caregiver's permission, take the child outside and ask them to identify five things in nature they like to see, four things they like to touch, three things they like to hear, two things they like to smell, and one thing they like to taste.

4. Next, beginning at number 5, ask the client to trace each number and to breathe slowly while doing so. Once they get to number 1, ask them to notice what is going on around them. Ask them what they notice and how they feel.

5. Explain that they are practicing mindfulness and congratulate them on their great work!

---

* Intervention by Lauren Mosback, LPC

"I Spy" Mindfulness Template*

Mindfulness is a fantastic skill for everyone to have! Mindfulness exercises help you learn how to slow down, relax, and enjoy the moment. They can also help you feel calmer and more collected when you are anxious or stressed.

The next time you're outside, give the following mindfulness exercise a try.

I spy . . .

5 Things in Nature I Like to See

4 Things in Nature I Like to Touch

3 Things in Nature I Like to Hear

2 Things in Nature I Like to Smell

1 Thing in Nature I Like to Taste

Now, beginning at number 5, trace each number and slowly breathe while you do so. Once you get to the number 1, notice what is going on around you. What do you notice? How do you feel?

You are practicing mindfulness. Great work!

---

* Reprinted from *Let's Grow on an Adventure: Finding Calm in the Joy of Nature* by Lauren Mosback (2024)

Rainbow Walk

Book

Let's Grow on an Adventure: Finding Calm in the Joy of Nature by Lauren Mosback, illustrated by Svitlana Holovchenko (2024)

Description

This is another wonderful nature-based mindfulness intervention that you can use alongside *Let's Grow on an Adventure*. Known as the rainbow walk, it involves going outside and asking the child to identify everything they can that corresponds with each color of the rainbow. Cherie L. Spehar introduced me to the concept of the rainbow walk many years ago, and since then, I have incorporated it into my therapy sessions and workshops—and I even enjoy my own rainbow walks! I also recommend that caregivers go on rainbow walks with their children at home, especially during those bewitching hours after dinner. The rainbow walk pauses the child's worries and calms their overactive brain by helping them mindfully focus on the present.

Treatment Goals

- Promote relaxation and stress reduction
- Increase attention span and heighten awareness
- Cultivate a connection with nature

Materials

- None needed

Directions

1. Read the story with the child.
2. With the caregiver's permission, take a walk with the child outside. Although a nature space is recommended, you can go anywhere outdoors as long as it is safe.
3. Ask the child if they know the colors of the rainbow: red, orange, yellow, green, blue, and purple (or indigo and violet).
4. Then ask the child to identify everything they can that corresponds with each color of the rainbow. For example: "We are going to start our rainbow walk with the color red. I want you to look around and find everything you can that is red." Then continue the same process with the remaining colors of the rainbow. Note that the order of the colors doesn't really matter; allow the child to go in whatever order they want.
5. To heighten the sensory experience as you complete your rainbow walk, the child can also touch or smell the items they identify, if appropriate.

6. Use the following questions to process the activity:
   - What did you like most about the walk?
   - Were there things you saw today that you never noticed before?
   - Did you think about your worries (e.g., your spelling test) when we were on the walk?
7. Encourage the child to use the rainbow method whenever they need to. For example, if they are feeling anxious at school, they can use this as a grounding technique while sitting in the classroom. All they have to do is notice the different colors in the room to give themselves a brain break if their anxious brain is particularly loud.

"In My Body" Drawing*

Book
In My Body, I Feel: A Story About the Felt Sense of Emotions by Jackie Flynn (2020)

Description
In My Body, I Feel helps children identify the various emotions they might experience, including how those emotions show up within the body. This intervention, which involves asking the client to trace a life-size image of their own body and decorate it to reflect how they feel, expands on the book and offers a means for self-expression. You can implement this activity over multiple sessions based on how much the child wants to color and decorate their outline. Completion may also vary based on how much psychoeducation you provide from the book regarding regulation and the "felt sense" of emotions. This intervention can be completed with the child alone or with their parents.

Treatment Goals
- Gain somatic awareness and recognize where emotions are felt in the body
- Recognize warning signs and triggers for certain emotions
- Appreciate and accept all parts of the body and all feelings

Materials
- Large roll of paper to trace a body (or construction paper)
- Coloring utensils
- Any other arts and crafts materials the child desires (e.g., pom-poms, stickers, glitter)

Directions
1. Read the book with the child.
2. Have the child lie down and trace an outline of their body. Ask the child if they would like to be traced by you or their caregiver (if they are participating in session). I recommend having a caregiver do the outlining for safety and touch issues as well as to educate the family about body awareness.
3. If the child is uncomfortable having their body traced, you can draw a simple body outline on a piece of construction paper to represent the child's body.
4. Allow the client to choose colors to represent their feelings (e.g., blue for sadness, red for anger) and have them decorate their body wherever they feel that particular emotion in the body. They can also represent different emotions using specific materials, images, and so forth.
5. Allow the child to continue decorating their body tracing with various art materials and other expressive media. They can choose to add clothes, hair, facial expressions, and so forth. They can

---
* Intervention by Christine Wheeler-Case Jones, MA, LPC

also decorate it with anything else they desire or feel is fitting. For example, the child can place objects and images that represent what they do to regulate when they feel big emotions.

6. When the child is finished with their creation, they can take it home and hang it on a wall if desired. This can encourage further discussion between the child and their caregivers regarding the topic.

Thank You Breath

Book
Thank You Breath: Finding Peace and Power from the Inside Out by Jennifer Cohen Harper, illustrated by Karen Gilmour (2022)

Description
Thank You Breath is a great book to help kids recognize and appreciate their breath as a superpower. Rather than just telling kids to "take a deep breath" when they're upset or dysregulated, it provides them with tools to use their breath in an intentional manner based on the state of their nervous system. For example, it allows kids to use their breath to gain energy when they're feeling tired or to slow down when they're feeling overwhelmed. This intervention draws on the book by helping children bring awareness to the breath and body. I also recommend that you check out Cohen Harper's other books, including *Thank You Body, Thank You Heart* (2019), *Thank You Mind* (2020), and *Little Flower Yoga for Kids* (2013).

Treatment Goals
- Teach mindful breathwork
- Increase gratitude, self-compassion, and self-awareness
- Calm and quiet the mind and body

Materials
- Art supplies
- Note cards or thank-you notes
- Envelope
- Writing utensil
- Sand tray and miniatures (optional)

Directions
1. Read the book with the child.
2. Ask the child, "How is your breath a superpower? How does it work?"
3. Then invite the child to draw a picture or create a sandtray of how their breath can help them stay calm and problem-solve, or how it can make them feel less stuck.
4. Next, encourage the client to write a thank-you note to their breath, thanking it for all the ways it has helped them when they needed it.
5. Once the child is done with their note, they can decorate it however they'd like. You can then put the card in an envelope and address it—To: My Breath, From: [*child's name*].

Listening to My Body: Feelings and Sensations

Book
Listening to My Body by Gabi Garcia, illustrated by Ying Hui Tan (2017a)

Description
This is one of my favorite books to help children bring awareness to their bodies and learn about their sensations and emotions in a fun way. It guides readers through a variety of interactive questions and activities to help them connect their physical sensations with their accompanying emotions, along with additional suggested activities in the back of the book. It is important for children to have the knowledge and language to differentiate between their internal body cues and their emotions so they can enhance their self-regulation skills. This intervention expands on the book with a useful worksheet that differentiates between feelings and sensations and allows kids to identify what sensations are linked to certain feelings.

Treatment Goals
- Promote emotion regulation and self-awareness
- Provide psychoeducation about sensations and feelings
- Help the child recognize how feelings and sensations are connected to one another
- Illustrate the mind-body connection

Materials
- Coloring utensils and the *Listening to My Body* worksheet (included at the end of this intervention)

Directions
1. Read the book with the child.

2. Introduce the worksheet by explaining the difference between sensations and feelings: "Sometimes our feelings, or emotions, can make our bodies feel certain ways, and sometimes our bodies can make us feel different ways. For example, if my tummy is hurting, I may get nervous and wonder if I am sick or if I am about to throw up. Or I might feel nervous about my school concert and then get a tummy ache. Our minds and bodies are connected."

3. Then use the worksheet to help the child identify what sensations may lead them to experience certain feelings (or vice versa). To help illustrate this, on your own copy of the worksheet you might draw lines from several sensations in the left-hand column and connect them with the "overwhelmed" emotion in the right-hand column. You can then explain to the child, "When I feel overwhelmed, my heart starts pounding, and I am jittery and tense."

4. Ask the child to do the same, discussing any instances that have made them feel this way in their body and mind. They can use different colors when drawing the lines to help show the various connections.

Listening to My Body*

Use different colors of markers to connect what feelings and sensations go together for you. There can be multiple answers.

Sensations	Feelings
Headache	Nervous
Cold	Angry
Tense	Excited
Sweaty	Safe
Dizzy	Scared
Hungry	Cranky
Out of breath	Proud
Heart pounding	Overwhelmed
Thirsty	Calm
Focused	Happy
Stomachache	Silly
Calm	Annoyed
Relaxed	Loving

* Based on *Listening to My Body* by Gabi Garcia, illustrated by Ying Hui Tan (2017a)

I Am Peace: Fun with Music

Book
I Am Peace: A Book of Mindfulness by Susan Verde, illustrated by Peter H. Reynolds (2017)

Description
I Am Peace is part of the *I Am* series, which includes many wonderful books, like *I Am Human* (2018) and *I Am Love* (2019). It can be difficult to explain mindfulness to young children, but Susan Verde has the most beautiful way of doing so alongside Peter H. Reynolds's sweet and lovable illustrations. In the book, readers will learn tools to slow down and ground themselves in the present moment. The following intervention uses Emily Arrow's wonderful "I Am Peace" song, which is based on the book, to teach kids the same mindfulness messages. Music is such a fun, playful way to help kids move their bodies, regulate, and connect with the words of the book more easily. You'll find that this sweet song fills the love tank of your littlest clients just like the book does.

Treatment Goals
- Teach mindfulness skills
- Quiet the mind
- Build self-awareness of feelings and body sensations through movement

Materials
- Variety of musical instruments
- Computer, phone, or other device to play the music video
- Enough space to move and dance

Directions
1. Read the book with the child.
2. Play the video, which is available at: https://www.youtube.com/watch?v=uqkPdIjjSFI.
3. Invite the child (and their caregivers, if they are participating) to use the instruments and their bodies to play and dance to the song. They can follow the instructor's prompts in the video as they move along to the song.
4. Replay the video and ask the child to be the instructor of the dance. What movements would they use for the prompts?
5. As an added bonus, you can encourage the child to create their own song inspired by the book.

Radar Senses*

Book
Calm and Peaceful Mindful Me: A Mindfulness How-To Guide for Toddlers and Kids by Andrea Dorn (2021)

Description
Mindfulness is an important tool that can support healthy emotional development throughout the lifespan. Though this can be a challenging topic for children to learn, *Calm and Peaceful Mindful Me* breaks down mindfulness into simple steps and introduces its benefits to children in a concrete and interactive way. The following intervention is designed to expand children's mindfulness practice by encouraging them to use their internal "senses radar" to stay present and attentive to their surroundings, and to take deep belly breaths whenever they need to calm down or refocus. This intervention is suitable for any phase of treatment and can be done with the caregiver as well.

Treatment Goals
- Teach mindfulness skills and highlight the benefits of being present in the moment
- Empower the child to learn how to focus their awareness
- Encourage the child to integrate mindfulness into their daily routine

Materials
- Paper or a copy of the *Radar Senses* handout (included at the end of this intervention)
- Coloring utensils

Directions
1. Read the book with the child and review the three essential mindfulness steps outlined in the book: stop, breathe, and notice.
2. Introduce the concept of an internal "senses radar." Explain that we have a natural ability to sense things close to us and far away, just like how a radar device can detect planes, birds, or even clouds by sending out special signals that reach the target and bounce back, letting the machine know it is there. Our internal radar involves our senses and brain working together to focus our attention and sense our surroundings.
3. Help the child practice attentional awareness with their senses radar: Ask the child to pick one of their senses. With that sense, encourage them to set their radar to scan things nearby. Invite them to stop, take a deep breath, and notice what they're experiencing with that sense close by them.

---
* Intervention by Andrea Dorn, MSW

4. Next, guide the child to expand their awareness by scanning for things far away while continuing to notice what they're experiencing with that same sense.
5. Use the *Radar Senses* handout (or a blank piece of paper) to help the child write or draw what they noticed both close by and far away.
6. Repeat the intervention with as many senses as desired.
7. If you would like to encourage discussion afterward, you might draw from the following questions:
    - What did you notice when you focused your senses radar on something nearby? And far away?
    - Was it challenging or easy to expand your awareness and scan things far away? Why?
    - How did using your senses radar help you become more mindful and present in the moment?
    - Can you think of a time when using your senses radar could be helpful in your life?
    - How can you use the three mindfulness steps (stop, breathe, notice) in your daily life to become more mindful and calm?
    - Did you learn anything new about your senses and how they work together to sense your surroundings?
    - What sense was the easiest to focus on? The most difficult? Why do you think that was?

Adaptation for Telehealth

- Use the whiteboard feature on your chosen telehealth platform as a drawing space for step 5 of the intervention.

Radar Senses

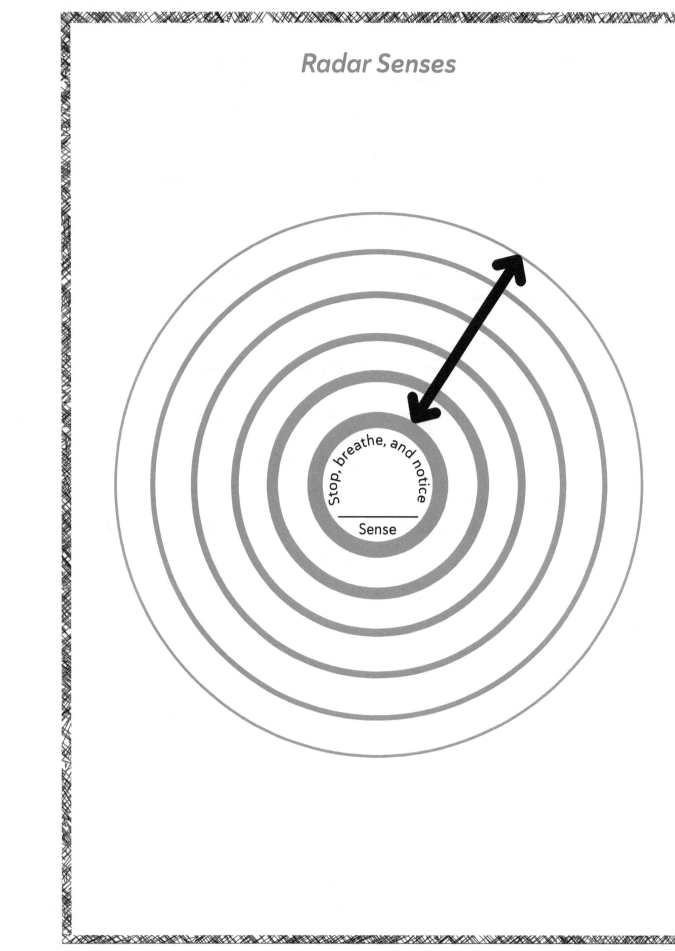

Breathing Power*

Book
The Power in Me by Meaghan Axel, illustrated by Michelle Simpson (2020)

Description
Our thoughts can be overwhelming and consuming at times. *The Power in Me* is an educational and practical tool that empowers children to mindfully notice what is happening in their brains and bodies when big feelings of worry arise. Through empowering mantras and deep-breathing exercises, this book provides easy-to-incorporate alternative thoughts that build self-esteem, self-worth, and inner strength. This intervention utilizes the therapeutic relationship to support validation, self-esteem, co-regulation, safety, and connection within the therapeutic setting and family unit. It allows the child to feel a sense of being supported through struggles, which strengthens the attachment bond between the child and their caregiver.

Treatment Goals
- Provide the child with a sense of empowerment as well as mindful strategies to manage stress
- Support co-regulation and connection within the family

Materials
- Expandable ball
- A favorite toy or stuffed animal

Directions
1. Introduce the book and activity as follows:
    - "Sometimes our brains feel like they are running around everywhere, and they need a little help to not run so fast. When this happens to me, I have a special ball that reminds me to help my brain walk instead of run. I wonder if you have a favorite toy or stuffed animal that helps you when your brain is running fast. This book can teach us how to use these favorite things to help our brains. Would you like to read it with me?"
2. If the child consents, read the book *The Power in Me* with them. If the child can read, they may choose to read it themselves or be read to.
3. While reading the book, utilize voice intonations and body movements to match the storyline and make the reading interactive.
4. Invite the child to demonstrate how their brain and body experiences feelings of anxiety and calm.

---

* Intervention by Fiona Hill, LPC, RPT

5. Demonstrate and practice the three breathing techniques in the book together during session, utilizing the expandable ball and the child's favorite toy or stuffed animal:
    - Three-count breath
    - Bunny breath
    - Belly breath
6. If time allows, invite the child to imagine a real-life situation in which they experienced anxiety, and breathe with them through that situation. Process their feelings before and after the breathing exercise.

Variation

- After reading the book and practicing breathing techniques, invite the caregiver into session and support the child in teaching their new skills to the caregiver. This supports co-regulation and attunement, and it also builds empowerment by affording the child an opportunity to teach and demonstrate knowledge.

Catching Thoughts*

Book
Catching Thoughts by Bonnie Clark, illustrated by Summer Macon (2020)

Description
Catching Thoughts tells the story of a girl who can't escape a nagging thought in her head—no matter where she goes, it seems to follow her everywhere. Using the metaphor of a balloon to represent thoughts, the book helps children understand that they can mindfully let go of thoughts that don't serve them and catch new, beautiful thoughts that bring them joy, hope, and truth. This intervention expands on the book's message with three activity options, allowing you to customize it to meet the needs of each child. By adjusting the complexity of the materials, this activity can be helpful for young children through teenage clients.

Treatment Goals
- Increase mindfulness skills
- Identify and evaluate negative automatic thoughts
- Develop more helpful positive self-statements

Materials
- Option 1: Bubble mix and wand
- Option 2: Balloons in a variety of colors and a permanent marker
- Option 3: Art supplies (e.g., markers, paint, colored pencils) and paper

Directions

Option 1: Bubbles

1. Read the book with the child.
2. Begin by blowing bubbles with the child. Discuss how the bubbles are like our thoughts: Some are big and take up more space in our heads, some are smaller, and some can be confusing and stuck together. There are also some bubbles (or thoughts) that we want to keep and hold on to, and some we would like to let drop and fall.
3. Discuss with the child what thoughts they would like to let drop. After they identify these thoughts, blow more bubbles and ask the child to imagine that the bubbles represent these thoughts dropping to the ground. Help the child identify what thoughts and feelings they are having—and where these show up in the body—when they let these other thoughts go.

---
* Intervention by Ann Meehan, MS, LPCC, RPT-S

4. Next, identify thoughts that the child would like to keep—these are thoughts that make them feel good, joyful, or accepted. Blow more bubbles and ask the child to catch a bubble (thought) that they would like to hold on to. Help the child identify what thoughts and feelings they are having—and where these show up in the body—when they hold on to the thoughts they would like to keep.

5. Process the difference between the two experiences.

Option 2: Balloons

1. Read the book with the child.
2. Have the child select one or more colors of balloons to represent the thoughts that bring them joy, clarity, hope, peace, and so forth.
3. Next, have them select colors of balloons to represent difficult or upsetting thoughts.
4. Process what it is about each color represents those thoughts for the child.
5. Blow up the balloons and have the child verbalize the corresponding thoughts. You can also write the thoughts on the outside of the balloons using a permanent marker.
6. Starting with the more difficult thoughts, play a game where the child attempts to keep the balloon in the air. Each time the child hits the balloon they have to say (out loud or in their head) the thought that the balloon represents.
7. Repeat the activity with the helpful or more positive thoughts.
8. Discuss the thoughts and feelings they are having—and where these show up in the body—focusing on each thought and on the difference between the difficult and helpful thoughts.

Option 3: Art Supplies

1. Read the book with the child.
2. Invite the child to select a medium (e.g., watercolor, crayons) and draw a balloon in the color of their choosing to represent the thoughts they want to let go of. Inside the balloon, have them write all the thoughts they want to let go of. Notice the size, shape, and color of this balloon.
3. Next, ask the child to draw balloons to represent thoughts that are helpful, are positive, and feel good. They can draw one or several balloons, choosing colors that feel right to them. Inside the balloons, ask the child to write all the specific thoughts they would like to hold on to. Notice the size, shape, and color of these balloons.
4. Process the differences between the difficult and helpful thought balloons and the experience of creating both.

Adaptation for Telehealth

- Send the materials to the child to use at home or see if the caregiver has them already. You could also do the art activity through your telehealth platform's whiteboard feature.

Special Stones

Book
Everybody Needs a Rock by Byrd Baylor, illustrated by Peter Parnall (1974)

Description
Everybody Needs a Rock is a beautifully illustrated book that helps children see the wonder, beauty, and magic of seemingly simple rocks. With its unique storyline, it provides children with a variety of amusing "rules" they can use to help them pick out a rock that's right for them. This book has had a huge impact on me and my work, as it reminds me that nature truly is the best remedy and that incorporating nature into my play therapy practice is so important! Mindfully connecting to the earth provides children with a way to ground themselves, co-regulate, and gain a deeper awareness of self.

Treatment Goals
- Improve the child's ability to stay in the present moment
- Enhance the child's awareness of their senses and surroundings
- Connect the child to their physical sensations and the environment
- Boost self-esteem and self-confidence
- Help the child bounce back from difficult experiences and setbacks encountered during play

Materials
- Rocks
- Paint, paint markers, or permanent markers
- Additional art supplies (e.g., glitter, googly eyes)

Directions
1. Read the book with the child.
2. Invite the child to pick a special stone from your basket, or go outside to collect one if you have a nature space available. (Remember: If going outside, you must ask the caregiver's permission and have them sign a special release form. Caregivers are also always welcome to come along!) You can ask the child to select a stone or, as I like to say, "Let the stone pick you."
3. They can then get to know their stone by holding it quietly in their hand, feeling it, and perhaps dancing with it. The child might whisper to it and listen for the stone to whisper back. You can ask, "Does your stone have a special message for you? Do you have a special message for your stone?"
4. The child can then paint or decorate the stone if they choose. This is their special stone to put in a special place at home. If it can fit in their pocket, they can use it to ground themselves when they are feeling anxious or dysregulated by putting their hand in their pocket and touching the stone, paying attention to its texture and feel.

CHAPTER 10

Bullying, Boundaries, and Kindness

There are so many children who are bullied every day, leaving them feeling isolated and depressed. Others may perceive that they are being bullied because they struggle to understand social cues or they view the world through an egocentric lens, leading them to believe that other children are intentionally leaving them out. These highly sensitive children feel deeply and lack resilience, often sitting with their pain in silence. Many children who are bullies may have a significant amount of anxiety and engage in this behavior as a way of seeking control, as they may think, "If I bully others, no one can hurt me."

In these situations, one of our most important roles is to help kids learn the value of kindness and empathy so we can create a world with no place for hate. I like to use Carol McCloud's (2015) analogy of "bucket fillers" and "bucket emptiers" when introducing the topic of empathy: We can choose to fill up other people's buckets with love and kindness instead of emptying them with unkind actions and words. This simple terminology helps kids understand the value of kindness and allows them to share how it feels when others are unkind and don't value or respect their thoughts and feelings.

We must also teach children at a young age the importance of having physical and social boundaries. This helps them develop the self-awareness they need to respect themselves and to respect other people's space. Children are naturally curious about their bodies and other people's bodies, but they need to know the importance of appropriate touch and inappropriate touch. Since many adults are uncomfortable talking about this subject, books offer an easy way to help children learn about healthy boundaries and how they can keep their bodies (and other people's bodies) safe. With these tools, you can give them a voice to be assertive and speak up when they see someone engaging in hurtful or inappropriate behavior. In this chapter, I offer several of my go-to books on these topics. Make sure you have a few on your own shelf, as they are an essential part of a therapeutic library.

Suggested Materials

- Aggressive and emotional release toys (e.g., pool noodles, army soldiers, toy weapons)
- Nurturing toys (e.g., baby dolls, play food, baby bottles)
- Bandages and doctor's kits
- Dolls and puppets
- Stuffed animals
- Sandtray miniatures to represent boundaries and connections (e.g., fences, string, walls, bridges)
- Hula-hoops
- Painters tape to create boundaries on the floor

Suggested Books

Featured in This Chapter

- *An Exceptional Children's Guide to Touch: Teaching Social and Physical Boundaries to Kids* by Hunter Manasco, illustrated by Katharine Manasco (2012)
- *Let's Talk About Body Boundaries, Consent and Respect: Teach Children About Body Ownership, Respect, Feelings, Choices and Recognizing Bullying Behaviors* by Jayneen Sanders, illustrated by Sarah Jennings (2016)
- *The Not-So-Friendly Friend: How to Set Boundaries for Healthy Friendships* by Christina Furnival, illustrated by Katie Dwyer (2021)
- *Body Boundaries Make Me Stronger* by Elizabeth Cole (2022)
- *Dare! A Story About Standing Up to Bullying in Schools* by Erin Frankel, illustrated by Paula Heaphy (2012a)
- *Tough! A Story About How to Stop Bullying in Schools* by Erin Frankel, illustrated by Paula Heaphy (2012b)
- *Weird! A Story About Dealing With Bullying in Schools* by Erin Frankel, illustrated by Paula Heaphy (2012c)
- *The Boy, the Mole, the Fox and the Horse* by Charlie Mackesy (2019)
- *Each Kindness* by Jacqueline Woodson, illustrated by E. B. Lewis (2012)
- *That Rule Doesn't Apply to Me!* by Julia Cook, illustrated by Anita DuFalla (2016)
- *Shubert's BIG Voice* by Becky A. Bailey and Leigh Ann Burdick, illustrated by James Hrkach (1999)
- *My Super Skills: Animals and Affirmations* by Lauren Mosback, illustrated by Chiara Savarese (2020)
- *Zero* by Kathryn Otoshi (2010)
- *One* by Kathryn Otoshi (2008)

Also Recommended

- *Have You Filled a Bucket Today? A Guide to Daily Happiness for Kids* by Carol McCloud, illustrated by David Messing (2006/2015)
- *Listening with My Heart: A Story of Kindness and Self-Compassion* by Gabi Garcia, illustrated by Ying Hui Tan (2017b)
- *Bullying Is a Pain in the Brain* by Trevor Romain, illustrated by Steve Mark (2016)
- *My New Best Friend* by Sara Marlowe, illustrated by Ivette Salom (2016)
- *Monty the Manatee* by Natalie Pritchard, illustrated by Natalie Merheb (2018)
- *A Friend for Lakota: The Incredible True Story of a Wolf Who Braved Bullying* by Jim Dutcher and Jamie Dutcher (2015)
- *The Pout-Pout Fish and the Bully-Bully Shark* by Deborah Diesen, illustrated by Dan Hanna (2017)
- *Tease Monster: A Book About Teasing vs. Bullying* by Julia Cook, illustrated by Anita DuFalla (2013)
- *Personal Space Camp: A Picture Book About Respecting Others' Physical Boundaries* by Julia Cook, illustrated by Carrie Hartman (2007)

Boundary Sandtray

Books
- *An Exceptional Children's Guide to Touch: Teaching Social and Physical Boundaries to Kids* by Hunter Manasco, illustrated by Katharine Manasco (2012)
- *Let's Talk About Body Boundaries, Consent and Respect: Teach Children About Body Ownership, Respect, Feelings, Choices and Recognizing Bullying Behaviors* by Jayneen Sanders, illustrated by Sarah Jennings (2016)

Description
An Exceptional Children's Guide to Touch and *Let's Talk About Boundaries, Consent and Respect* are resources designed to educate children with special needs about personal boundaries, touch, and consent. You can read either of these books for this intervention, which uses sandtray miniatures to help children identify whom they feel comfortable having in their personal space (their "space bubble") and whom they prefer to have at a farther distance. This intervention also serves as a diagnostic tool for obtaining more information regarding the child's attachment relationships. For example, a child who is struggling in math may place the miniature representing their math teacher far away in the sand tray. This can give you more insight into relationships that lack connection and lead to discomfort and anxiety.

Treatment Goals
- Define what physical boundaries are
- Identify the child's space bubbles
- Understand the proximity of different attachment relationships

Materials
- Sand tray and miniatures
- Miniature fences (optional)

Directions
1. Read either of the books with the child.
2. Invite the child to pick a miniature that represents themselves and miniatures that represent the various people in their life (e.g., family members, teachers, friends, "frenemies," bullies).
3. Have the child place the miniature of themselves in the middle of the sand tray and draw a circle around their miniature in the sand. They may like to put a fence around their figure for added safety.
4. Ask the child to place other people in the sand tray in the proximity that feels "just right" to them. Process the placement of these miniatures with questions like:
    - How close can this person be to you?
    - Are there times when you need this person to be father away and times when you want them closer? Share those times.

Popsicle Stick Boundary Setting*

Book
The Not-So-Friendly Friend: How to Set Boundaries for Healthy Friendships by Christina Furnival, illustrated by Katie Dwyer (2021)

Description
The Not-So-Friendly Friend tells the story of a young girl who bravely stands up to a school bully by setting boundaries in a kind yet assertive way. This book supports children in developing healthy friendships, recognizing the traits of a good friend (as well as the actions of mistreatment), and knowing that their voice matters and deserves to be heard. This intervention also helps clients understand the difference between kind and unkind words and actions, and it is a great way to begin the conversation about boundaries. The end of the book contains additional conversation starters and discussion questions you can use with the caregiver to help broaden their awareness of their own attitude toward setting boundaries.

Treatment Goals
- Explain what a boundary is
- Teach the child to recognize signs of mistreatment
- Help the child practice saying a simple boundary out loud

Materials
- Paper
- Coloring utensils
- Popsicle sticks
- Glue

Directions
1. Read the book with the child.
2. Talk about how a boundary is a barrier between two things, like a fence between a house and the road. In this case, the boundary protects the house. When it comes to people, we set boundaries with our words to let others know what we do or do not like in how they are treating us or others. Setting a boundary shows that we love and care for ourselves.
3. Ask the child to describe how they would feel if they were not being treated well.
    - What feelings would come up?

---

* Intervention by Christina Furnival, MS, LPCC

- What unkind actions might others do that would lead to these feelings?
- What kind actions might you see in healthy friendships?

4. Fold a piece of paper in half and reopen it. On the left-hand side, have the child write or draw actions or words of mistreatment. On the right-hand side, have the child write or draw actions or words that show friendship and kindness.

5. Then provide the child with popsicle sticks and invite them to decorate the sticks however they would like. They might use their favorite color, draw things they like, or draw something to represent themselves on the sticks.

6. Glue the popsicle sticks onto the paper as a boundary between the signs of mistreatment and the signs of friendship and kindness.

7. Remind the child that they matter—that their feelings, thoughts, wants, and needs matter—and that setting boundaries is a way for them to be true to themselves while also protecting themselves.

8. Share an example of setting a boundary, such as "I deserve to be treated with kindness. If you are going to hurt my feelings or body, I will not play with you. I will play with you again when you're ready to be kind." Have the child practice saying this boundary.

Adaptation for Telehealth

- Draw a line down the middle of the screen using the whiteboard feature on your telehealth platform. Have the child identify kind versus unkind words and actions on either side of the screen. The child can then draw a fence or wall along the line to represent their boundaries.

Hula-Hoop Boundaries

Book
Body Boundaries Make Me Stronger by Elizabeth Cole (2022)

Description
Body Boundaries Make Me Stronger is a great book to help kids understand boundaries and unwanted touch. It follows the story of Little Nick, who encounters several touch-related situations that make him uncomfortable, such as a friend who tickles him too much. After talking with his mom, Little Nick learns that it's okay to say no when we feel like our body boundaries are being crossed. The pictures are engaging and the rhyming story helps kids remember this very important message. The book also introduces the idea of a "body safety team," which are trusted adults that children can talk to about their concerns. Since many parents and therapists feel uncomfortable talking about boundaries, I highly recommend including this book as part of your therapeutic repertoire. The following intervention expands on the ideas of a body bubble and body safety team.

Treatment Goals
- Provide a basic understanding of the body, private parts, and personal space
- Identify and name trusted adults the child can talk to about concerns or inappropriate touch
- Assist the child in establishing personal boundaries and understanding that it's okay to say no when they feel uncomfortable

Materials
- *Body Boundaries* worksheet (included at the end of this intervention)
- Notecards or other small pieces of paper
- Writing utensil
- Hula-hoop (or anything else that can work to create a circle around the child, such as string or, if you are able to go outside, sidewalk chalk)
- Sandtray miniatures (optional)

Directions
1. Read the book with the child.
2. Introduce the *Body Boundaries* worksheet and have the child draw or list who is a part of their body safety team. Then fill out the rest of the worksheet by having the child identify the types of touch that feel most comfortable to them.
3. Ask the child to either write the names of their safety team on separate notecards or to pick out a miniature to represent each person.

4. Then ask the child to write down names of people who are *not* on their body safety team or to pick out miniatures to represent them.

5. Have the child stand inside the hula-hoop and let them know that this is their special body space bubble that keeps them out of trouble.

6. Go through the names of the people the child identified and ask the child who should be inside the bubble (hula-hoop) with them. Place anyone on the child's body safety team inside the hula-hoop and place anyone who is not on this team outside the hula-hoop.

7. Ask the child what makes them feel uncomfortable about the people outside of the bubble. Suggest potential ways the child can interact with these people while still remaining in their bubble. For example, you can pretend to be one of these people and ask, "Can I come inside your bubble for a hug?" The child can practice kindly saying, "I don't want a hug and I need my space, but we can high-five or fist-bump."

8. Finally, have the child sit in the hula-hoop with the names or miniatures of the people on their body safety team. Ask, "What makes you feel comfortable with them?" You can ask for specific instances of touch that make them feel safe with these people. For example: "Do you like it when Mommy snuggles with you?" or "Do you like it when your big sister holds your hand when you cross the street?" Help the child identify and verbalize, or "show," you what makes them feel most comfortable or at ease.

Body Boundaries*

Draw or write who is part of your trusted body safety team.

Safety Rules

- My body is my own and I will say no to uncomfortable touch.
- I always get permission before I touch someone.
- I will listen to how my body feels when a situation makes me feel uncomfortable.
- I will talk to my body safety team when I have concerns or questions.
- I will not keep secrets.

Mark what feels most comfortable to you. You can add your own in the blank spaces, too!

- ❏ Fist bump
- ❏ High five
- ❏ Wave
- ❏ Thumbs-up

- ❏ Handshake
- ❏ Elbow bump
- ❏ _____
- ❏ _____

* Based on the book *Body Boundaries Make Me Stronger* by Elizabeth Cole (2022)

Bullying and Perspective Taking

Books
- *Dare! A Story About Standing Up to Bullying in Schools* by Erin Frankel, illustrated by Paula Heaphy (2012a)
- *Tough! A Story About How to Stop Bullying in Schools* by Erin Frankel, illustrated by Paula Heaphy (2012b)
- *Weird! A Story About Dealing With Bullying in Schools* by Erin Frankel, illustrated by Paula Heaphy (2012c)

Description
This is a series of three wonderful books that tell the story of a third grader being bullied from different perspectives: the bully, the bystander, and the child being bullied. *Weird!* follows Luisa's bullying experience and offers options at the end of the book to inspire confidence. *Dare!* tells the same story from the perspective of a bystander, Jayla, who learns to speak up for her friend. The end of this book offers suggestions to help readers develop courage. *Tough!* follows the perspective of the bully, Sam, and provides suggestions to cultivate kindness. In this intervention, your client will learn how to see the same story from three different perspectives and decide whether they want to be part of a confidence, courage, or kindness club.

Treatment Goals
- Enhance perspective taking
- Build resilience for children who are bullied, the bystander, or the bully
- Build empathy, understanding, and self-awareness

Materials
- Puppets, art materials, or sand tray and miniatures
- Construction paper
- Coloring utensils

Directions

Activity 1

1. Read the three books with the child.

2. Invite the child to create a bullying scenario involving three characters: the bully, the victim, and the bystander. They can choose or create puppets (or miniatures) to represent each of the three characters.

3. Have the child be the narrator of the story and put on a puppet show, telling the story through the puppets from three different perspectives.

Activity 2

1. Let the child choose which "club" they would like to join: confidence, courage, or kindness (or they can create their own).

2. Invite them to create a sign with the rules of the club. Maybe it has a special saying or motto. Maybe there is a special handshake. Invite the child to be creative and act as the president of this important club.

The Boy, the Mole, the Fox, the Horse, and the Sand Tray

Book
The Boy, the Mole, the Fox and the Horse by Charlie Mackesy (2019)

Description
The Boy, the Mole, the Fox and the Horse is a story about friendship, kindness, bravery, and compassion. As the boy meets these new animal friends, they walk through the wilderness together and talk about what is important in life and what their dreams are. Although it is recommended for children seven years and up, you can read out some of the quotes and shorten it for little ones, since *everyone* needs to hear these sweet messages that travel deep into the heart. In this intervention, you'll find a variety of suggested quotes you can use to explore the topics of kindness, compassion, patience, and bravery. I also recommend checking out the animated movie *The Boy, the Mole, the Fox and the Horse*, which is based on the book and may be one of my favorite movies. I watched with pure delight as it opened my heart and expanded my compassion.

Treatment Goals
- Teach kindness, compassion, and bravery
- Recognize the important of friendship

Materials
- Sand tray and miniatures (or paper and coloring utensils)

Directions
1. Read the book with the child.
2. Pick a quote from the book and invite the client to create a sandtray exploring that theme. For example, ask the child to create a sandtray of a time when they refused to give up:

    "What is the bravest thing you've ever said?" asked the boy.

    "Help," said the horse.

    "Asking for help isn't giving up," said the horse. "It's refusing to give up."

3. You can also ask the child to create a sandtray of how they make a difference in this world:

    "I'm so small," said the mole.

    "Yes," said the boy, "but you make a huge difference."

4. Or a sandtray of when they feel lost and the things that bring them home:

    "Sometimes I feel lost," said the boy.

    "Me too," said the mole, "but we love you, and love brings you home."

5. Or a sandtray that represents kindness:

    "What do you want to be when you grow up?"

    "Kind," said the boy.

6. If you don't have a sand tray available, you can ask the child to create drawings to represent these same themes.

Kindness Ripples

Book
Each Kindness by Jacqueline Woodson, illustrated by E. B. Lewis (2012)

Description
Each Kindness is a book about a little girl named Chloe, who has the opportunity to befriend a new peer at school but chooses to be unkind and rejecting instead. With time and guidance from her teacher, Chloe learns that each little act of kindness we do can have a ripple effect out into the world. Teaching children about the ripple effect of acts of kindness is a wonderful way to instill empathy, compassion, and a sense of community. It helps children understand that their actions, no matter how small, have the power to create a positive chain reaction that can make the world a better place. In this intervention, you'll help your client see the impact of their kindness as they place rocks in a bowl of water, with each rock representing a simple act of kindness. If they struggle to identify an example of a kind act they have done, point out kind moments you have witnessed in the playroom (e.g., putting away toys, agreeing to participate in an activity, keeping the sand in the sand tray, making a bracelet for a friend or sibling). You can do this intervention with the child during any phase of treatment and can include the caregiver as well.

Treatment Goals
- Identify acts of kindness
- Demonstrate and teach the importance of empathy
- Help the child understand the impact of their behaviors

Materials
- Bowl
- Pitcher of water
- Rocks
- Paper or copy of the *Kindness Ripples* worksheet (included at the end of this intervention)
- Writing utensil

Directions
1. Read the book with the child.
2. Fill a pitcher of water and have the child pour it into the bowl.
3. Ask the child to place rocks, one by one, in the water. As the child places each rock in, invite them to describe an act of kindness that they have done. Point out how the ripples in the water extend out, signifying how their acts of kindness spread to the world.

4. Present the client with the *Kindness Ripples* worksheet and have them write their answers to the following questions in each ripple:
   - How do you show kindness?
   - What is the ripple effect of this kindness?
   - How could your kindness make the world a better place? (Have them use their imagination!)
   - (*If the caregiver is participating*) How do you see your child showing kindness?

5. Additionally, you can extend this activity and create a pond for others to build empathy. Print additional worksheets for other people in the child's life and ask the child, "How does your [*mom, friend, sibling, teacher, etc.*] show kindness?"

Adaptation for Telehealth

- Share the *Kindness Ripples* worksheet online or ask the client to use a blank piece of paper to create ripples. If using the virtual whiteboard, make circles with the annotate feature. Ask the same questions and have the child write (or draw) their answers in the circles.

Kindness Ripples: Example

The teacher was so happy and inspired by Sam's help; they even cleaned out extra items to donate to children in need.

Sam was happy and volunteered to help the teacher organize the toys in the classroom.

Katie felt happier and shared her favorite toy with Sam at recess.

Katie was feeling sad, and I told her I liked her art project.

Kindness Ripples

Write or draw in the bottom circle how you show kindness.
Write or draw in the other circles the ripple effect of this kindness
and how your kindness could make the world a better place.

Smartie Pants Activity*

Books
That Rule Doesn't Apply to Me! by Julia Cook, illustrated by Anita DuFalla (2016)

Description
That Rule Doesn't Apply to Me! is a story about a boy named Norman—also known as Noodle—who frequently gets into trouble because he believes he is above the rules. With the help of his mother, Noodle learns that rules do apply to him and comes to realize that rules actually protect and help him. This intervention draws on the book by helping children use their brains to take accountability for their behaviors and make smarter decisions. It can be used to address areas concerning impulse control, difficulty following directions, bullying, and other social skills, as it helps children recognize the consequences of being disrespectful or not following rules.

Treatment Goals
- Enhance decision-making skills
- Promote responsibility for one's thoughts and behaviors
- Address the importance of following rules

Materials
- Smarties® candy**
- Slips of paper
- Writing utensil
- Hat, box, bag, or other container

Directions
1. Before the session, write down a variety of questions on slips of paper to help the client reflect on making good decisions. You can individualize the questions for your particular client. For example:
    - Is it a good idea to hit someone when you are angry?
    - Is it okay to lie about something to get your way?
    - Is it a good decision to not listen to your peers about things?
    - Is it a good idea to get in someone's personal space or "bubble"?
    - Is it okay to talk to a teacher when you think someone is being bullied?
2. Fold the slips of paper and place them into a hat or other container.

---

* Intervention by Christine Wheeler-Case Jones, MA, LPC
** Always ask permission from the caregiver to allow food in the session. Never give a child food without permission. Children may have allergies or parents may restrict certain foods from the child.

3. In the session, read the book with the child.

4. Discuss the importance of making good decisions, then invite the client to draw a question from the hat, read it, and share their thoughts. Each time the client answers one of the prompts, give them a piece of Smarties candy to eat.

5. You and the caregiver, when appropriate, can then use humor to reinforce the child's ability to make decisions by calling them a "smartie pants." Encourage the child and their caregiver to make good decisions throughout the week and point these out to each other.

Shubert's BIG Voice*

Book
Shubert's BIG Voice by Becky A. Bailey and Leigh Ann Burdick, illustrated by James Hrkach (1999)

Description
Shubert's BIG Voice is about a lightning bug who is excited to meet his new teacher and wants to make a good impression. When he gets to school, though, he is confronted with another student who is unkind to him. The teacher shows Shubert how to stand up for himself, which helps him feel better about himself and empowers him to use his voice again. In this intervention, your client will have an opportunity to act out a situation in which they were bullied and then imagine reenacting that same situation with the help of a supportive person who makes them feel confident and powerful.

Treatment Goals
- Help the child stand up to bullying behaviors
- Enhance self-esteem
- Empower the child to use their voice

Materials
- Sand tray and miniatures
- Miniature megaphone (can also be drawn or made out of Shrinky Dink® paper)

Directions
1. Read the book with the child.
2. Have the child pick out a miniature to represent themselves and a miniature to represent their bully, then place both figures in the tray.
3. Invite the child to use the sand tray to act out a situation between them and the bully as it happened.
4. When they're done, ask the child to pick another miniature to represent someone who helps them feel confident and powerful, then have them place that figure in the sand tray.
5. Present the megaphone miniature to the client and talk about how Shubert practices a phrase with his teacher that he then uses to confront the bully: "I don't like it when you push me. Give me back my apple." Invite the client to practice standing up for themselves by replaying the situation from before, while adding the megaphone in at the end and tailoring Shubert's words to fit their own situation: "I don't like it when _____. I need _____."
6. If time allows, the client can act out other situations in which they could stand up for themselves.
7. At the end of the activity, the child can take the megaphone miniature with them as a reminder to assert themselves in the face of a bully.

---
* Intervention by Erika Walker, LSCSW, LCSW, LICSW, RPT-S

Create Your Own Super Animal*

Book
My Super Skills: Animals and Affirmations by Lauren Mosback, illustrated by Chiara Savarese (2020)

Description
My Super Skills is a story about a young boy named David, who is having a rough time, so his sister Lily swoops in to save the day! She shows him some tips and tricks to help him feel better, each of which is paired with an animal behavior that the siblings have fun practicing (e.g., pausing to slow down like a sloth). In this book-inspired activity, your client will design their own "super animal" and assign it a coping skill that will help them manage their emotions. This intervention works well in one-on-one sessions, with the entire family, or in a classroom or group setting.

Treatment Goals
- Introduce children to coping skills and self-care strategies in fun and empowering ways
- Normalize the experience of all emotions

Materials
- Variety of arts and crafts supplies (e.g., construction paper, coloring utensils, boxes, ribbon, bottle caps, scissors, glue)

Directions
1. Read the book with the client.

2. Invite the client to use the art supplies to create their own "super animal" by pairing an animal with a "superpower"—a coping skill that will help them manage their emotions. For example, they might create a brave lion who practices affirmations, a horse who takes deep breaths, or a bird who likes to sing. They can also use their imagination to create their own animal and corresponding coping skill.

3. Invite the client to take their super animal home and, whenever they start feeling overwhelmed by feelings, they can hold or visualize their animal and practice their chosen coping skill.

---
* Intervention by Lauren Mosback, LPC

Everyone Counts

Books
- *Zero* by Kathryn Otoshi (2010)
- *One* by Kathryn Otoshi (2008)

Description
Zero and *One* are two of my favorite books on bullying. *Zero* introduces readers to a character named Zero, who feels empty inside because she has a hole in the center of her body. She wonders how a number that adds up to nothing can be worth something. She eventually learns to find value in herself and others, realizing that the number 10 wouldn't exist without her! *One* tells the story of a bunch of colors who have different personalities. Red is a bully who is unkind and cruel, especially to Blue, but the other colors don't step in to stop the bullying behavior. It isn't until One joins the group that the colors find the strength to speak out against Red's actions. Both stories are about accepting differences, standing up for yourself, and standing up to bullies. I recommend reading both books, maybe in two different sessions.

Treatment Goals
- Empower the child to use their voice to stand up for themselves
- Promote respect for diversity and tolerance of differences
- Help the child develop empathy and understand the impact of their actions on others

Materials
- Sand tray and miniatures
- Paper
- Coloring utensils

Directions

Zero

1. Read the book *Zero* with the client and read aloud the quote: "Everyone counts. Zero wanted to count and find a purpose."
2. Invite the child to draw a picture or do a sandtray of how they count and why they are important.
3. Process the activity with the following questions:
    - When was a time that you felt like you counted or mattered?
    - When did you feel like you were an important part of the group?
    - What makes you important at school?
    - What makes you important at home or in your friend group?

- How do you make others feel like they matter?
- Who has made you feel like you matter? In what ways?
4. If the child struggles to answer these questions, point out examples of specific situations. For example: "Did you feel important when you scored a goal in soccer?" or "Did you feel like you mattered when you helped your friend feel better on the playground by sharing the swing?"

One

1. Read the book *One* with the client. Questions for reflection might include:
   - Do you know someone like Red?
   - Have you ever felt like Red, getting bigger and bigger?
   - Does anyone ever comfort you?
   - Does anyone stick up for you?
   - Have you ever noticed people not speaking up and the bully got bigger and bigger?
   - Have you ever stood up to someone? How did it feel, or how do you think it would feel?
   - Let's pretend you are One in the book and you are standing up to Red. What would you say?
2. Invite the client to draw a picture or create a sandtray of what it looks like to stand up for themselves and others. Process the child's creation by asking, "Is it easier to stand up for others and not yourself?" and "What does it feel like to be bullied and not stand up for yourself?"

Acknowledgments

I would like to give a special shout-out to Deanne Gruenberg for introducing me to the wonderful world of children's books. I also want to acknowledge my dear friends and colleagues who have continued to ignite my fire for this work, as well as my clients, who have been my inspiration and whose wisdom has been my teaching guide.

I am so grateful to my friends and family, including my amazing and magical daughter, Gabby, my brilliant and talented son, Aden, and my supportive and loving life partner, Neal King, who have been my rocks. They make me a better person and fill my heart with so much love and gratitude.

List of Contributors

Rachel Altvater, PsyD, RPT-S
Sophia Ansari, LPCC, RPT-S
Jessica Biles, LCSW-R, RPT
Margot Burke, PsyD
Isabella Cassina, MA, TPS, CAGS, PhD candidate
Cherie Catron, LPCC-S, RPT-S
Janet A. Courtney, PhD, RPT-S
Jodi Crane, PhD, NCC, LPCC-S, RPT-S
Dorothy Derapelian, MEd, LCMHC
Andrea Dorn, MSW
Kelsey Dugan, MPS, ATR-BC, LCPAT
Jackie Flynn, EdS, LMHC-S, RPT
Theresa Fraser, CYC-P, CPT-S, MA, RP, RCT
Karen Fried, PsyD, MFT
Christina Furnival, MS, LPCC
Paris Goodyear-Brown, LCSW, RPT-S
Robert Jason Grant, EdD, LPC, NCC, RPT-S
Dora Henderson, LMHC, RPT-S, CTP, CST
Fiona Hill, LPC, RPT
Sandra Holloway, LPC, RDMT, LBS
Sueann Kenney-Noziska, MSW, RPT-S
Neal King, LCSW
Rose LaPiere, LPC, RPT-S, ACS
Jennifer Lefebre, PsyD, TCTSY-F, RYT-500, RCYT, NASM-CPT, ATA-AIT
Liana Lowenstein, MSW, RSW, CPT-S
Ann Meehan, MS, LPCC, RPT-S
Lauren Mosback, LPC
Jodi Ann Mullen, PhD, LMHC, RPT-S
Amy Nelson, LCSW, LSCSW, RPT-S
Rebecca O'Neill, LCSW, CAS
Mary Anne Peabody, EdD, LCSW, RPT-S
Kelly Pullen, MA, LPC-S, RPT
Briana Quinlan, LCSW-C
Laci Radford, CPC student
Lisa Remey, LPC-S, RPT-S
Beth Richey, LCSW, RPT-S
Rachael Scott, MA, LPC, RPT
Lisa Shadburn, PsyD, RPT-S
Sarah Stauffer, PhD
Jessica Stone, PhD, RPT-S
Jennifer Taylor, LCSW-C, RPT-S
Lyla Tyler, LMFT, RPT-S
Erika Walker, LSCSW, LCSW, LICSW, RPT
Christine Wheeler-Case Jones, MA, LPC
Sarah Wintman, RPT, LICSW
Lynn Louise Wonders, LPC, CPCS, RPT-S
Dana Wyss, PhD

References

Alcott, A. (2021). *When things get too loud: A story about sensory overload*. Tiny Horse Books.

Anonymous. (2007). *Motherbridge of love* (J. Masse, Illus.). Barefoot Books.

Ashworth, M. (2016). *Step one, step two, step three and four: A picture book story about blending children from two families to one* (A. Chele, Illus.). Big Belly Book Co.

Atkinson, C. (2017). *Where Oliver fits*. Tundra Books.

Avis, H. (2021). *Different—A great thing to be!* (S. Mensinga, Illus.). WaterBrook.

Axel, M. (2020). *The power in me* (M. Simpson, Illus.). Belle Isle Books.

Axiline, V. M. (1964). *Dibs in search of self: The renowned, deeply moving story of an emotionally lost child who found his way back*. Houghton Mifflin.

Bailey, B. A. (2000). *I love you rituals*. William Morrow Paperbacks.

Bailey, B. A., & Bailey, L. A. (1999). *Shubert's big voice* (J. Hrkach, Illus.). Loving Guidance.

Bailey, K. D. (2019). *Some days I flip my lid: Learning to be a calm, cool kid* (H. Bailey, Illus.). PESI Publishing & Media.

Bailey, K. D. (2021). *Some days I breathe on purpose: Learning to be a calm, cool kid* (H. Bailey, Illus.). PESI Publishing.

Bailey, K. D. (2022). *Some days I make mistakes: How to stay calm and cool when your day is not so great* (H. Bailey, Illus.). PESI Publishing.

Baldacchino, C. (2014). *Morris Micklewhite and the tangerine dress* (I. Malenfant, Illus.). Groundwood Books.

Bassiri, K., & Bassiri, A. (2022). *Congratulations, you're autistic!* (D. Zinn, Illus.). Authors.

Baylor, B. (1974). *Everybody needs a rock* (P. Parnall, Illus.). Atheneum Books for Young Readers.

Betker McIntyre, B. (2000). *Jungle journey: Grieving & remembering Eleanor the elephant* (M. O. Henderson, Illus.). Traverse.

Biles, J., & Kelly-Wavering, J. (2022). *My grief is like the ocean: A story for children who lost a parent to suicide* (J. Biles, Illus.). Loving Healing Press.

Birtha, B. (2017). *Far apart, close in heart: Being a family when a loved one is incarcerated* (M. Kastelic, Illus.). Albert Whitman & Company.

Booth, P. B., & Jernberg, A. M. (2010). *Theraplay: Helping parents and children build better relationships through attachment-based play* (3rd ed.). Jossey-Bass.

Byers, G. (2018). *I am enough* (K. A. Bobo, Illus.). Balzer + Bray.

Carle, E. (1995). *The very lonely firefly*. World of Eric Carle.

Carlson, N. (1988). *I like me!* Puffin Books.

Carr, J. (2010). *Be who you are!* (B. Rumback, Illus.). AuthorHouse.

Cassina, I. (2020). *The magic home: A displaced boy finds a way to feel better*. Loving Healing Press.

Cave, K. (2003). *You've got dragons* (N. Maland, Illus.). Peachtree Publishing Company.

Chandler, R. K. (2017). *You make your parents super happy! A book about parents separating*. Jessica Kingsley Publishers.

Cherry, M. A. (2019). *Hair love* (V. Harrison, Illus.). Kokila.

Clark, B. (2020). *Catching thoughts* (S. Macon, Illus.). Beaming Books.

Cohen Harper, J. (2013). *Little Flower Yoga for kids: A yoga and mindfulness program to help your child improve attention and emotional balance*. New Harbinger.

Cohen Harper, J. (2019). *Thank you body, thank you heart: A gratitude and self-compassion practice for bedtime* (K. Gilmour, Illus.). PESI Publishing.

Cohen Harper, J. (2020). *Thank you mind: Understanding my big feelings on tricky days* (K. Gilmour, Illus.). PESI Publishing.

Cohen Harper, J. (2022). *Thank you breath: Finding peace and power from the inside out* (K. Gilmour, Illus.). PESI Publishing.

Colagiovanni, M. (2017). *The reflection in me* (P. H. Reynolds, Illus.). [Video]. FableVision. https://www.fablevisionstudios.com/reflection

Cole, E. (2022). *Body boundaries make me stronger*. Author.

Cook, J. (2007). *Personal space camp: A picture book about respecting others' physical boundaries* (C. Hartman, Illus.). National Center for Youth Issues.

Cook, J. (2008). *It's hard to be a verb!* (C. Hartman, Illus.). National Center for Youth Issues.

Cook, J. (2013). *Tease monster: A book about teasing vs. bullying* (A. DuFalla, Illus.). Boys Town Press.

Cook, J. (2016). *That rule doesn't apply to me!* (A. DuFalla, Illus.). Boys Town Press.

Courtney, J. A. (2013a). *The Magic Rainbow Hug©: A fun interactive storyteller-child activity*. Author.

Courtney, J. A. (2013b). *The Magic Rainbow Hug activity book*. Author.

Courtney, J. A., Langley, J. L., Wonders, L. L., Heiko, R., & LaPiere, R. (Eds.). (2022). *Nature-based play and expressive therapies: Interventions for working with children, teens, and families*. Routledge.

Crenshaw, D. A., & Mordock, J. B. (2007). *Understanding and treating the aggression of children: Fawns in gorilla suits*. Jason Aronson.

Crenshaw, K., & Meschke, A. (2020). *Her body can* (L. Liu, Illus.). Authors.

Crenshaw, K., & Meschke, A. (2021). *His body can* (L. Liu, Illus.). Authors.

Deak, J. (2010). *Your fantastic elastic brain: A growth mindset book for kids to stretch and shape their brains* (S. Ackerley, Illus.). Little Pickle Press.

Deak, J., & Deak, T. (2022). *Good night to your fantastic elastic brain: A growth mindset bedtime book for kids* (N. Daggett, Illus.). Little Pickle Press.

Delahooke, M. (2019). *Beyond behaviors: Using brain science and compassion to understand and solve children's behavioral challenges*. PESI Publishing & Media.

Delahooke, M. (2022). *Brain-body parenting: How to stop managing behavior and start raising joyful, resilient kids*. HarperCollins.

Derapelian, D. (2015). *Core Attachment Therapy©: Secure attachment for the adopted child*. Author.

Derapelian, D. (2017). *Letting us into your heart* (S. Toh, Illus.). Author.

Derapelian, D. (2019). *Your love is hope: Parent companion of Core Attachment Therapy©*. Author.

Diesen, D. (2017). *The pout-pout fish and the bully-bully shark* (D. Hanna, Illus.). Farra, Straus and Giroux.

Diggs, T. (2011). *Chocolate me!* (S. W. Evans, Illus.). Feiwel & Friends.

Doerrfeld, C. (2018). *The rabbit listened*. Scallywag Press.

Dorn, A. (2021). *Calm and peaceful mindful me: A mindfulness how-to guide for toddlers and kids*. PESI Publishing.

Dorn, A. (2022). *When someone dies: A children's mindful how-to guide on grief and loss*. PESI Publishing.

Doyle Bailey, K. (2019). *Some days I flip my lid: Learning to be a calm, cool kid* (H. Bailey, Illus.). PESI Publishing & Media.

Doyle Bailey, K. (2021). *Some days I breathe on purpose: Learning to be a calm, cool kid* (H. Bailey, Illus.). PESI Publishing.

Doyle Bailey, K. (2022). *Some days I make mistakes: How to stay calm and cool when your day is not so great* (H. Bailey, Illus.). PESI Publishing.

Dr. Seuss. (1990). *Oh, the places you'll go!* Random House Children's Books.

Dutcher, J., & Dutcher, J. (2015). *A Friend for Lakota: The incredible true story of a wolf who braved bullying*. National Geographic Kids.

Empson, J. (2012). *Rabbityness*. Child's Play International.

Faber, A., & Mazlish, E. (2012). *Siblings without rivalry: How to help your children live together so you can live too*. W. W. Norton. (Original work published 1987)

Feder, T. (2021). *Bodies are cool*. Rocky Pond Books.

Flynn, J. (2020). *In my body, I feel: A story about the felt sense of emotions*. Author.

Flynn, J. (2022a). *Being human: A polyvagal informed story about the states of the nervous system*. Author.

Flynn, J. (2022b). *I am octopus: Playful projections to strengthen one's sense of self* (A. Flynn, Illus.). Author.

Forman, R. (2020). *Curls* (G. Bowers, Illus.). Little Simon.

Forman, R. (2021). *Glow* (G. Bowers, Illus.). Little Simon.

Forman, R. (2022). *Bloom* (T. Skyles, Illus.). Little Simon.

Frankel, E. (2012a). *Dare! A story about standing up to bullying in schools* (P. Heaphy, Illus.). Free Spirit Publishing.

Frankel, E. (2012b). *Tough! A story about how to stop bullying in schools* (P. Heaphy, Illus.). Free Spirit Publishing.

Frankel, E. (2012c). *Weird! A story about dealing with bullying in schools* (P. Heaphy, Illus.). Free Spirit Publishing.

Fraser, T., & Fraser, E. E. W. (2019). *We're all not the same, but we're still family: An adoption and birth family story*. Loving Healing Press.

Fried, K., & McKenna, C. (2020). *Healing through play using the Oaklander model: A guidebook for therapists and counselors working with children, adolescents and families*. Authors.

Friend, K. (2018). *The greatness chair*. Words Matter Publishing.

Furnival, C. (2021). *The not-so-friendly friend: How to set boundaries for healthy friendships* (K. Dwyer, Illus.). PESI Publishing.

Furnival, C. (2022). *Fear not! How to face your fear and anxiety head-on* (K. Dwyer, Illus.). PESI Publishing.

Furnival, C. (2023). *The big feelings flip chart: A psychoeducational in-session tool to help kids learn about and understand their many emotions*. PESI Publishing.

Garcia, G. (2017a). *Listening to my body* (Y. H. Tan, Illus.; 2nd ed.). Skinned Knee Publishing.

Garcia, G. (2017b). *Listening with my heart: A story of kindness and self-compassion* (Y. H. Tan, Illus.). Skinned Knee Publishing.

Garcia, G. (2018). *I can do hard things: Mindful affirmations for kids* (C. Russell, Illus.). Skinned Knee Publishing.

Garcia, G. (2020). *Find your calm: A mindful approach to relieve anxiety and grow your bravery* (M. Pineda, Illus.). Skinned Knee Publishing.

Ghosh Ippen, C. (2016). *Once I was very very scared.* (E. Ippen Jr., Illus.). Piplo Productions.

Ghosh Ippen, C. (2019a). *Holdin Pott.* (E. Ippen Jr., Illus.). Piplo Productions.

Ghosh Ippen, C. (2019b). *You weren't with me.* (E. Ippen Jr., Illus.). Piplo Productions.

Ghosh Ippen, C. (2020). *Mama's waves.* (E. Ippen Jr., Illus.). Piplo Productions.

Ghosh Ippen, C. (2021). *Daddy's waves.* (E. Ippen Jr., Illus.). Piplo Productions.

Ghosh Ippen, C. (2022). *Argo and me: A story about being scared and finding protection, love, and home.* (E. Ippen Jr., Illus.). Piplo Productions.

Gliori, D. (2014). *No matter what.* Bloomsbury. (Original work published 1999)

Gobbel, R. (2023). *Raising kids with big, baffling behaviors: Brain-body sensory strategies that really work.* Jessica Kinglsey Publishers.

Gomi, T. (2020). *Everyone poops.* Chronicle Books. (Original work published 1977)

Goodyear-Brown, P. (2003). *Gabby the gecko* (B. Hull, Illus.). Author.

Goodyear-Brown, P. (2016). *A safe circle for little U* (E. Gott, Illus.). Author.

Goodyear-Brown, P. (2018). *Penelope the peacock* (E. Gott, Illus.). Author.

Goodyear-Brown, P. (2022). *Big behaviors in small containers: 131 trauma-informed play therapy interventions for disorders of dysregulation.* PESI Publishing.

Grant, R. J. (2024). *Play interventions for neurodivergent children and adolescents: Promoting growth, empowerment, and affirming practices* (2nd ed.). Routledge.

Gray, K. (2009). *Mom and Dad glue* (L. Wildish, Illus.). BES Publishing Co.

Green, A. (2008). *The nose that didn't fit.* Monsters in My Head.

Green, A. (2011). *Don't feed the worrybug: A children's book about worry.* Monsters in My Head.

Greening, R. (2020). *The very hungry worry monsters* (L. Ede, Illus.). Make Believe Ideas.

Griswold, D. (2022). *My zoo: A book of feelings* (E. Reisfeld, Illus.). Magination Press.

Guber, T., & Kalish, L. (2005). *Yoga pretzels: 50 fun yoga activities for kids & grownups* (S. Fatus, Illus.). Barefoot Books.

Gutiérrez, J. (2023). *Too much! An overwhelming day* (A. Chang, Illus.). Harry N. Abrams.

Hall, M. (2015). *Red: A crayon's story.* Greenwillow Books.

Hanh, T. N. (2012). *A handful of quiet: Happiness in four pebbles.* Plum Blossom.

Harris, N. (2023). *My brain is a race car: A children's guide to a neuro-divergent brain.* Author.

Henderson, D. (2022). *Neuro & the Ception Force friends: A special team of receptor neurons that help your body & brain with regulation* (H. Worley, Illus.). Author.

Henderson, R. (2019). *I see, I see.* Chronicle Books.

Herman, S. (2020). *Two homes filled with love: A story about divorce and separation.* DG Books Publishing.

Herthel, J., & Jennings, J. (2014). *I am Jazz* (S. McNicholas, Illus.). Dial Books.

Higgins, M. (2013). *The night Dad went to jail: What to expect when someone you love goes to jail* (W. Kirwan, Illus.). Picture Window Books.

Holmes, M. M. (2000). *A terrible thing happened* (C. Pillo, Illus.). Magination Press.

Honig-Briggs, R. (n.d.). *Two-hug day* (M. Nelson, Illus.). Sesame Workshop. https://sesameworkshop.org/resources/transitioning-between-parents

Hoopmann, K. (2020a). *All cats are on the autism spectrum* (Rev. ed.). Jessica Kingsley.

Hoopmann, K. (2020b). *All dogs have ADHD* (Rev. ed.). Jessica Kingsley.

Hussain, N. (2021). *My monster and me: A reassuring story about sharing worries* (E. Bailey, Illus.). Viking Books for Young Readers.

Hutton, J. S. (2016). *ADH-me!* (L. Griffin, Illus.). Blue Manatee Press.

Jeffers, O. (2010). *The heart and the bottle.* Philomel Books.

Jimenez-Pride, C. (2019). *Amir's brave adventure: Exploring confidence, mindfulness and attachment* (T. Varcelija, Illus.). Author.

Joosse, B. M. (1996). *I love you the purplest* (M. Whyte, Illus.). Chronicle Books.

Karst, P. (2018). *The invisible string* (J. Lew-Vriethoff, Illus.). Little, Brown Books for Young Readers. (Original work published 2000)

Karst, P. (2020). *You are never alone: An Invisible String lullaby* (J. Lew-Vriethoff, Illus.). Little, Brown Books for Young Readers.

Karst, P., & Wyss, D. (2019). *The Invisible String workbook: Creative activities to comfort, calm, & connect* (J. Lew-Vriethoff, Illus.). Little, Brown Books for Young Readers.

Kasza, K. (1999). *A mother for Choco.* Puffin Books. (Original work published 1982)

Kates, B. (1992). *We're different, we're the same* (J. Mathieu, Illus.). Random House.

Kennedy, B. (2022). *Good inside: A guide to becoming the parent you want to be.* Harper Wave.

King, N. (2022). *Where's my pajommy, Mommy Mommy? A tongue twisterommy* (E. John, Illus.). Author.

Kitze, C. A. (2003). *I don't have your eyes* (R. Williams, Illus.). EMK Press.

Lefebre, J. (2021). *The fabulous fight or flight stress system: Neuroscience & polyvagal theories through animal metaphors*. Author.

Lefebre, J. (2022). *A body-based journey through nature & animal metaphors: Trauma-sensitive yoga & embodied play to support the fabulous fight or flight stress response system*. Author.

Lefebre, J. (2023). *Seven sensational senses for little sprockets: Part of the fabulous fight or flight stress system series*. Author.

LeMaire, C. (2014). *I have two homes* (M. Saumell, Illus.). Author.

LeMaire, C. (2015). *I have a stepmom* (M. Saumell, Illus.). Author.

LeMaire, C. (2016). *I have a stepdad* (M. Saumell, Illus.). Author.

LeMaire, C. (2019a). *I have two dads* (M. Saumell, Illus.). Author.

LeMaire, C. (2019b). *I have two moms* (M. Saumell, Illus.). Author.

Lester, J. (2005). *Let's talk about race* (K. Barbour, Illus.). Amistad.

Letourneau, J. (2019). *A kids book about shame*. A Kids Book About.

Levinson Gilman, J. (2008). *Murphy's three homes: A story for children in foster care* (K. O'Malley, Illus.). Magination Press.

Levitt, T. (2017). *Happiness doesn't come from headstands*. Wisdom Publications.

Llenas, A. (2018). *The color monster: A story about emotions*. Little, Brown Books for Young Readers.

Lowenstein, L. (2013). *Cory helps kids cope with divorce: Playful therapeutic activities for young children*. Champion Press.

Mackesy, C. (2019). *The boy, the mole, the fox and the horse*. HarperOne.

MacLean, K. L. (2004). *Peaceful piggy meditation*. Albert Whitman & Company.

MacLean, K. L. (2009). *Moody cow meditates*. Wisdom Publications.

Maguire, N. (2020). *My body sends a signal: Helping kids recognize emotions and express feelings* (A. Zababashkina, Illus.). Author.

Manasco, H. (2012). *An exceptional children's guide to touch: Teaching social and physical boundaries to kids* (K. Manasco, Illus.). Jessica Kingsley Publishers.

Marler, J. (2012). *Lily hates goodbyes* (All military ed.). (N. Stoltenberg, Illus.). Quincy Companion Books.

Marlowe, S. (2016). *My new best friend* (I. Salom, Illus.). Wisdom Publications.

Masurel, C. (2001). *Two homes* (K. MacDonald Denton, Illus.). Candlewick Press.

McCloud, C. (2015). *Have you filled a bucket today? A guide to daily happiness for kids* (D. Messing, Illus.). Bucket Fillers. (Original work published 2006)

Mills, J. C. (1993). *Gentle willow: A story for children about dying* (C. Pillo, Illus.). Magination Press.

Moore-Mallinos, J. (2005). *When my parents forgot how to be friends* (M. Fabrega, Illus.). Sourcebooks Trade.

Mosback, L. (2020). *My super skills: Animals and affirmations* (C. Savarese, Illus.). Empowering Kids Media.

Mosback, L. (2021). *Transforming anxiety: Grow resilience and confidence* (C. Savarese, Illus.). Empowering Kids Media.

Mosback, L. (2022). *In Grandpaw's pawprints: A story of loss, life & love* (N. Aptsiauri, Illus.). Empowering Kids Media.

Mosback, L. (2024). *Let's grow on an adventure: Finding calm in the joy of nature* (S. Holovchenko, Illus.). PESI Publishing.

Nelson, A. (2023). *Every bunny can learn: A tail of inclusion* (Y. Mahajan, Illus.). Emotional Milestones.

Nichols, L. (2014). *Maple & Willow together*. Nancy Paulsen Books.

Niner, H. L. (2004). *Mr. Worry: A story about OCD* (G. Swearingen, Illus.). Albert Whitman & Company.

Novesky, A. (2016). *Three little words* (G. Lee, Illus.). Disney Press.

Nyong'o, L. (2019). *Sulwe* (V. Harrison, Illus.). Simon & Schuster Books for Young Readers.

Oaklander, V. (1978). *Windows to our children: A gestalt approach to children and adolescents*. Gestalt Journal Press.

Oaklander, V. (2006). *Hidden treasure: A map to the child's inner self*. Routledge.

Oelschlager, V. (2010). *A tale of two daddies* (K. Blackwood & M. Blanc, Illus.). VanitaBooks.

Oelschlager, V. (2011). *A tale of two mommies* (M. Blanc, Illus.). VanitaBooks.

Otoshi, K. (2008). *One*. KO Kids Books.

Otoshi, K. (2010). *Zero*. KO Kids Books.

Parets Luque, C. (2018). *A handful of buttons*. Catacric Catacrac.

Parr, T. (2001). *It's okay to be different*. Little, Brown Books for Young Readers.

Parr, T. (2003). *The family book*. Little, Brown Books for Young Readers.

Parr, T. (2007). *We belong together*. Little, Brown and Company.

Parr, T. (2015). *The goodbye book*. Little, Brown Books for Young Readers.

Parr, T. (2016). *Be who you are*. Little, Brown Books for Young Readers.

Penn, A. (2006). *The kissing hand* (R. E. Harper & N. M. Leak, Illus.). Tanglewood Press. (Original work published 1993)

Perkins, M. (2019). *Between us and Abuela: A family story from the border* (S. Palacios, Illus.). Farrar, Straus and Giroux.

Perry, B. D., & Dobson, C. L. (2013). The neurosequential model of therapeutics. In J. D. Ford & C. A. Courtois (Eds.), *Treating complex traumatic stress disorders in children and adolescents: Scientific foundations and therapeutic models* (pp. 249–260). The Guilford Press.

Perry, B. D., & Szalavitz, M. (2006). *The boy who was raised as a dog and other stories from a child psychiatrist's notebook: What traumatized children can teach us about loss, love, and healing.* Basic Books.

Perry, B. D., & Winfrey, O. (2021). *What happened to you?: Conversations on trauma, resilience, and healing.* Flatiron Books.

Pett, M., & Rubinstein, G. (2011). *The girl who never made mistakes* (M. Pett, Illus.). Sourcebooks Jabberwocky.

Porges, S. W. (2017). *The pocket guide to the polyvagal theory: The transformative power of feeling safe.* W. W. Norton.

Prince Guttman, A. (2021). *Wherever you'll be* (G. Godbout, Illus.). Flamingo Books.

Pritchard, N. (2018). *Monty the manatee* (N. Merheb, Illus.). Author.

Qiu, Y. (2022). *I am an amazing Asian girl: A positive affirmation book for Asian girls* (J. Le, Illus.). Author.

Quinlan, B. (2022). *Family forest* (P. F. Braga, Illus.). Ingram Spark.

Reynolds, P. H. (2003). *The dot.* Candlewick Press.

Reynolds, P. H. (2004). *Ish.* Candlewick Press.

Reynolds, P. H. (2011). *I'm here.* Atheneum Books for Young Readers.

Reynolds, P. H. (2012). *Sky color.* Candlewick Press.

Reynolds, P. H. (2017). *Happy dreamer.* Orchard Books.

Ricci, I. (1997). *Mom's house, Dad's house: Making two homes for your child.* Fireside. (Original work published 1980)

Ricci, I. (2006). *Mom's house, Dad's house for kids: Feeling at home in one home or two.* Touchstone.

Richardson, B. L., & Rehr, E. (2001). *101 ways to help your daughter love her body.* Quill.

Richey, B., & Wood, P. (2019). *When a grown-up you love hurts you: A book for children who have experienced physical abuse.* Warren Publishing.

Richey, B., & Wood, P. (2021). *Understanding neglect: A book for young children.* Warren Publishing.

Romain, T. (2016). *Bullying is a pain in the brain* (S. Mark, Illus.). Free Spirit Publishing.

Rossner, R. (2020). *I love you like no otter* (S. Hanson, Illus.). Sourcebooks Wonderland.

Saltz, G. (2005). *Amazing you! Getting smart about your private parts* (L. Cravath, Illus.). Dutton Children's Books.

Saltzberg, B. (2010). *Beautiful oops!* Workman Publishing Company.

Sanders, J. (2016). *Let's talk about body boundaries, consent and respect: Teach children about body ownership, respect, feelings, choices and recognizing bullying behaviors* (S. Jennings, Illus.). Educate2Empower Publishing.

Schaefer, C. E., & Drewes, A. A. (2013). *The therapeutic powers of play: 20 core agents of change.* John Wiley & Sons.

Schwiebert, P., & DeKlyen, C. (2005). *Tear soup: A recipe for healing after loss* (T. Bills, Illus.). Grief Watch. (Original work published 1999)

Shadburn, L. (2022). *I've got this! A child's guide to lifting yourself up when you're feeling down* (R. Noonan, Illus.). Author.

Shah, O. (2023). *Ash's handwashing adventure.* Author.

Sheppard, C. H. (1998). *Brave Bart: A story for traumatized and grieving children.* Institute for Trauma and Loss in Children.

Siegel, D. J. (2022). *NowMaps Jr.: Adventure stories to help young kids navigate everyday challenges & grow in caring and kind ways.* PESI Publishing.

Siegel, D. J., & Payne Bryson, T. (2011). *The whole-brain child: 12 revolutionary strategies to nurture your child's developing mind.* Delacorte Press.

Sileo, F. J. (2017). *A world of pausabilities: An exercise in mindfulness* (J. Zivoin, Illus.). Magination Press.

Sileo, F. J. (2023). *The small and tall ball: A story about diversity and inclusion* (K. Dwyer, Illus.). PESI Publishing.

Silver, G. (2009). *Anh's anger* (C. Krömer, Illus.). Plum Blossom.

Sister Susan. (2002). *Each breath a smile: Based on teachings by Thich Nhat Hanh* (T. H. Nguyen & D. Nguyen, Illus.). Plum Blossom.

Skolmoski, S. (2006). *A paper hug* (A. Bennion, Illus.). Author.

Smith, T. E. (2019). *Here and there* (E. Daviddi, Illus.). Barefoot Books.

Smitten, R. (2021). *The secret life of Rose: Inside an autistic head.* Author.

Sooful, P. (2023). *My brain is magic: A sensory-seeking celebration* (G. Ladi, Illus.). Soaring Kite Books.

Sotomayor, S. (2019). *Just ask! Be different, be brave, be you* (R. López, Illus.). Philomel Books.

Stead, R. (2020). *The list of things that will not change.* Wendy Lamb Books.

Stockly, L. (2020). *Be mindful of monsters: A book for helping children accept their emotions* (E. Surrey, Illus.). Bumble Press.

Stockly, L. (2022). *Mindfulness is your superpower: A book about finding focus and cultivating calm* (Z. Grzeszkowiak, Illus.). Rockridge.

Stuart, S. (2021). *My shadow is pink.* Larrikin House.

Thomas, N. (2020). *Some brains: A book celebrating neurodiversity* (C. MacInnes, Illus.). Black.

Tyler, M. (2005). *The skin you live in* (D. L. Csicsko, Illus.). Chicago Children's Museum.

Vail, R. (2005). *Sometimes I'm Bombaloo* (Y. Heo, Illus.). Scholastic Paperbacks.

Van Hollander, T. (2018a). *Casey's greatness wings: Teaching mindfulness, connection & courage to children* (A. Wilkinson, Illus.). Author.

Van Hollander, T. (2018b). Greatness sticks. In C. Mellenthin (Ed.), *Play therapy: Engaging & powerful techniques for treatment of childhood disorders* (pp. 107–109). PESI Publishing & Media.

Verde, S. (2015). *I am yoga* (P. H. Reynolds, Illus.). Abrams Books for Young Readers.

Verde, S. (2017). *I am peace: A book of mindfulness* (P. H. Reynolds, Illus.). Abrams Books for Young Readers.

Verde, S. (2018). *I am human: A book of empathy* (P. H. Reynolds, Illus.). Abrams Books for Young Readers.

Verde, S. (2019). *I am love: A book of compassion* (P. H. Reynolds, Illus.). Abrams Books for Young Readers.

Viorst, J. (1972). *Alexander and the terrible, horrible, no good, very bad day* (R. Cruz, Illus.). Atheneum.

Walvoord Girard, L. (1984). *My body is private* (R. Pate, Illus.). Albert Whitman & Company.

Ward, L. (2017). *Brobarians.* Two Lions.

Watt, M. (2006). *Scaredy squirrel.* Kids Can Press.

Watt, M. (2007). *Scaredy squirrel makes a friend.* Kids Can Press.

Watt, M. (2008). *Scaredy squirrel at the beach.* Kids Can Press.

Watt, M. (2009). *Scaredy squirrel at night.* Kids Can Press.

Watt, M. (2011). *Scaredy squirrel has a birthday party.* Kids Can Press.

Watt, M. (2012). *Scaredy squirrel prepares for Christmas.* Scholastic Inc.

Watt, M. (2013). *Scaredy squirrel prepares for Halloween.* Kids Can Press.

Watt, M. (2021). *Scaredy squirrel goes camping.* Random House Books for Young Readers.

Watt, M. (2022). *Scaredy squirrel visits the doctor.* Random House Books for Young Readers.

Wilgocki, J., & Kahn Wright, M. (2022). *Maybe days: A book for children in foster care* (A. I. Geis, Illus.). Magination Press.

Willard, C., & Rechtschaffen, D. (2019). *Alphabreaths: The ABCs of mindful breathing* (H. Clifton-Brown, Illus.). Sounds True.

Willems, M. (2019). *Because.* Hyperion Books for Children.

Winkler Tyson, B. (2019). *A grandfamily for Sullivan* (A. Walker-Parker, Illus.). Author.

Wonders, L. L (2019). *When parents are at war: A child therapist's guide to navigating high conflict divorce & custody cases.* Author.

Wonders, L. L. (2021a). *Miss Piper's playroom: Helping Danny with his parents' divorce* (U. Barabash, Illus.). Author.

Wonders, L. L. (2021b). *Miss Piper's playroom: Helping Lily with her loss* (U. Barabash, Illus.). Author.

Wonders, L. L. (2022a). *Miss Piper's playroom: Helping Aiden with his ADHD* (U. Barabash, Illus.). Author.

Wonders, L. L. (2022b). *Miss Piper's playroom: Helping Sal with social anxiety* (U. Barabash, Illus.). Author.

Woodson, J. (2012). *Each kindness* (E. B. Lewis, Illus.). Nancy Paulsen Books.

Yamada, K. (2014). *What do you do with an idea?* (M. Besom, Illus.). Compendium.

Yamada, K. (2016). *What do you do with a problem?* (M. Besom, Illus.). Compendium.

Yamada, K. (2018). *What do you do with a chance?* (M. Besom, Illus.). Compendium.

Yamada, K. (2019). *Maybe* (G. Barouch, Illus.). Compendium.

Young, K. (2017). *Hey warrior: A book for kids about anxiety* (N. Dovidonyte, Illus.). Hey Sigmund Publishing.

About the Author

Tammi Van Hollander, LCSW, RPT-S™, is a licensed clinical social worker and registered play therapist supervisor with over 25 years of experience working with infants, children, families, and adults of all ages. She specializes in attachment, sandtray play therapy, and sensory integration. She holds a Master of Social Work from the University of Pennsylvania and has had extensive training and supervision from the Family and Play Therapy Center in Philadelphia. She is a certified advanced trainer for the Nurtured Heart Approach®, a certified FirstPlay® practitioner, and a founding board member of the World Association for Sand Therapy Professionals.

Tammi's work and creative interventions in the field of play therapy have been published and internationally recognized. She is the author of a multi-sensory, attachment-based children's book titled *Casey's Greatness Wings: Teaching Mindfulness, Connection & Courage to Children*. The success of the book inspired her to create Casey's Greatness Sticks and Greatness Cards to be used in schools, therapy offices, and the home.

Tammi also teaches monthly virtual sandtray classes and played a pivotal role in co-teaching the inaugural sandtray therapy class in China, effectively introducing this therapeutic modality to the country. She is an internationally sought-after presenter and gave her first TEDx Talk, *Stories in the Sand: Healing Trauma, Anxiety, and Grief*, in October 2023.